"*Cracks in the Schoolyard* provides powerful accounts of the ways in which Latina/o students achieve in spite of formidable obstacles."
   Amanda Datnow, associate dean of social sciences and
   professor of education, University of California, San Diego

"Conchas has provided readers with an important gift: authentic stories, authentic struggles, authentic strategies, and authentic success. This work debunks the deficit discourse around Latina/o education with a complex analysis of how race, community strengths, and identity become assets for educational excellence. The cases presented are rich, powerful, compelling, and inspiring. Essential reading for social justice advocates!"
   Tyrone Howard, professor of education at the University of California,
   Los Angeles, and author of *Why Race and Culture Matters in Schools*

"Conchas' provocative and compelling case studies in education position him once again as a leading voice in challenging common sense notions of Latina/o school failure."
   Kris D. Gutiérrez, professor of education, University of California, Berkeley

"Latina/os compromise the country's largest ethnic minority group and school-age youth are the fastest-growing sector of this dynamic population. In *Cracks in the Schoolyard*, Conchas and his colleagues provide educators, policymakers, community based organizations, and philanthropy a compelling lens on the challenges we face—and must address—in improving the academic and social outcomes for Latina/o youth."
   Peter Rivera, senior program officer, California Community Foundation

"*Cracks in the Schoolyard* convenes a dynamic group of scholars committed to transforming our schools. Using the latest theories and methodological approaches, it offers crucial frameworks to understanding Latina/os and schooling. It's a must-read book, especially for practitioners, researchers, and policymakers."
   Gilda L. Ochoa, professor of Chicana/o-Latina/o Studies at Pomona College and
   author of *Academic Profiling: Latinos, Asian Americans, and the Achievement Gap*

"Through rich, detailed, and rigorous case studies, Conchas and his contributors highlight numerous locations of Latina/o youth agency and success within diverse educational contexts. This is a must-read volume for anyone interested in finding ways to address the deeply-rooted inequalities that exists in America's educational system."
   Lisa Garcia Bedolla, Chancellor's Professor of education and political science,
   University of California, Berkeley, and author of *Latino Politics*

"Conchas ushers in a new paradigm for understanding Latina/o student achievement. The authors in this volume collaboratively and compellingly demonstrate the importance of understanding Latina/o educational achievement by analyzing assets and agency in the lives of youths and their families. This volume provides educators, policymakers, and scholars the critical hope and pragmatic agenda for developing a more just educational system—the authors cogently teach us to identify and understand the plethora of contributions that Latina/o students make to our educational system on a day-to-day basis."
   Victor M. Rios, professor of sociology, University of California, Santa Barbara,
   and author of *Punished*

D0775208

Cracks in the Schoolyard—Confronting Latino Educational Inequality

Edited by

Gilberto Q. Conchas

with Briana M. Hinga

Foreword by
Amanda Datnow

TEACHERS COLLEGE PRESS
TEACHERS COLLEGE | COLUMBIA UNIVERSITY
NEW YORK AND LONDON

Published by Teachers College Press, 1234 Amsterdam Avenue, New York, NY 10027

Figure 3.1 courtesy of Nancy Acevedo-Gil. @ 2013 by Nancy Acevedo-Gil. Used by permission.

Figure 9.1 is from Wikipedia, Creative Commons Free Share.

Library of Congress Cataloging-in-Publication Data

Cracks in the schoolyard : confronting Latino educational inequality / edited by Gilberto
    Q. Conchas ; with Briana M. Hinga ; foreword by Amanda Datnow
        pages ; cm
    Includes bibliographical references.
    ISBN 978-0-8077-5703-1 (paperback)—ISBN 978-0-8077-5704-8 (hardcover) ISBN
    978-0-8077-7413-7 (ebook)
    1. Hispanic Americans—Education. 2. Discrimination in education—United States. 3.
    Educational equalization—United States. I. Conchas, Gilberto Q.
    LC2669.C73 2015
    371.829'68073—dc23

                                                                                2015033789

ISBN 978-0-8077-5703-1 (paperback)
ISBN 978-0-8077-5704-8 (hardcover)
ISBN 978-0-8077-7413-7 (ebook)

Printed on acid-free paper
Manufactured in the United States of America

22 21 20 19 18 17 16 15   8 7 6 5 4 3 2 1

To those who courageously opened the doors to us and to the hard work that needs to be done to keep those doors wide open.

And, special praise to my thought partner—Briana M. Hinga—who will labor alongside us to keep the doors always open.

Finally, I wish to acknowledge Estela Zarate for her work, which was not only instrumental in the writing of Chapter 1, but also contributed to the conceptual framework for this book.

Contents

PART III: CRITICAL CASE STUDIES EXPLORING
ETHNICITY, IDENTITY, AND IMMIGRATION

Foreword

Latinos are the fastest growing population in U.S. schools today. This makes the fact that their educational achievement continues to lag behind that of White students—from the early years through college—highly problematic (Gandara & Contreras, 2009), especially since this lesser achievement impacts their success in the workforce. Consider that community college is an important gateway to higher education for Latino students in California. But even though more Latino students are enrolling in community college than before, their university transfer and completion rates have not improved at anywhere close to the same rate (Solorzano, Acevedo-Gil, & Santos, 2013). Many Latino students find themselves unprepared for college coursework and are hamstrung in developmental education courses. Only 14% of Latinos who enroll in a community college will transfer to a 4-year university, and most will leave community college without a certificate or a degree (Solorzano et al., 2013). An even smaller number will receive a bachelor's degree, only 6% by age 26 (Terriquez, 2012).

There are ways to increase Latino educational achievement. We know that when Latino youth attend well-resourced high schools that offer college preparatory courses, they graduate and enter college at higher rates (Rogers & Freelon, 2012). They also gain important opportunities from mentoring and college advising. And when Latinos do complete college, the labor market returns on this investment are substantial, particularly for Latino males (Ashtiani, Burciaga, & Feliciano, 2013). We just haven't quite figured out how to make this a reality for more Latino students.

Institutions at both the K–12 and higher education levels have launched a variety of initiatives to help Latino students. These are no doubt important but not enough to increase their rate of college entry. We must do better to aid them in completing college. Also, many programs supporting college access and retention for Latino students have fallen short of their desired goals, due mostly perhaps to the fact that they exist within a highly unequal and stratified society in which Latino young people face persistent racism and discrimination. It will take substantial political will and social change to address this unfortunate reality.

Cracks in the Schoolyard—Confronting Latino Educational Inequality provides powerful accounts of the ways in which Latino students achieve despite formidable obstacles. The chapters herein, all written by Latino/a scholars, give insight into the ways in which we can better ensure educational success for Latino students.

The authors in this volume use a critical lens acknowledging racial disparities, a strengths-based approach, and they ground their work in the lived experience of Latino students with their families, in their communities, and within the social institutions they attend. The authors present case studies of educational initiatives, student-led efforts, community-based reforms, and other important topics.

How might we apply what we learn from these cases? First, we must listen to the voices of Latino youth. Within each of these studies, there are important lessons about the lived experience of Latino students and the institutional agents that are attempting to make a difference in their lives. By listening closely, we can learn what helps students achieve their educational goals. The studies also highlight that Latino students in California are a diverse group, with varied backgrounds and life experiences. Understanding the variations in their experiences can enable educators to better plan educational reforms that respond to Latino students' needs and support their success.

Second, if we are to apply the lessons embedded in these cases, we must remember to focus on principles, not just practices (Datnow & Park, 2015). We cannot simply adopt what has worked well in one location and expect it to work in another. We must attend to contextual differences. Many efforts to scale up educational reforms have failed because they have not addressed the fact that reforms must be localized. Each of the studies provides a powerful account of the context in which the efforts to ameliorate the outcomes of Latinos take place, and there are important lessons here about how such efforts may vary in different locations. Improving educational outcomes for Latino students does not just involve implementing a set of innovative practices; it is driven by an important set of principles that can be distilled from these cases.

It is important to underscore that the chapters in this volume are written by Latino scholars who have likely overcome many of the same barriers they write about. In fact, the book begins with Gilberto Conchas, the son of Mexican immigrant farmworkers, describing his own personal journey of persevering in school and ultimately earning degrees and getting positions at top universities in the United States. He credits numerous mentors for helping to pave the path of his success. I have known Gil for the past 20 years of his journey and have witnessed how he has in turn opened doors for students and colleagues in his institutions and elsewhere. The generosity of spirit that he experienced is what he now bestows on others. Gil's research has not only been influential among researchers, but also among practitioners. Through most of his career, he has been committed to working alongside educational practitioners to bridge the gap between research and practice, so that all students have the opportunity to achieve at high levels. This commitment to transformational educational research is also exhibited by the other scholars who wrote chapters for this volume, and it makes the work all the more powerful.

This book will undoubtedly be of substantial value to scholars of Latino education, urban education, sociology of education, and social justice education. But this book is much more than a volume for academics. It is also highly useful for policymakers and practitioners whose goal is to improve education for Latino students—and indeed all students. Quite simply, taken in its entirety, this book is a must-read that can be an important catalyst for educational and social change.

Amanda Datnow

REFERENCES

Ashtiani, M., Burciaga, E., & Feliciano, C. (2013). Labor market outcomes and postsecondary educational attainment of low-income youth (*Pathways to Postsecondary Success, Policy Report, 9*). Retrieved from http://pathways.gseis.ucla.edu/publications/LaborMarkets.pdf

Datnow, A., & Park, V. (2015). Data use for equity. *Educational Leadership, 72*(5), 49–54.

Gandara, P., & Contreras, F. (2009). *The Latino education crisis: The consequence of failed social policies.* Cambridge, MA: Harvard University Press.

Rogers, J., & Freelon, R. (2012). Unequal experiences and outcomes for Black and Latino males in California's public education system (*Pathways to Postsecondary Success, Research Brief, 5*). Retrieved from http://pathways.gseis.ucla.edu/publications/201209_rojersfreelonRB.pdf

Solorzano, D., Acevedo-Gil, N., & Santos, R. (2013). Latino/a community college students: Understanding the barriers of developmental education (*Pathways to Postsecondary Success, Policy Report, 10*). Retrieved from http://pathways.gseis.ucla.edu/publications/DevEdPolicyBrief.pdf

Terriquez, V. (2012). Educational and employment profile of California youth (*Pathways to Postsecondary Success, Research Brief, 4*). Retrieved from http://pathways.gseis.ucla.edu/publications/201207_terriquezRB.pdf

CHAPTER 1

Introduction

Educational Inequality and the Construction of Latina/o Achievement Cases

Gilberto Q. Conchas

So let there be no doubt: The future belongs to the nation that best educates its citizens—and my fellow Americans, we have everything we need to be that nation. We have the best universities, the most renowned scholars. We have innovative principals and passionate teachers and gifted students, and we have parents whose only priority is their child's education. We have a legacy of excellence, and an unwavering belief that our children should climb higher than we did.

And yet, despite resources that are unmatched anywhere in the world, we've let our grades slip, our schools crumble, our teacher quality fall short, and other nations outpace us. . . . And year after year, a stubborn gap persists between how well white students are doing compared to their African American and Latino classmates. The relative decline of American education is untenable for our economy, it's unsustainable for our democracy, it's unacceptable for our children—and we can't afford to let it continue. . . . What's at stake is nothing less than the American Dream.

—President Obama to the Hispanic Chamber of
Commerce Washington, DC, March 10, 2009

I had no need to apologize that the look-wider, search-more affirmative action that Princeton and Yale practiced had opened doors for me. That was its purpose: to create the conditions whereby students from disadvantaged backgrounds could be brought to the starting line of a race many were unaware being run.

—Supreme Court Justice Sonia M. Sotomayor

When it comes to inequality, the United States of America has no equal. When it comes to opportunity, yet again, the United States of America has no equal. Therein lies the contradictory paradox of American society and culture. At the center of this complex dilemma is P–20 public education as the best remaining hope for disenfranchised populations. As President Obama astutely proclaimed to the Hispanic Chamber back in 2009: "And yet, despite resources that are unmatched anywhere in the world, we've let our grades slip, our schools crumble, our teacher quality fall short, and other nations outpace us . . . . And year after year, a stubborn gap persists between how well white students are doing compared to their African American and Latino classmates" (Hispanic Chamber of Commerce, 2009). Today, the American dilemma is the complex and opposing nature of inequality and opportunity that run deep through the majority of institutions in society—namely, in education.

THE BARRIO SCHOOLBOY

My academic and social experiences attest to the complex and contradictory nature of the American dilemma. I am the son of Mexican immigrant farmworkers. I am a "barrio" schoolboy. I am a tenured professor in the University of California. I embody inequality and opportunity.

I was born in East Los Angeles, California, to proud and hardworking parents. My father ventured into unknown territory during the early 1960s as part of the *Bracero* Program—an unjust and exploitative labor policy that brought in low-skilled, low-paid agricultural workers to the United States. His was a life of sweat, toil, and outright discrimination. My mother then followed with my two older brothers as undocumented and unwanted sojourners. However, when I was born in the winter of 1969, immigration policy allowed my family to become legal residents. Legal residents but permanent brown and uneducated foreigners in a raced, classed, and gendered society.

When I was 5 years old, we moved to the pleasant central coast of Ventura, California. Both my father and mother secured employment in the local plant harvesting mushrooms in substandard working conditions. Like my father, my mother worked long hours but was burdened with the second shift. As a woman, she was expected to work outside of the home and within the home. She had the opportunity to work for pay but experienced the harsh reality of a patriarchal society. I vividly remember that on her day off, I would accompany my mother to the local laundromat to wash clothes; we would then shop for groceries, clean the house, and eventually cook. She did not drive and we did not own a washing machine or dryer, so we pushed more than 20 loads of clothes in grocery carts and did the same when we shopped for food. At the time, we were a family of seven. My mother and father never complained.

Both of my parents instilled in me a sense of motivation, high aspirations, and dedication to succeed. My story, however, is not one of resilience. I did not do it alone, for my parents were the institutional agents who, despite limited opportunity, provided me with my first positive sense of social and cultural capital. I eventually met other key institutional structures and agents that further launched my young academic career.

Although my father did not live to hear about my academic work as a sociologist or to see his son as a Harvard professor, as a tenured professor in the University of California, and as a senior program officer with the Bill & Melinda Gates Foundation, my teaching and my research represent my parents' commitment and perseverance for equity and equality. My parents opened the door for me, and my undergraduate experience provided the social scaffolds to acquire and activate the necessary social capital to further expand on the limited opportunities afforded the son of immigrant laborers with plenty of cultural wealth but with limited financial resources.

All of this would not have been possible without the support and guidance I experienced as an undergraduate at the University of California, Berkeley. I was fortunate to have been part of three significant institutional processes that laid the foundation for my eventual matriculation at the University of Michigan's prestigious graduate program in sociology. The first came from living in the Chicano/Latino theme house, Casa Joaquin Murrietta, on the Berkeley campus. At Casa, I was fortunate to have received the structural and cultural aspects of the undergraduate experience that privileged classes all too often take for granted. I was exposed to caring and supportive adults, peer mentoring, cultural activities, and, above all, a safe and high-achieving atmosphere. It was this climate that exposed me to my second and perhaps strongest influence.

Through contacts gleaned from living at Casa, I was introduced to professor of sociology Denise Segura at the University of California, Santa Barbara (UCSB) after my sophomore year. Professor Segura was a good friend with the Casa director, who secured for me an internship at UCSB. The summer program, Summer Academic Research Institute, forever changed my identity. Under the tutelage of Professor Segura, I embraced graduate school and wholeheartedly embraced an identity as a sociologist. One sunny day on the UCSB campus, Professor Segura suggested that I apply for the American Sociological Association's Minority Opportunity Summer Training (MOST). I was chosen to participate in MOST on the Berkeley campus the following summer.

MOST represents the third scaffold during my undergraduate experience. MOST sought to recruit, prepare, and help admit the next generation of graduate students of color into top doctoral programs in sociology. I had the honor to not only work with renowned sociologists like Robert Blauner and Mike Hout, but to be exposed to equally impressive peers. It was not enough to emphasize enrollment, but completion and eventual acquisition of the PhD. To date, Professors Segura, Blauner, and Hout remain my strongest advocates. Moreover, many fellow MOST peers are close colleagues throughout academia. Most of us successfully secured tenure and are well-respected national scholars. Unfortunately, MOST no longer exists.

America is fraught with both inequality and opportunity. I represent that complicated dilemma. My individual determination was not enough to complete college, obtain a PhD, and acquire tenure. I benefited from institutional processes and social policies like Affirmative Action that mediated my engagement and success. As Justice Sonia Sotomayor passionately stated, she did not need to apologize for Affirmative Action policies that created opportunity for her at both Princeton and Yale. It all began with my parents' hard work, the institutional agents, and the various policies along the way that paved the path for me. I too have no need to apologize! This is indeed at the heart of this important volume on Latina/o education—the need to create achievement cases amidst inequality.

CRACKS IN THE SCHOOLYARD

This book is a collection of Latina/o achievement cases in communities and schools. The case study is increasingly becoming essential to the study of educational phenomena and, in particular, schooling systems. This volume provides an understanding of the complexity and diversity of case studies as a method to investigate sensitive and important phenomena in American everyday life. The focus on case studies, per se, is secondary to what the case studies signify—namely, their capacity to illustrate the ways in which inequality and opportunity operate in the communities in question.

Cracks in the Schoolyard—Confronting Latino Educational Inequality challenges deficit models of schooling among Latinas/os and turns school failure on its head. It shows how education can work despite inequality in and outside of the schoolyard. The various achievement cases depict Latinas/os as active actors in the quest for social and economic mobility instead of hopeless victims. These counter-spaces begin to fill the cracks in the schoolyard that create disparity, failure, and marginalization. Therein lies the power and utility of the achievement case model.

Why a focus on California? California, as the most populous and ethnically diverse state in the nation, has been a leader in promoting school policy reform. Over the years, however, Californians have voted against the influx of immigrants, bilingual education, and affirmative action, and states such as Texas, Michigan, Washington, DC, and Arizona—to name a few—have followed California's attempt to change important civil rights policy. In light of the dismantling of affirmative action, education policy desperately needs new ways to increase the college enrollment and academic success of nondominant students—such as low-income, single mothers; boys of color; immigrants; lesbian, gay, bisexual, transgender, and queer (LGBTQ) people; and the undocumented. In this regard, California can once again be a leader and this volume illuminates various examples that tackle educational inequality head on.

POSITIONALITY AND REFLEXIVITY IN RESEARCH
ON LATINA/O EDUCATION

An important component of the role of the researcher in critical research is reflection into the position of the researcher within society and within the research. Key understandings of Latina/o education experiences have come from the explicit questioning of whose perspectives are valued and legitimized through the research process. Insights from Latina/o scholars and Latina/o communities have been an important source of expertise into Latina/o education.

Reflexivity among Latina/o scholars has shed insight into important questions and research dynamics into Latina/o education. One example of this type of research is Villenas and Foley's (2002) review of critical ethnography, where they argued that in order to "reveal oppressive relations of power" researchers must sometimes collaborate with research gatekeepers while simultaneously moving away from scientific notions of detached objectivity in research.

Echoing Anzaldúa's (1999) call for a *mestiza* consciousness that skillfully negotiates multiple borders, Villenas and Foley (2002) described a critical ethnographer's journey as one that straddles academic and working-class Chicano identities. This often means addressing the limitations of being both the colonized and the colonizer (Cordova, 1998; Villenas, 1996). Such tensions are not uncommon in Latina/o education research. Bringing such tensions to the forefront has highlighted the importance of reflexivity through the research process.

Through such research, perspectives of Latina/o researchers have added to important methodological insights. This is in part due to scholars' own exploration of their insider knowledge, subjectivities, and standpoints to formulate new research queries, provide new frameworks for examining the educational experiences of Latina/o students, and reexamine previous assumptions dominant in education research methodologies.

We do not presume that insider status based on ethnic membership alone provides a clearance to make unchecked assumptions about research subjects. Zavella (1996) cautioned against assuming that insider status does not diminish class, education, or identity differences that exist and that may permeate the researchers' interactions with the subjects. Peshkin (1988) offered that it is not sufficient to simply acknowledge researcher subjectivity; it is also important to "systematically identify" subjectivities so that researchers can critically and methodically "attend to it" throughout the research process. Rather, we acknowledge important insights Latina/o scholars can have through the research process. This falls in line with Maxwell's (1996) and Hammersley and Atkinson's (1983) argument that researchers' background and cultural identity offer an acceptable source of theoretical insights and valid interpretations to findings. Indeed, scholars' personal experiences provide a valuable source of methodological developments.

Latina/o scholars are in unique positions to understand the lived experiences of Latina/o students because their own lived experiences have involved negotiating different voices, strategies, and identities for survival in educational institutions

(Anzaldua, 1999; Delgado Bernal, 1998; Gonzales, 1999; Villenas & Foley, 2002). Delgado Bernal (1998) argued that Chicanas have "unique viewpoints that can provide 'cultural intuition.'" This "cultural intuition" derives from personal and professional experiences, existing literature, and the analytical process. For Delgado Bernal (1998), cultural intuition allows Chicanas to draw on their own experiences and form the basis of an epistemology that allows Chicana/o scholars to reclaim their own knowledge.

Moreover, in his book *The Color of Success*, Conchas (2006) similarly disclosed his "subjugated knowledge" when referring to research subjectivity. The following excerpt clearly speaks to his stance as a Chicano social scientist:

> Another issue with which I dealt related to my politics. I chose to concentrate more on programs that best represented the racial and ethnic composition of the school and that made strong steps toward dismantling inequality. I firmly believe that racial inequality must be addressed. Thus, my sympathies lie with the teachers who held similar views. . . . I cannot hide the fact that I was less sympathetic to individuals that maintained the status quo. As a racial minority researcher, I strongly believe that schools should be places of fairness and equal participation. My critical stance, I hope, has allowed me to illuminate agents, those individual and group behaviors, involved in seeking to improve the quality of schooling for urban youth. (p. 127)

Delgado Bernal's (1998) and Conchas's (2006) arguments are pivotal methodological turns because they grant legitimacy to the experiential knowledge of the researcher in developing the research objective, theoretical framework, and methodology of a study when existing paradigms do not capture the nuances of Latina/o educational experiences.

LATINA/O ACHIEVEMENT CASES AROUND THREE THEMES

The methodological developments considered in this volume reveal previously overlooked Latina/os' educational experiences, perspectives, and struggles. We argue that critical methodologies with various origins and diverse applications have the potential to depict and contest the structural oppression often faced by Latina/os in schools and in society. In what follows, we adopt and extend Zarate and Conchas' (2010) critical methodology framework. In so doing, we survey the development of methodologies along three key themes that are particularly important to understanding educational experiences of Latina/o youth.

Theme 1: Centering on Race, Racism, and Inequality

We start with a discussion of the importance of critical methodology in exposing the deeply embedded and often unacknowledged role of race and racism within the U.S. educational system. Frequently, race or ethnicity in education research is a variable or factor to be considered alongside other factors relevant to education experience (Hurtado, Gonzales, & Vega, 1996; Perna, 2000; Portes & Rumbaut, 2001; Saenz, Oseguera, & Hurtado, 2007). For example, in addressing racial differences in access to college, Perna (2000) and Hurtado et al. (1996) used race or ethnicity as a category for which to compare outcomes across racial and ethnic groups. Such an approach focuses on capturing individual-level experiences and "testing" existing theories of access to higher education.

Similarly, Portes and Rumbaut (2001) and Conchas (2006) employed racial and ethnic categories to compare immigrant and U.S.-born youth experiences. In their work, the unit of analysis is also the student, and both used research designs driven by established theoretical frameworks. For Portes and Rumbaut (2001) and Conchas (2006), the theoretical frameworks guiding their work allows them to frame their research within the political landscape of immigration and school hierarchies, respectively. Portes and Rumbaut's (2001) segmented assimilation framework combined with quantitative analysis leads to a discussion of how different immigrant groups socially and psychologically adapt to their immigrant status. Conchas (2006), on the other hand, used an inductive analytical method combined with social capital theory that lends to a discussion of structural and institutional dimensions of students' racialized experiences.

In these examples, comparing outcomes and experiences across immigrant groups captures Latina/o students' learning and schooling experiences differently from other groups. In addition to establishing statistical or empirical differences in outcomes across groups, such differences are then explained as cultural phenomena or the results of policy (Hurtado et al., 1996; Perna, 2000; Portes & Rumbaut, 2001). The authors also provide many references and evidence to suggest that the national status of race relations has a lot to with the predicament of students of color. Although racial differences are remarkable in the studies, the impact of racism as a political or institutional condition is not discussed due to the parameters of a methodology that focuses on documenting individual-level outcomes. Racism, per se, is difficult to capture unless the theoretical framework directly addresses race issues.

Critical Race Theory (CRT) has emerged as a theoretical and methodological instrument that has been useful to centering education research on race and racism. Briefly, proponents of CRT challenge dominant notions of racial progress and color-blind institutions in a commitment toward bringing about a more just society. CRT scholars center the experiential knowledge of peoples of color to expose everyday forms of racial violence, placing these experiences within a collective historical context. Most recently, Latina/o Critical Race Theory (or LatCrit) has emerged to "complement" CRT by including other forms of oppression unique to Latina/os' experiences in its analysis of racism in schools and education.

Methodologies informed by CRT delve head on into issues of race and racism in schools, families, and communities. This perspective has helped shed light on the educational experiences of Latina/o students in higher education (Solorzano & Villalpando, 1998), affirmative action (Aguirre, 2000; Solorzano & Ornelas, 2004), scholars of color in the academy (Solorzano & Yosso, 2001), and student teachers aiming to teach in underrepresented communities (Smith-Maddox & Solorzano, 2002). Critical race theory has also been used alongside concepts such as racial microaggression (Solorzano, Ceja, & Yosso, 2000), marginality (Solorzano & Villalpando, 1998), transformational resistance (Solorzano & Delgado Bernal, 2001), and Freire's problem-posing methodology (Smith-Maddox & Solorzano, 2002) to further understand the impact of overt and subtle forms of racism on Latina/o students and scholars.

A specific methodology that is closely aligned with CRT is counter-storytelling (Aguirre, 2000; Delgado, 2000; Solorzano & Delgado Bernal, 2001; Solorzano & Yosso, 2001), and it is true to the theme of experiential knowledge in CRT. Counter-stories are narratives that can be either autobiographical or composite sketches emanating from research subjects and autobiographical accounts (see Conchas & Vigil, 2012). There is no one single method associated with counter-storytelling. The counter-stories can draw on interviews, observations, historical records, or the researchers' experiences (Aguirre, 2000; Solorzano & Delgado Bernal, 2001; Solorzano & Yosso, 2001). Counter-storytelling is an important methodological contribution to education research because it gives voice to previously suppressed stories or narratives of oppression not captured in educational research. It emphasizes the subjects' standpoint when existing theoretical frameworks do not shed light on racist school culture. Counter-stories with a CRT framework are able to place these alternative narratives explicitly within the context of racist educational practices and institutions.

Much of the educational research using CRT has focused on exposing the unique and racialized educational experiences of students of color. To a lesser extent, CRT has also been employed to explore macro-policy issues, such as anti-affirmative action voter initiatives and the relative unavailability of advanced placement (AP) classes in high schools with high concentrations of Latina/o and African American students (Solorzano & Ornelas, 2004; Taylor, 2000). Research designs that compare racial and ethnic groups using a variety of measurements are valuable to illustrate inequitable access to quality education. However, CRT is a methodological contribution because it moves discourse on racial differences to discussions about racism in institutional practices. Such research has been key to exposing deeply rooted problems within the system that need to be addressed if real change within the system can occur.

Theme 2: Family, Cultural Resources, and Community Strengths

Racism embedded within educational systems has spurred researchers to use critical methodologies to counter deficit notions of Latina/o culture. Historically, the educational attainment levels of Latina/os and other people of color have been explained by cultural deficit frameworks (Conchas, 2001; Valencia, 1997). Latina/o families—and their kin—are often "blamed" for the academic failures of their children. Valencia (1997) and Gándara (1995)

comprehensively reported on this topic over 10 years ago and discussed its eu-
genics roots and its application in explaining low academic achievement among
Latina/os. Although it is not as common to hear blatant denigration of a racial
group in public discourse, it remains acceptable to insidiously blame "Latina/o
culture" for their low academic achievement (Conchas, 2006; Conchas & Vigil,
2012; Rowland, 2007).

We can see many examples of how a deficit framework shapes education agendas. For example, Pearl (1997) argued that some federal programs, such as Head
Start, are based on the premise that Latina/o families are not raising their children
with the "correct" family values. As another example, some college outreach programs assume that Latina/o students do not want to be educated and need to be
convinced of the merits of education. These assumptions exist despite the abun-
dance of evidence that Latina/o parents and students value and aspire to higher
education (Conchas, 2001; Tornatsky, Cutler, & Lee, 2002). Also, support or tolerance for non-English language use in official and school settings in the United
States has ebbed and flowed, depending on popular opinion toward the non-
English speaking group (Dicker, 1996).

Such examples have spurred diverse forms of rich research to expose and
combat this deficit narrative. For one, "funds of knowledge" are conceptualized
by researchers Moll, Amanti, Neff, and Gonzalez (2001) to "refer to the historically
accumulated and culturally developed bodies of knowledge and skills essential for
household or individual functioning and well-being" (p. 133). In their work, the
Latina/o household, therefore, is proposed as a fundamental and necessary source
of cultural knowledge. These important works speak more broadly about the critical methodologies that have been used to counter deficit thinking by excavating
Latina/o families' cultural knowledge and cultural/linguistic and literacy practices
and highlighting these as strengths.

Additionally, in the past 2 decades, ethnographic studies of Latina/o families
have powerfully depicted ways that Latina/o families support education that are
not recognized (or supported) by education systems. This research highlights a
problematic role of the education system, rather than deficits in Latina/o culture.
For example, the concept of *educación* has been posed to explain how Latina/o
parents interface with formal education. Methodologies that have allowed the researcher to depict how Latina/o families view schooling, education, and *educación*
have been a critical development in educational research of Latina/os because it
has highlighted the many ways that Latina/o families support formal education,
albeit in ways that vary from mainstream expectations of parental support (Lopez,
2001; Zarate, 2007).

Common themes of Latina/o family support have been so influential through
this research that Hidalgo (1999) proposed a shift in research paradigms for
studying Latina/o families, where "families, not individuals are placed at the center of the analysis" (p. 108). The family, as the unit of analysis, is then examined
within the social context of the family's experiences, including "ethnic, race, class,
and gender systems of power" (p. 109). According to Hidalgo (1999), the research

then yields an "understanding and interpretation of forms of Latina/o family cultural knowledge grounded in the experiences and adaptations they make" (p. 117).

Delgado-Gaitan (1994) first discussed *consejos* (cultural narratives providing guidance and direction) as practices that often capture the importance of schooling and education.She presented this cultural practice as a problem-solving strategy used by parents to support their children's education, advocate for their children, and instill a sense of independence and self-determination in their children. Perhaps not openly visible to schools or outside observers of Latina/o students, *consejos* are one such example of discursive practices that demonstrate how some Latina/o families are involved in their child's education. Delgado-Gaitan (1994) deliberately examined her observations and interviews with the research subjects from a perspective that acknowledges power hierarchies in schools. By not neutralizing school sites, she could examine parent-school relationships critically and give voice to families' strategies for underscoring the important of education in the household.

Like Delgado-Gaitan (1994), Valdes (1996) and Reese, Balzano, Gallimore, and Goldberg (1995) introduced new concepts that challenge cultural deficit pathologies of Latina/o families. Valdes (1996) introduced one of the most extensive ethnographic studies that sought to document how a group of Latina/o immigrant parents, as the central unit of analysis, participated in their children's education while struggling to survive in a hostile new setting. However, unlike middle-class parents who may engage in academic tasks with their children to advance educational outcomes, the parents in the study used moral teachings, such as *consejos* (advice catered to a specific behavioral objective) and *respeto* (respect) for others, to prepare their children to be worthy individuals in society. In this ethnography, Valdes (1996) deliberately set out to illustrate how Latina/o families participate in education outside the dominant classifications of parental involvement and within unfavorable schooling structures.

Also employing ethnography as a research method, Reese et al. (1995) explored the concept of *educación* in their study of more than 100 Latina/o immigrant families. But rather than compartmentalize *educación* as the moral counterpart to formal education, Reese et al. (1995) described it as an essential aspect of formal education. In dissecting how *educación* is evidenced in the parents' upbringing of their children, the authors found that *educación* permeates every aspect of raising children, including how parents shape their educational aspirations for their children. Unlike Valdes (1996), Reese et al. (1995) did not engage or examine the structural constraints faced by Latina/o families in their interactions with schools. Nonetheless, their ethnographic approach allowed the subjects to challenge mainstream definitions of familial participation in education and weaken prevailing assumptions about Latina/o families' "values."

Both Reese et al. (1995) and Valdes (1996) emphasized that schools should not perceive Latina/o families' values about education and *educación* as necessarily problematic for American schooling practices. Rather, the conflict arises when school policy or practices are ignorant of parenting practices and may design interventions that inadvertently seek to change the families' commitment to moral upbringing. Reese (2001), Reese et al. (1995), and Valdes (1996) all documented the way Latina/o immigrant families seek to adapt familial practices to incorporate American ideas of prosperity, opportunity, and economic demand. Reese (2001) and Valdes (1996) both questioned why schools and U.S. educational practices do not do more to recognize and make use of the value that parents place on *educación* and moral identity. These "how" and "why" questions that directly speak to processes are precisely what quantitative studies are not able to capture, thus rendering a culturally deficient understanding of Latina/o families and educational achievement while ignoring the structural factors that promote inequality.

The results of the studies of Delgado-Gaitan (1994), Reese et al. (1995), and Valdes (1996) have illustrated how some Latina/o cultural practices related to education are undervalued in mainstream educational institutions. This is an important methodological contribution because it shifts blame for deficit educational practices to the institutions and reaffirms Latina/o families' commitment to education.

Many such studies use ethnographic methods for data collection, but they draw from diverse methodological approaches and theoretical frameworks, such as cognitive anthropology, sociocultural reproduction, cultural and social capital, and assimilation theories. To be clear, ethnographies and open-ended interviews alone do not contest dominant and simplistic representations of Latina/o families (Paredes, 1984). Rather, it is a combination of centering Latina/o families in the design of the study and working with families to understand their perspectives. Without the constraints of predefined measurements of family involvement, Delgado-Gaitan (1994), Reese et al. (1995), and Valdes (1996), for instance, help us understand how Latina/o families in their studies experience schooling institutions. The analytical contribution of these studies has been to move away from dominant interpretive lens of school involvement and allow for new paradigms of family–education connections to emerge. The aim is to situate Latina/o families as experts on their experiences and their culture, and to expose problematic deficit models that promote structural and cultural forces of inequity instead of social mobility.

Theme 3: Exploring Ethnicity, Identity, and Immigration

The critical exploration of ethnicity, identity, and immigration has also been important to understand the Latina/o educational experience. Studies examining Latina/o student identities have relied on a variety of methods and research designs to understand how Latina/o students negotiate their status as immigrants or racial minorities (Hurtado, Gonzales, & Vega, 1996; Lopez & Stanton-Salazar, 2001; Portes & Rumbaut, 2001; Zentella, 1997). This research has included both research designs that seek to "test" associations between ethnic identity and educational outcomes as well as research designs that rely on a grounded approach to understand the dynamic nature of ethnic identity (Vigil, 1997; Vila, 2000).

A grounded analytical process allows for an understanding of how ethnic identity is a nuanced and a political reflection of adolescents' lived experiences. Such an approach has also moved us to capture even more labels considered by adolescents. Instead of researchers defining labels a priori, researchers have incorporated the subjects' standpoints and subjectivities to acknowledge the subjects' characterization of various ethnic labels. We argue that both a grounded analysis and incorporation of subjects' standpoints have moved the discussion of ethnic identity forward by pointing out how assimilation or acculturation is not a linear and stepwise process.

Similarly, many theoretical frameworks have been used to interpret the implications of adolescents' ethnic identity on education. A socio-psychological interpretation of Latina/o adolescents' ethnic identity has been used most consistently over the years to understand how immigrant and minority youth adapt to their marginal status in schools or communities (Hurtado, 2003; Lopez & Stanton-Salazar, 2001; Portes & Rumbaut, 2001; Suarez-Orozco & Suarez-Orozco, 1995). Such a perspective has been useful to generalize how individual students negotiate different influences in their identity formation (e.g., family, school culture, or community), and how this can influence their academic success. On the other hand, such an approach limits researcher claims of *how* macro-policy, institutions, and school practices influence students' ethnic identity formation. It is our opinion that postmodern concepts of identity formation have best been able to document how institutions influence the ethnic identity of Latina/os (Torres & Valle, 2000; Vila, 2000). This perspective has been important because it moves the discussion of ethnic identity away from individual interactions to the broader political and cultural climate and captures how public discourse can influence Latina/o students' engagement in schools.

The broader political and cultural climate opens a discussion of Latina/o identity, in recent decades, as tied to the backlash against increased immigration from Latin America and Mexico. This conversation includes a public discourse reflecting a fear of a "cultural invasion" from south of the border. Public debate for and against immigration control has inspired historical and massive public demonstration supporting immigrants and their economic contribution to the nation. Although we have yet to document the impact of this discourse and movements on Latina/o adolescents, we can guess that Latina/o youth will incorporate these public events in their formation of their ethnic identity. For many Latina/o students, their race and ethnic identity has emerged from their own or their parents' immigrant status, public opinions on ethnic minorities, current immigration policy, peer group associations, and many other factors that color students daily experiences. Ethnic identity has been a particularly useful analytical construct for scholars seeking to map the adaptation of immigrant Latina/o youth in the United States and to investigate whether acculturation or assimilation is indeed related to educational attainment of Latina/o youth in the United States (Conchas, 2006; Hurtado, Gonzales, & Vega, 1996; Lopez & Stanton-Salazar, 2001; Portes & Rumbaut, 2001; Vigil, 1997).

A critical and pivotal methodological and epistemological development that has influenced research on Latina/o identity is Anzaldua's (1999) eloquent description of borderlands, *mestiza* consciousness, and *fronteras*. Anzaldua's discussion of Chicano identities resembles Du Bois's (1995) use of "double consciousness" to describe Black identity in a predominantly White nation, and postmodernists' discussions of hybrid identities. However, Anzaldua (1999) placed her discussion of Chicano identity within a historical and geographical context that captures Mexico's and Mexicans' relation(s) to the United States. The *mestiza* consciousness, as Anzaldua (1999) presented it, is the result of living in between and within plural cultures with sometimes contradictory Mexican, indigenous, and U.S. influences. As a result of these experiences, a *mestiza* consciousness allows for greater skill at negotiating boundaries, deconstructing rigid frameworks, and building new paradigms: "She copes by developing a tolerance for contradictions, a tolerance for ambiguity" (p. 79).

According to Anzaldua (1999), a Chicana with a *mestiza* consciousness can critically examine inherited, imposed, and acquired cultures to develop a theoretical framework that captures her experiences as a border crosser. Anzaldua's (1999) hybrid identities, *mestiza* consciousness, and plural feminisms have been useful to educational research because it has (1) moved forward the exploration of hybrid/bicultural/bilingual identity among Latina/o students and beyond assimilationist paradigms of immigrant adaptation, and (2) provided a stepping-stone for addressing methodological concerns regarding the role of the researcher's ethnic identity in education research.

Studies on Latina/o identities have highlighted that Latina/o students must negotiate different worlds and identities in institutions that have historically marginalized their experiences (Conchas, 2001; Hurtado, 2003; Portes & Rumbaut, 2001; Valenzuela, 1999; Vigil, 1997). Studies confirm Anzaldua's argument that a Latina/o identity cannot be captured by rigid categories or spectrums. Ethnic identity is situational, constantly malleable, historically produced, and politically positioned (Anzaldua, 1999; Gonzales, 1997; Hurtado, 2003; Oboler, 1995; Valenzuela, 1999).

ORGANIZATION OF THE ANTHOLOGY

Part I, *Critical Case Studies Centering on Race, Racism, and Inequality*, positions the deeply embedded and often unacknowledged role of race, racism and inequality within the U.S. educational system. In Chapter 2, Gilberto Q. Conchas, Leticia Oseguera, and Isiaah Crawford detail the theoretical underpinnings at play in challenging college students' perceptions by describing an undergraduate course that utilizes service learning in Latina/o communities as a medium for transforming misconceptions about race, racism, and inequality in the United States. In Chapter 3, Nancy Acevedo-Gil examines the racialization processes in school culture, climate, and college choice using critical race theory. In the final chapter of this part—Chapter 4—Irene I. Vega, Leticia Oseguera, and Gilberto Q. Conchas illustrate an achievement case study on race, brotherhood, and educational engagement among Black and Latina/o boys in an urban high school.

Part II, *Critical Case Studies Documenting Family, Cultural Resources, and Community Strengths*, examines research into family, cultural resources, and community strengths that has grown largely out of the need to combat structural inequalities, including racism inherent in the educational system. In Chapter 5, Louie F. Rodriguez foregrounds student voice and community strengths in the use of participatory action research to engage Latina/o student intellectuals in transforming race and school inequality deep in the San Bernardino sun. In Chapter 6, Eduardo Mosqueda and Kip Téllez elevate agency and examine a nontraditional high school's quest to combat marginalization and Mexican immigrant youth failure through the lens of social capital theory. Lastly, in Chapter 7 Alejandra S. Albarran and Gilberto Q. Conchas uncover the role of community-based organizations in Los Angeles in embracing Latina/o parent cultural wealth and empowering them to advocate for their children in and outside of the school context.

Part III, *Critical Case Studies Exploring Ethnicity, Identity, and Immigration*, provides a critical lens into ethnicity, identity, and immigration as an avenue into important perspectives of Latina/o students and communities along three integral components integrally tied to the Latina/o educational experience. In Chapter 8, Cindy Cruz provides a powerful case study of lesbian, gay, bisexual, transgender, and queer homeless youth in a large American city and reframes Latina/o immigrant and U.S.-born youth narratives through a lens of infrapolitics—reimagining what might count as resistance. In Chapter 9, Leo R. Chavez examines postsecondary education and two related factors, Spanish and English language usage and income, among the children of Mexican undocumented immigrants in the greater Los Angeles area. Finally, in Chapter 10, Edelina M. Burciaga draws on months of participant observation of the Coalition for Safer Schools and shows how community members are building a foundation for long-term change in school policies and practices that disproportionately impact youth of color, including undocumented immigrant youth.

Briana M. Hinga and Gilberto Q. Conchas conclude with Chapter 11. The concluding chapter informs ways to understand assets and agency of Latina/o youth, their families, and their communities. Such perspectives counter a deficit perspective on Latina/o youth and thus provide windows into a critical hope toward authentic transformation in the education system beyond the schoolyard. In doing so, the achievement cases in this edited book foster a critical hope toward a more just educational system. Critical hope acknowledges injustice while pushing for transformation—critical hope, in essence, begins to fill the cracks in the schoolyard.

PAVING NEW DIRECTIONS

The following achievement cases highlight needs and promises within Latina/o education through critical methodologies. We hope to have made our point clear:

that transformational education research need not be associated with one method of research only or with a finite set of theoretical frameworks.

This book highlights how different types of methodological approaches can paint a more vivid picture of problems and promises within the system. Research in Latina/o education still has many areas of inquiry left unexplored, and this volume proposes several considerations for scholars to engage in ongoing discussion. We hope that organizing this discussion within the three themes fosters productive understanding, discussion, and movement toward key components of educational experiences for Latina/o youth. The aim is to construct Latina/o achievement cases despite educational inequality.

The case studies in this volume provide a critical examination of the sources and types of inequity that continue to plague disenfranchised populations, as well as the value of the case study method for illuminating the same. In so doing, this volume goes beyond presenting critical case studies of social inequality and education, and (1) takes a rare look at in-school and out-of-school school success stories on a comparative level, instead of those depicting only failure; (2) explores the social and cultural processes that enable Latina/o youth and young adults to escape the unequal structures of public schooling to perform well in school; (3) illuminates how educators and schools can address these issues by becoming increasingly attuned to the sociocultural worlds in which their students live; and (4) paves the way toward overcoming challenges so that historically disadvantaged groups may receive equitable, high-quality educations.

These poignant case studies represent the dismantling of inequality and the struggle to expand opportunity in Latina/o education to generations to come. The achievement cases provide a roadmap toward Latina/o opportunity and success in communities and schools. We believe that the case studies will make you think and hopefully make you act. We ask that you join the journey with us and help us reclaim education as truly the best hope to achieve the American dream.

REFERENCES

Aguirre, A. (2000). Academic storytelling: A critical race theory story of affirmative action. *Sociological Perspectives, 43*(2), 319–339.

Anzaldua, G. (1999). *Borderlands (La frontera): The new mestiza* (2nd ed.). San Francisco, CA: Ann Lute Books.

Conchas, G. (2001). Structuring failure and success: Understanding the variability in Latino school engagement. *Harvard Educational Review 70*(3), 475–504.

Conchas, G. Q. (2006). *The color of success: Race and high-achieving urban youth.* New York, NY: Teachers College Press.

Conchas, G., & Vigil, J. D. (2012). *Streetsmart schoolsmart: Urban poverty and the education of adolescent boys.* New York, NY: Teachers College Press.

Cordova, T. (1998). Power and knowledge: Colonialism in the academy. In C. Trujillo (Ed.), *Living Chicana theory* (pp. 17–44). Berkeley, CA: Third Woman Press.

Delgado, R. (2000). Storytelling for oppositionists and others: A plea for narrative. In

R. Delgado & J. Stefancic (Eds.), *Critical race theory: The cutting edge* (pp. 60–70). Philadelphia, PA: Temple University Press.

Delgado Bernal, D. (1998). Using Chicana feminist epistemology in educational research. *Harvard Educational Review, 68*, 555–581.

Delgado-Gaitan, C. (1994). Consejos: The power of cultural narratives. *Anthropology and Education Quarterly, 25*(3), 298–316.

Dicker, S. J. (1996). *Languages in America: A pluralist view*. Philadelphia, PA: Multilingual Matters Ltd.

Du Bois, W. E. B. (1995). *The souls of Black folk / W.E.B. Du Bois; With a new introduction by Randall Kenan*. New York, NY: New American Library/Signet.

Gándara, P. (1995). *Over the ivy walls: The educational mobility of low-income Chicanos.* Albany, NY: State University of New York Press.

Gonzales, F. E. (1999). Formations of Mexicananess: Trenzas de identidades multiples (Growing up Mexicana: Braids of multiple identities). In L. Parker, D. Deyhle, & S. Villenas (Eds.), *Race is . . . race isn't: Critical race theory and qualitative studies in education* (pp. 125–154). Boulder, CO: Westview Press.

Gonzalez, D. J. (1997). Chicana identity matters. *Aztlan, 22*(2), 124–138.

Hammersley, M., & Atkinson, P. (1983). *Ethnography: Principles in practice.* New York, NY: Routledge.

Hidalgo, N. M. (1999). Toward a definition of Latino family research paradigm. In L. Parker, D. Deyhle, & S. Villenas (Eds.), *Race is . . . race isn't: Critical race theory and qualitative studies in education* (pp. 101–124). Boulder, CO: Westview Press.

Hispanic Chamber of Commerce. (2009). Remarks of the President to the United States Hispanic Chamber of Commerce. Retrieved from https://www.whitehouse.gov/the-press-office/remarks-president-united-states-hispanic-chamber-commerce.

Hurtado, A. (2003). *Voicing Chicana feminisms: Young women speak out on sexuality and identity.* New York, NY: New York University Press.

Hurtado, A., Gonzales, R., & Vega, L. (1996). Social identification and the academic achievement of Chicano students. In R. Figueroa, E. Garcia, & A. Hurtado (Eds.), *Latino eligibility study* (pp. 57–73). Santa Cruz, CA: University of California.

Lopez, G. (2001). The value of hard work: Lessons on parental involvement from an (im) migrant household. *Harvard Educational Review, 71*(3), 416–437.

Lopez, D. E., & Stanton-Salazar, R. D. (2001). Mexican Americans: A second generation at risk. In R. G. Rumbaut & A. Portes (Eds.), *Ethnicities: Children of immigrants in America* (pp. 57–90). Berkeley, CA: University of California Press.

Maxwell, J. A. (1996). *Qualitative research design: An interpretive approach.* Thousand Oaks, CA: Sage Publications.

Moll, L., Amanti, C., Neff, D., & Gonzalez, N. (2001). Funds of knowledge for teaching: Using a qualitative approach to connect homes and classrooms. *Theory Into Practice, XXXI*(2), 132–141.

Oboler, S. (1995). *Ethnic labels, Latino lives: Identity and the politics of (re)presentation in the United States.* Minneapolis, MN: University of Minnesota Press.

Paredes, A. (1984). On ethnographic work among minority groups: A folklorists perspective. In R. Romo & R. Paredes (Eds.), *New directions in Chicano scholarship* (pp. 1–31). Santa Barbara, CA: Center for Chicano Studies.

Pearl, A. (1997). Cultural and accumulated environmental deficit models. In R. R. Valencia (Ed.), *The evolution of deficit thinking: Educational thought and practice* (pp. 211–240). London, England: The Falmer Press.

Perna, L. W. (2000). Differences in the decision to attend college among African Americans, Hispanics, and Whites. *The Journal of Higher Education, 71*(2), 117–141.

Peshkin, A. (1988). In search of subjectivity—one's own. *Educational Researcher, 17*(7), 17–21.

Portes, A., & Rumbaut, R. G. (2001). *Legacies: The story of the immigrant second generation.* Berkeley, CA: University of California Press.

Reese, L. (2001). Morality and identity in Mexican immigrant parents' visions of the future. *Journal of Ethnic and Migration Studies, 27*(3), 455–472.

Reese, L., Balzano, S., Gallimore, R., & Goldberg, C. (1995). The concept of *educación*: Latino family values and American schooling. *International Journal of Educational Research, 23*(1), 57–61.

Rowland, K. (2007, August 18). Successful on the field, not so in the classroom. *News Register.* Retrieved from http://www.newsregister.com/news/results.cfm?story_no = 225178

Saenz, V. B., Oseguera, L., & Hurtado, S. (2007). Losing ground? Exploring racial/ethnic enrollment shifts in freshman access to selective institutions. In G. Orfield, P. Marin, S. M. Flores, & L. M. Garces (Eds.), *Charting the future of college affirmative action: Legal victories, continuing attacks, and new research* (pp. 79–104). Los Angeles, CA: University of California, Los Angeles, The Civil Rights Project.

Smith-Maddox, R., & Solorzano , D. G. (2002). Using critical rate theory, Paulo Freire's problem-posing method, and case study research to confront race and racism in education. *Qualitative Inquiry, 8*(1), 66–83.

Solorzano, D. G., Ceja, M., & Yosso, T. (2000). Critical race theory, racial microaggressions, and campus racial climate: The experiences of African American college students. *The Journal of Negro Education, 69*(1/2), 60–73.

Solorzano, D. G., & Delgado Bernal, D. (2001). Examining transformational resistance through a critical race theory and LatCrit theory and framework: Chicano and Chicana students in urban context. *Urban Education, 36*(3), 308–342.

Solorzano, D. G., & Ornelas, A. (2004). A critical race analysis of Latin and African American advanced placement enrollment in public high schools. *High School Journal, 87*, 15–26.

Solorzano, D. G., & Villalpando, O. (1998). Critical race theory: Marginality and the experience of students of color in higher education. In *Sociology of education: Emerging perspectives* (pp. 211–224). Albany, NY: State University of New York Press.

Solorzano, D. G., & Yosso, T. (2001). Maintaining social justice hopes within academic realities: A Freirean approach to critical race/LatCrit pedagogy. *Denver University Law Review, 78*(4), 595–621.

Suarez-Orozco, C., & Suarez-Orozco, M. M. (1995). *Transformations: Immigration, family life, and achievement motivation among Latino adolescents.* Palo Alto, CA: Stanford University Press.

Taylor, E. (2000). Critical race theory and interest convergence in the backlash against affirmative action: Washington State and Initiative 200. *Teachers College Records, 102*(3), 539–560.

Tornatsky, L. G., Cutler, R., & Lee, J. (2002). *College knowledge: What Latino parents need to know and why they don't know it.* Los Angeles, CA: Tomas Rivera Policy Institute.

Torres, R. D., & Valle, V. M. (2000). *Latino metropolis.* Minneapolis, MN: University of Minnesota Press.

Valdes, G. (1996). *Con respeto: Bridging the distances between culturally diverse families and schools.* New York, NY: Teachers College Press.

Valencia, R. R. (Ed.). (1997). *The evolution of deficit thinking: Educational thought and practice.* London: The Falmer Press.

Valenzuela, A. (1999). *Subtractive schooling: U.S.–Mexican youth and the politics of caring.* Albany, NY: State University of New York Press.

Vigil, D. (1997). *Personas Mexicanas: Chicano high schoolers in a changing Los Angeles.* Orlando, FL: Harcourt Brace and Company.

Vila, P. (2000). *Crossing borders, reinforcing borders: Social categories, metaphors, and narrative identities on the U.S.-Mexico frontier.* Austin, TX: University of Texas Press.

Villenas, S. (1996). The colonizer/colonized Chicana ethnographer: Identity, marginalization, and co-optation in the field. *Harvard Educational Review, 66*(4), 711–731.

Villenas, S., & Foley, D. E. (2002). Chicano/Latino critical ethnography of education: Cultural productions from la frontera. In *Chicano school failure and success: Past, present, and future* (2nd ed., pp. 195–225). London, England: Routledge/Falmer.

Zarate, M. E. (2007). *Understanding Latino parental involvement in education.* Los Angeles, CA: Tomas Rivera Policy Institute.

Zarate, M. E., & Conchas, G. G. (2010). Contemporary and critical methodological shifts in research on Latino education. In E. G. Murillo, S. A. Villenas, R. T. Galván, J. S. Muñoz, C. Martínez, & M. Machado-Casas (Eds.), *Handbook of Latinos and education: Theory, research, and practice* (pp. 90–107). New York, NY: Routledge.

Zavella, P. (1996). Feminist insider dilemmas: Constructing identity with "Chicana" informants. In D. L. Wolf (Ed.), *Feminist dilemmas in fieldwork.* Boulder, CO: Westview.

Zentella, A. C. (1997). *Growing up bilingual: Puerto Rican children in New York.* Malden, MA: Blackwell.

PART I

CRITICAL CASE STUDIES CENTERING ON RACE, RACISM, AND INEQUALITY

College Student Perspectives on Racial Inequality and Opportunity in Latina/o Communities

Exploring the Role of Multicultural Curriculum and Service Learning at a Large Public University

Gilberto Q. Conchas, Leticia Oseguera, & Isiaah Crawford

Success comes with the support systems that are available to help a person succeed. Certain communities have more support systems both inside the school and in the home. Schools in LAUSD that are primarily Latina/o and African American have far less resources than schools of affluent areas. Family situations—students worried about their home stability, taking care of younger siblings, etc.—takes a toll on a student's success vs. a student who has to focus solely on getting good grades.

—College student

Though their educational experiences are currently facing massive budget cuts that take away, as the school site coordinator put it, "basic necessities," the kids were trying their best with the given resources. Their families cannot provide them with economic resources to send them to school with supplies. [The service-learning site coordinator] also added that kindergarten was always the first to receive budget cuts, and soon it might not even be mandatory.

—College student

College students are potentially the next generation of leaders to take on the social responsibility of changing public opinion about the causes and effects of inequality in the United States. Challenging college students' (mis)conceptions about class, culture, and race can be a daunting but important and necessary task. This chapter details the theoretical underpinnings at play in challenging students' perceptions by describing an undergraduate course that uses service learning in Latina/o communities as a medium for transforming misconceptions about inequality in the United States. In this chapter, we argue that in order to invoke real change in the perceptions and experiences of undergraduate students in a large and diverse university regarding social inequality and education among Latina/os, a well-structured articulation of curriculum that challenges the status quo, with the simultaneous implementation of service-learning goals, is necessary.

Despite efforts from government entities, school systems, and political activists to improve the conditions of disadvantaged and ethnic minority groups, social inequality remains abundantly pervasive. In the United States, inequality is especially rampant in the educational arena. However, the underlying causes for inequality have long been equated to ethnic cultural differences or, rather, a resistance to cultural assimilation. Recent research argues that social inequality can be more holistically explained through structural barriers (Chavez, 2008; Conchas, 2006; Feliciano, 2006; Lee, 1996; Noguera, 2003; Perez, 2009; Vigil, 2002). Such structural barriers that prevent upward mobility for ethnic and marginalized groups include unequal access to educational resources, low socioeconomic status, citizenship and immigration status, neighborhood demographics, historical factors, social relationships in and out of schools, developmental factors, and family dynamics, often are dismissed by the general public as a reason for social inequality. Moreover, the general public attributes social inequality to their own perceptions based on limited interactions with other cultures and media portrayals of different ethnic minority populations. Transforming public opinion about the roots of social inequality is needed in order to enact policies and practices that will support the psychosocial development of disadvantaged and marginalized students.

The audiences that need the most objective and researched guidance are college undergraduates who come in with preconceived notions of how the world is and ought to be—often from privileged positions in society. College students are potentially the next generation of leaders, and challenging and complicating their (mis)conceptions can be a daunting but an important and necessary task. This chapter details the theoretical underpinnings at play in complicating these perceptions by describing an undergraduate course that uses service learning in low-income Latina/o communities as a medium for change. The chapter applies text analysis to students' writings about their service-learning experiences as a means to assess undergraduate student perceptions on inequality and opportunity in America.

The students were asked at the beginning of the course why they were taking the course, and a pre-reflection on their views on educational inequality was collected. Many students believed that the Latina/o culture explained educational achievement and thus the goal of the course was to transform students' beliefs about race, culture, inequality, and school success. Throughout the course, lectures, readings, and documentaries allowed students to critically reflect and compare the ideas with their experiences in their field placement. However—as evidenced in their essays and in-class discussions—many students still explained the achievement/opportunity gap through negative cultural representations. Thus, the fact that the course's goals were not met for all of the students indicates that more needs to be done throughout the learning process.

We therefore argue that in order to invoke real change in the perceptions and experiences of undergraduate students in a large and diverse university regarding social inequality and education among Latina/os, a well-structured articulation of curriculum that challenges the status quo and the implementation of service-learning goals is necessary. This has tremendous implications for the creation of diverse leaders who embrace a racially just society.

THEORIES OF SOCIAL CHANGE AND SERVICE LEARNING

A proposed remedy to the narrow view of inequality as a consequence of an ethnic group's culture is service learning. Service learning in higher education institutions aims to integrate the surrounding community into classroom discourse by providing students with an opportunity to apply course content to authentic tasks that mutually benefit both the community and student (Deeley, 2010). Service learning also has other benefits such as fostering civic engagement and reducing the perpetuation of stereotypes (Schmidt, Marks, & Derrico, 2004). The student has to be careful not to become paternalistic or equate community-based learning as charity (Peterson, 2009). Approaching the communities in which they will work or serve with deficit notions of need within the community will undermine, if not prevent, their learning. Learning occurs through reflective practices that lead students to examine their belief systems and the social cultural forces that have shaped their attitudes and behaviors. Without reflection, transformation of thinking cannot occur (Ethridge & Branscomb, 2009).

Masucci and Renner (2001) argued that when service learning is part of the curriculum, four components must be present to make it an effective educational tool: (1) pre-reflection on reasons for taking the course, (2) taking action in the surrounding communities, (3) immersion in social theory, and (4) critical reflections on experiences in the course. Other purposes for service learning are to enact change in perceptions and to engender a willingness to continue to participate in civic engagement as a lifelong practice. It is hoped that through the service-learning experience students will be motivated to continue their work in the community and broadly promote the pursuit of social justice.

The type of reflection a student undertakes will determine the amount of deep learning that will occur through service-learning coursework. Sporadic reflection that does not require the student to engage in critical thinking does not provide enough structure to lead to learning. However, questions and inquiries that require students to synthesize and cite specific evidence for their beliefs and perspectives lead to transformative thought (Ash & Clayton, 2004; Gutiérrez, 2002). Moreover, the ways students participate in their service-learning projects also contribute to their learning. Passive participants or observers gain very little insight beyond what they see. The more active participants who engage in the work at their sites are more apt to theorize the connections between their service learning and their course materials (Kronick, 2007).

The nuances in participants' attributions of their statements to their experiences with their service-learning experience are also significant. Through a triangulation model of student-agency-adult, students reflect on their service-learning experiences in contrast or comparison to the knowledge they are being encouraged to learn and critique. The way in which students attribute their experiences to refute or support their claims based on course ideas is also significant. Students who are enrolled in the same classroom with a service-learning component, we argue, conceptualize the concept of inequality in a specialized way. They become a community of interest that develops its own specialized way of knowing and doing (Collins & Halverson, 2009). Thus, they create a common way of seeing and noticing. They participate in

> discursive practices [that] are used by members of a profession to shape events in the domains subject to their professional scrutiny. The shaping process creates the objects of knowledge that become the insignia of a profession's craft: the theories, artifacts, and bodies of expertise that distinguish it from other professions. (Goodwin, 1994, p. 606)

In this case, their profession is that of a critical and active member of a course conducting preliminary research on social inequality or action in educational settings—as we term it, "a socio-educational researcher."

The students are asked to craft a "professional vision lens" via classroom materials, discussions, and service learning in an attempt to articulate this vision in reflective practices such as journals, essays, and service-learning notes. These practices, expressed in Goodwin's professional vision parlance include: (1) highlighting or calling attention to specific instances of inequality or unjust educational practices in a contextually sensitive and constructive manner, (2) coding or articulating the observations and instances with the correctly applied terms of the sociologist/educational researcher, and (3) ultimately communicating or representing the observations in a manner and style consistent with socio-educational research and theory.

Thus, the professional vision framework provides another theoretical concept from which to view and analyze student-generated documents, such as essays, in an effort to address their developing professional vision as observers of socio-educational events—in effect, they are developing a socio-educational vision. The professional vision construct is based on practice theory (Bourdieu, 1977; Chaiklin & Lave, 1993; Hanks, 1987; Lave & Wenger, 1991) and activity theory (Duranti & Goodwin, 1992; Gutiérrez, 2002; Vygotsky, 1978) and includes the "field of conversation analysis [which] has developed the most powerful resources currently available for the analysis of the interactive organization of emerging action with actual settings" (Goodwin, 1994, p. 629). Together, these concepts provide a context from which social practices can be examined.

Professional vision analysis organizes the activities of professional fields by analyzing three practices: highlighting, coding, and producing and articulating material representations. Goodwin (1994) used the fields of archeology and law to demonstrate the use of the respective highlighting, coding, and representations in those fields. These three practices are an inherent part of many college-level courses when viewing the undergraduate process as professional development for emerging professionals within education or sociology. As such, evaluation of the students (emerging socio-educational professionals) can demonstrate their developing professional vision and thus will be reflected in a summative assessment as a representation of their experiences. These essays, as a summative assessment, need not agree or challenge the instructor's or the sociological theories on the educational culture, but should model the professional vision demonstrated in the course by effectively highlighting, coding, and representing their experiences consistent with a professional vision as presented throughout the course.

Course term papers or essays are the summative assessment of choice in most college classes. We argue that the reasons or attributions for statements students make about any concept, such as inequality, further give insight into the students' conceptualization of why the concept matters (i.e., why social inequality exists). Moreover, when making attributions about negative experiences, college students tended to lay the blame on external factors outside of their locus of control (Morewedge, 2009). When put in a situation where the participants lost in a game of cards but expected to win, participants attributed their losses to external factors. When they expected to win at the game and succeeded in doing so, they attributed the accomplishment to internal causes such as strategy, knowledge of the game, and good decisionmaking. Much in the same way, students who view their field experiences negatively may attribute the concept of social inequality to cultural bias, though a pervasive part of life, as outside the control of the after-school program. Whereas those who participated and viewed their field experiences as a refutation of the common notion of race as a reason for social inequality attribute success to factors that are controllable such as student motivation, engaging curriculum, staff self-efficacy, and parent involvement. The following will critically examine the ways undergraduate students conceptualize Latina/o school inequality and what they attribute as to its origins.

THE COURSE AND LEARNING PROCESS

Drawing on Masucci and Renner's (2001) service-learning framework and Goodwin's (1994) concept of professional vision, the authors will describe how a multicultural education course with a service-learning component centered on social inequality fared. The two salient questions that shape this study on service learning are: (1) How do university students explain social inequality and education in their reflective essays? and (2) How did their service-learning experiences contribute to their reasons for explaining why some ethnic minority children do well in school and others do not?

This multieducational undergraduate course has been offered at a large and diverse Research I university in southern California for 6 years. The course syllabus outlines the purpose of the course as the following:

> The purpose of this course is to addresses how demographic, economic, historical, political, and social forces impact race and ethnic populations with respect to their performance in schools. Particular emphasis will be placed on understanding the educational plight of low-income Asian Americans, African Americans, and Chicano/Latina/os in urban school contexts. The experiences of these groups in schooling and their attempts to gain social mobility will be critically assessed. The aim is to examine how structures of domination and subordination are reproduced and resisted through the "cultural practices" of distinct student populations. Special attention is given to the transformative practices that enable students to dismantle inequality and struggle for a more democratic society.

The course further challenges students by requiring them to participate in after-school programs in a neighboring Latina/o community for a total of 20 hours over the span of 8 weeks. At the beginning of the quarter, students were asked to reflect on why they took the course and their initial thoughts on education and inequality.

At the end of the quarter the students were asked to reflect on their experiences both in the field and the classroom in the form of an essay that addresses the following concepts related to the course: (1) the identification of factors that shape inequality in schools, and (2) the integration of their service-learning experiences with the socio-educational theories they were exposed to during the course to frame discussion points. Based on these prompts, the students create a final essay that attempts to integrate the three concepts of inequality, service learning, and theory into one cohesive reflective product.

The students in this study were a "particular social group," all of whom were, by virtue of their enrollment in this course, in training to become socio-educational observers. The objective of the course was, through the use of literature, lecture, and a service-learning placement, to develop a socio-educational professional vision of multicultural education. They were assigned to read seven books that put forth an argument that structural barriers are more likely the reason for social inequality than supposed ethnic cultural differences. The students were also assigned to service-learning placements in various Latina/o communities; these placements were organized by a large after-school community-based agency in order to observe and witness the *in vivo* socio-educational process discussed in lecture and addressed in the readings. During these placements, the students would hopefully encounter the salient phenomenon that would illustrate the concepts discussed in the course. The last of the three practices unique to the professional vision construct is the "producing and articulating of the material representation"—that is, students' term papers serve as a demonstration of their ability to communicate as a professional socio-educational observer through their written reflections.

Most of the literature in the field of service learning, and the process of discernment associated with it, connects student reflections to their experiences in the field (Ash & Clayton, 2004; Kronick, 2007). This chapter aims to contribute to this methodology by including the third component of classroom discourse and materials to better triangulate data. Moreover, the consideration of Goodwin's professional vision to theorize what students learned from this service-learning course is also a new way to approach these data as they collectively form a codified way of viewing social inequality. Students were given the essay assignment at the beginning of the quarter. They had approximately 5 weeks to write, edit, and submit the paper.

More than 400 student essays were collected over the course of 2 years—the students were diverse with respect to ethnicity, SES, and gender; however, the majority of students were Asian (40%) and Caucasian (25%), but the placements were in predominantly low-income Latina/o communities. All essays were de-identified by a member of the research team not involved in the courses. For this study, a total of 55 essays were randomly selected from the larger sample. All authors read the essays in detail for contextual purposes. From the sample of 55 essays, a random number generator selected 14 of the de-identified essays for deep discourse analysis.

We applied text analysis guided by the professional vision lens that allowed for ideas and themes to emerge (Merriam, 2009; Patton, 2002). Following field conventions, a core category or conceptual framework was discovered by constant comparison among the sample of papers and study authors and by theoretical sampling by looking at different parts of the essays. The data were also analyzed using content-categorical methods to identify common themes (Lieblich, Tuval-Mashiach, & Zilber, 1998). As essays were examined, sentences that related to student service learning or related to concepts in class were identified.

CO-CONSTRUCTING STUDENT THEMES

We read each essay and identified themes by applying content-categorical analysis methods. It was understood that themes could be at the sentence level or at the paragraph level. If a theme was the topic within the essay or was highlighted by the student, the highlighted theme was noted for analysis. All themes presented by each student were identified for each essay. Compiling the unique list from each essay into a pooled theme list generated a total list of themes. The total pool consisted of 56 themes from which 20 distinct highlighted themes were identified in the sample of essays (see Figure 2.1 for a complete table of the identified themes).

**Figure 2.1. Overall Themes in Sample (Number of
Essays Discussing Theme in Parentheses)**

1. After-School Programs (1)
2. **Culture (5)**
3. Deficit Thinking (3)
4. Gender (3)
5. Homework (4)
6. Hyper-segregation (1)
7. **Inequality (6)**
8. Language Barriers (4)
9. **Limited Resources (7)**
10. Media (3)
11. Parent Involvement (1)
12. Physical Space (3)
13. Professional Youth Development (3)
14. Race (4)
15. **Social Capital (6)**
16. Structural Barriers (1)
17. Student Engagement (1)
18. Urban School (1)
19. Violence (1)
20. **Deficit Thinking (5)**

Each student's discussion of a theme counted only once for each subject, and a total count over the 14 selected essays yielded a theme count that ranged from a single theme being mentioned across seven essays down to individual themes uniquely referenced in a single essay. The top five themes mentioned in the sample are identified below for analysis (and appear in bold in Figure 2.1).

The most prevalent themes identified in the sample of essays were Limited Resources (7 highlighted themes), Social Capital (6 hightlighted themes), Inequality (6 highlighted themes), Deficit Thinking (5 highlighted themes), and Culture (5 highlighted themes). Other themes (N = 15) were also identified, but there were not enough instances to determine whether they were consistent throughout most of the essays.

Limited Resources

Looking specifically at the theme of Limited Resources, seven of the essays mentioned this theme. Essays that addressed this theme were specifically highlighting instances in their field placements where a significant poverty of material resources was noted that impacted the students served in the field placement. Some of the essays described Limited Resources in relation to the instructional materials made available to the students receiving services/education at the field placement sites.

> Though the homework [assignment sheets] had many pictures, some of the pictures were disadvantagedly [sic] copied, resulting in an amorphous blob or the homework contained directions in a miniscule font on the side next to the staple. Sometimes the homework contained no directions at all. Disadvantagedly [sic] designed or mass-produced copies such as these only hinder the students, who do not know what they are doing, how they should do it, or what they are supposed to be learning. (Essay 105)

Essay 105 described the copied homework ditto in detail to highlight how this can be perceived as inadequate resources at the school site, which was also connected to student failure. So although this student focused on resources for activities done at the after-school program, other students wrote about Limited Resources in relation to general activities that involved having basic school supplies.

> Though their educational experiences are currently facing massive budget cuts which take away, as the school site coordinator put it, "basic necessities," the kids were trying their best with the given resources. Their families cannot provide them with economic resources to send them to school with supplies. [The coordinator] also added that kindergarten was always the first to receive budget cuts, and soon it might not even be mandatory. (Essay 154)

The economic resources of the family unit were mentioned, as well as the school's dependency on the federal government to provide funding for "basic necessities." There exists then a strong connection between the family and school as partners in providing students with adequate resources.

Another way Limited Resources was operationalized was through the physical description of the schools.

> The state of "Field Placement A" is in fair condition; the school is aged, small, and without modernized classrooms. Field Placement A is located in X, which is not a wealthy area. In Granada's lecture, he speaks of the capitalist economy and how the economic recession is impacting Chicano families and their children. He contends that education reform is required since these institutions are being used for business than for the needs of the children. (Essay 180)

Again, the student described the school to communicate that students attending Field Placement A are functioning under Limited Resources due to the condition of the school buildings. Moreover, the student was able to connect what occurred at the site to a theory lecture that was given during the course. Each of the seven essays used examples from their field experiences to explain the connection between school successes to the amount of resources that were available, or rather for most of them, not available. One essay also pointed out students who took the resources for granted.

Social Capital

The theme of Social Capital was highlighted in six of the essays. Unlike the Limited Resources theme, which was illustrated within the essays when discussing field placement activities, the theme of Social Capital was distributed within the essays sometimes relating to the course lecture or reading material and connected sometimes with placement activities. The overall manner in which Social Capital was contextualized involved family, nonfamilial ties, institutions, social context/networks, and language.

Essay 115 had Social Capital as an identified theme but only discussed this theme when providing background and support. This essay did not connect the highlighted theme of Social Capital back to experiences in the field. This lack of connection between the highlighted concept and the field experiences makes a good argument for how sometimes students know that a given topic is significant and worthy of discussion in a paper but their ability to integrate the topic with the activity is weak or, perhaps, there may not have been opportunities to see the concept actualized in the field. Essay 115 focused on both families and social networks as resources for students to draw upon as examples of Social Capital.

> Social capital is a sociological concept used in business, economics, organizational behavior, political science, public health and the social sciences in general to refer to connections within and between social networks. Though there are a variety of related definitions, which have been described as "something of a cure-all" for the problems of modern society, they tend to share the core idea "that social networks have value." (Essay 115)

By providing a definition of what Social Capital is (albeit incomplete), Essay 115 attempted to explain how pervasive this construct is, at the same time acknowledging its value. In contrast to Essay 115, Essay 162 integrated the Social Capital theme with experiences in the field and attributed social institutions as purveyors of such a construct.

> As evidence of [the] Professor['s] thesis, [the Homework Club from the field placement activity] increases the level of social capital available to these students, and in turn increases their likelihood for success . . . . Coaches for several of the school's sports . . . are requiring their students to attend the Homework Club on a consistent basis. (Essay 162)

Here, Essay 162 highlighted the important role social or public institutions play in providing students with positive role models or positive relationships with adults and the eventual acquisition of Social Capital. Essay 180 also pointed out the significance of this role and provided teachers, friends, and school officials with examples of positive social networks and ways of using them to succeed.

With the essay prompt devoid of any mention of the theme of Social Capital, its presence in the papers represents a more accurate representation of an incidence of professional vision. When coding, these students are participating in a "systematic practice used to transform the world into categories and events that are relevant to the work of the profession" (Goodwin, 1994, p. 608). Their essays code for Social Capital because they have used that to categorize what they saw happening in their field placements and what they understood from their lectures.

In reference to the course's socio-educational definition of Social Capital, many of the students referenced the pre-migration status of parents or the socioeconomic status of the family as a source for Social Capital. Other students connected Social Capital to institutions, networks, peers, and nonfamily connections. Essay 115 gave almost a textbook definition of Social Capital from the course:

> Social capital is a sociological concept used in business, economics, organizational behavior, political science, public health and the social sciences in general to refer to connections within and between social networks. . . . Social capital is the benefits obtained through relationships and social networks. (Essay 115)

Here the student coded the term, referencing other fields that also code the term in a similar way. The student then went on to explain how social capital is at play in the field placement when parents are mentioned as either a source of Social Capital or its absence. In all instances, the students explained how Social Capital is defined and applied this definition to their experiences.

Inequality

Inequality was also highlighted in six of the essays. Inequality was interesting in that it was expressly identified and queried as part of the essay prompt. Inequality as a theme was equally distributed between the supporting material and the service-learning experience illustrations of the essays. Specific references to Inequality provided representations that ranged from citing lack of evidence to referencing unequal resources in terms of access to people and spaces.

The writer of Essay 154 stated, "Inequality is created due to low teacher's expectations which unmotivated student[s] are discouraged by." The connection between the course literature and the field experience is the function of the sentence and the highlighted theme. This occurrence is in direct contrast with Essay 151, where a paragraph's topic sentence asserted, "There is a correlation between inequality and education" and then continued on a totally theoretical discussion of the inequalities with no reference or connection to their field experiences. Either way, both students highlighted the theme of Inequality in their essays—albeit in profoundly different ways (the former focused on access to people, and the latter focused on access to spaces). Both were consistent with the broad parameters of the assigned essay. Two students (Essay 138 and Essay 163) both stated that their field experiences refuted the notion of Inequality.

In addition, the following sentence from an essay included in its description the specific theme of Inequality from a socio-educational perspective:

> Moreover, insufficient teacher attention adds to the *inequality* reproduced in disadvantaged communities. (Essay 154, paragraph highlighted Limited Resources and coded for Inequality)

This student used the Inequality theme to explain why the students in the service-learning site have limited social capital that can lead to social reproduction of current conditions.

Deficit Thinking

Deficit Thinking was mentioned in five essays. Many students took away from the lecture a definition of Deficit Thinking that is evident across all of the papers that coded for Deficit Thinking. In this context, "*Deficit thinking* entails that the behavior of a student demonstrates the values of how the child truly is" (Essay 180). Other essays also focused on Deficit Thinking as connecting behavior to value. There were some differences in the way these students coded for this concept. Two of the papers focused on the actions of adults/professionals who held these convictions at the field site.

> The counselors came to class and explained some opportunities to get a head start in getting information about college. There was a college convention at the city convention center and there was bus transportation available. At first I thought this was a great idea until they said, "I know that none of you want to go." I thought this could not be any clearer to being *deficit thinking*. (Essay 160)

> Teachers are most often at blame for using *deficit thinking*. They too often assume that kids have problems or are a problem and decide to just give up on the students because "there is nothing [they] can do for them." (Essay 175)

The student from Essay 160 witnessed Deficit Thinking enacted by a counselor at the school when it came to promoting a college-going culture. The student from Essay 175 described the actor most likely to think of his or her students as unwilling learners who have strayed too far to be helped. Other ways Deficit Thinking was contextualized focused on the direct link between student behavior and how adults in the field perceived them, whereas another paper mentioned it to link to Professional Youth Development. Lastly, another essay used Deficit Thinking to rationalize why the field site made certain decisions regarding enrollment.

> While I never found out what happened to her, I find this particular case to be noteworthy because of the many socio-ecological problems with teachers and unruly

students who are recommended for medication or greater discipline. It is possible that the student was removed from the program on the basis of disruptive behavior, which seems to fall in line with [the guest lecturer] (2009) presentation on "*Deficit Thinking.*" (Essay 105)

Here the student focused on how Deficit Thinking may be at play when programs decide to bar a student from attending an after-school program; however Deficit Thinking was referenced, the students all connected the concept to their service-learning experiences.

The examples of the Deficit Thinking theme that have been highlighted demonstrate the ability of classroom discourse to create a codified way for students to view and describe their service-learning experiences. The results demonstrated quite clearly that the course motivated students to examine their placement experiences through a socio-educational lens.

Culture

The final distinctive theme from the sample is Culture. Five student essays were found to have focused on Culture in several notable ways; however, unlike Inequality and Social Capital, this theme was purely rooted in their field experiences, similar to the theme of Inequality. One student (Essay 176) spoke about the construct of Culture in the context of the after-school program as having both positive and negative effects.

> To draw parallels between the Colombian dance group and the 3rd grade class, the 3rd graders (except one) all shared a Latina/o background with a common goal of bettering their education. Therefore, they rarely fought with one another and were very willing to help each other. (Essay 176)

> On one occasion several of the students in the 3rd grade class asked me to read some Chinese characters they saw in a library book. I explained to them that I could not read it because I am Vietnamese. One of the boys asked me what "a Vietnamese" was while the rest insisted I was lying. . . . I attribute this lack of cultural awareness to a number of reasons. One reason is that society lumps diverse Asian ethnicities into one racial group. (Essay 176)

This student was able to explain how Culture can be an isolating construct but can also serve as a benefit in helping students feel familiar with one another and in turn support one another.

Other essays pointed out how Culture could prevent immigrant groups from assimilating with the mainstream culture. "Since everyone in the neighborhood is Latina/o and speaks Spanish, there is no reason for them to learn English" (Essay 175). In this instance, the student seemed to believe that the parents and children from the after-school program live in a homogeneous immigrant neighborhood and so became culturally isolated. Essay 162 pointed out the instant rapport that can be made between adults at the field site and students simply by sharing a common culture or ethnicity. One particular student explained how cultural factors influenced the way students in the after-school program behaved, which is consistent with previous research on the factors associated with generational change within ethnic groups. "To be more specific about the cultural change in students are that they can't speak Spanish, but they are Mexican and proud of it which is described in *Personas Mexicanas*" (Essay 160). Students in this after-school program demonstrated to her that they hold on to their cultural identities despite not knowing much of the language of their ancestors.

DISCUSSION AND CONCLUSION

This chapter suggests that the process of developing a professional vision starts in the course lectures and eventually is applied in the field. As students reflected on their experiences in their essays, it was important to find an approach that allowed the authors to dissect these essays in a reasonable way to decipher what students gained from the course. By utilizing methods rooted in discourse analysis and applying professional vision theories to pinpoint the themes and codes, the authors were able to see how students made sense of their service-learning placements and the course material. This process yielded three distinct conceptual strands: (1) a salience of common course content across student papers, (2) a prevalent theme different from the assigned theme from the prompt, and (3) a bias toward a certain code found across the samples. We claim that this may be an informative way to approach future data in other critical studies in adult learning and promote a more socially just understanding of society.

The assigned essay represents a material representation of students' field placement experience and an opportunity to demonstrate highlighting of concepts and appropriate codification of the socio-educational craft. Goodwin's (1994) professional vision explains how writing the essay became a "shaping process of objects of knowledge that become the insignia of a profession's craft" (p. 606). The college essays indicate that the students are developing their personal professional vision. However, it appears that not all students equally demonstrated a professional vision.

Looking back at the Masucci and Renner (2001) framework, we can trace the reasons for the different themes as mentioned by the students. Their service-learning placement (stipulation 2) requires that they are immersed in social theory (stipulation 3) and reflect critically on their experiences in the course and the community placement (stipulation 4). However, at any step, including stipulation 1 (pre-reflection on taking the course), students will come away with different beliefs and theories on why inequality exists.

To accurately capture what students took away from the course and the field assignment, students should be asked to reflect on their experiences throughout the quarter rather than only toward the end—this may lead more students to question what they are observing in their service-learning placement and to connect course topics and themes to their experiences. Also, students should be placed in distinct after-school programs. In addition, future studies to be conducted with these data and methods could involve more course analysis—lectures should be videotaped. Following some students to their sites could also be informative. Interviewing students or having focus groups can also help triangulate data in order to discover whether or not students are convinced that structural reasons explain the achievement gap better than cultural reasons. Considering the context of the students may also be helpful in analyzing these data by looking for associations associated with their demographics such as the students' socioeconomic status (SES), race or ethnicity, major, and prior experiences with after-school programs. Finally, conducting statistical analyses on the themes in pre- and postanalysis may provide a deeper understanding of what students took away from the course.

Nonetheless, the course proposes that race and social inequality is evident in the current climate of education. Moreover, social inequality cannot be explained by cultural factors alone. The course included readings on structural factors that contributed to success in nondominant students. It spoke about having high-quality teachers and rigorous and relevant curriculum to keep all students engaged. Other points made in this course are the presence of program partnerships among the school and community organizations and having the resources to support instructional programs and initiatives at the school site. In essence, the course allowed students to read critical research on education and to participate in lectures that challenged the racial disparity and the status quo. What became most salient to students is the notion that social inequality is important to consider when it comes down to Latina/o student engagement and school success.

REFERENCES

Ash, S., & Clayton, P. (2004). The articulated learning: An approach to guided reflection and assessment. *Innovative Higher Education, 29*(2), 137–154.

Bourdieu, P. (1977). *Outline of a theory of practice* (R. Nice, Trans.). Cambridge, England: Cambridge University Press.

Chaiklin, S., & Lave, J. (Eds.). (1993). *Understanding practice: Perspectives on activity and context.* Cambridge, England: Cambridge University Press.

Chavez, L. (2008). *The Latina/o threat: Constructing immigrants, citizens, and the nation.* Palo Alto, CA: Stanford University Press.

Collins, A., & Halverson, R. (2009). *Rethinking education in the age of technology.* New York, NY: Teachers College Press.

Conchas, G. Q. (2006). *The color of success: Race and high-achieving urban youth.* New York, NY: Teachers College Press.

Deeley, S. J. (2010). Service-learning: Thinking outside of the box. *Active Learning in Higher Education, 11*(1), 43–53.

Duranti, A., & Goodwin, C. (Eds.). (1992). *Rethinking context: Language as an interactive phenomenon*. Cambridge, England: Cambridge University Press.

Ethridge, E., & Branscomb, K. (2009). Learning through action: Parallel learning processes in children and adults. *Teaching and Teacher Education, 25*, 400–408.

Feliciano, C. (2006). *Unequal origins: Immigrant selection and the education of the second generation*. El Paso, TX: LFB Scholarly Publishing LLC.

Goodwin, C. (1994). Professional vision. *American Anthropologist, 96*(3), 606–633.

Gutiérrez, K. (2002). Studying cultural practices in urban learning communities. *Human Development, 45*(4), 312–321.

Hanks, W. (1987). Discourse genres in a theory of practice. *American Ethnologist, 14*(4), 668–692.

Kronick, R. (2007). Service learning and the university student. *College Student Journal, 41*(2), 296–304.

Lave, J., & Wenger, E. (1991). Situated learning: Legitimate peripheral participation. Cambridge, England: Cambridge University Press.

Lee, S. (1996). *Unraveling the model minority stereotype: Listening to Asian American youth*. New York, NY: Teachers College Press.

Lieblich, A., Tuval-Mashiach, R., & Zilber, T. (1998). *Narrative research: Reading, analysis, and interpretation*. Applied social research methods, vol. 47. London, England: Sage Publications.

Masucci, M., & Renner, A. (2001). *The evolution of critical service-learning for education: Four problematics* (Report No. ED456962). Retrieved from ERIC database.

Merriam, S. (2009). *Qualitative research: A guide to design and implementation*. San Francisco, CA: Jossey-Bass.

Morewedge, C. (2009). Negativity bias in attribution of external agency. *Journal of Experimental Psychology: General, 138*, 535–545.

Noguera, P. (2003). *City schools and the American dream*. New York, NY: Teachers College Press.

Patton, M. (2002). *Qualitative research and evaluation methods* (3rd ed.) London, England: Sage Publications.

Perez, W. (2009). *We are Americans: Undocumented students pursuing the American dream*. Sterling, VA: Stylus Publishing.

Peterson, T. H. (2009). Engaged scholarship: Reflections and research on the pedagogy of social change. *Teaching in Higher Education, 14*(5), 541–552.

Sacks, H. (1992). *Lectures on conversation*. (2 Vols.) (G. Jefferson, Ed.). Oxford, England: Basil Blackwell.

Schmidt, M., Marks, J., & Derrico, L. (2004). What a difference mentoring makes: Service learning and engagement for college students. *Mentoring & Tutoring: Partnership in Learning, 12*(2), 205–217.

Vigil, J. D. (2002). *Personas Mexicanas: Chicano high schoolers in a changing Los Angeles*. Belmont, CA: Wadsworth Custom Publishing.

Vygotsky, L. S. (1978). *Mind in society: The development of higher psychological processes*. Cambridge, MA: Harvard University Press.

CHAPTER 3

Critical Race Case Study on College Choice

Racialization in School Culture and Climate

Nancy Acevedo-Gil

This chapter presents a qualitative case study that examined the college-going processes of an under-resourced and highly racialized urban high school with a large Latina/o student population. At the organizational level, the study revealed the conceptualization and application of college-going efforts within the larger school culture. At the student level, the study identified how college-going efforts shaped the college choice, transition, and navigation pathways of Latina/o students who aspired to earn a bachelor's degree.

In California, Latinas/os represent 53% of the K–12 public school population and are the fastest growing group in the K–12 sector nationwide (California Department of Education, 2013; U.S. Census Bureau, 2012). However, schools with large populations of Latina/o students offer inferior academic resources (Rogers, Fanelli, Freelon, Medina, Bertrand, & Del Razo, 2010). Therefore, it is not surprising that Latinas/os are underrepresented in 4-year colleges and maintain the lowest educational outcomes among all racial groups (Fry, 2004; Solorzano, Villalpando, & Oseguera, 2005). The educational statistics result in one of education's most vexing problems because Latina/o students have high educational aspirations and want to attend college (NWLC & MALDEF, 2009; Pew Hispanic Center, 2005; Roderick, Nagaoka, & Allensworth, 2006; Venezia, Kirst, & Antonio, 2003). The lack of counselors in schools contributes to the problem and instead of receiving individual college guidance students obtain information in school group settings (Kimura-Walsh, Yamamura, Griffin, & Allen, 2008). Although schools aim to develop strong college-going cultures, the amount and type of resources available to a school influence the effectiveness of efforts that provide information to all students (Tierney, Corwin, & Colyar, 2003).

Given the increase in Latina/o population and educators resorting to a college-going culture, this chapter examines the college-going efforts of educators at Academies High School (AHS) and the college choice and integration processes of Latina/o students. With the study, I aimed to understand how educators in an under-resourced school developed a college-going climate and informed the post-secondary pathways of Latina/o students. The study was guided by the following research questions:

1. What is the structure and culture of Academies High School?
2. How do Academies High School educators utilize policies, resources, and practices to develop a college-going climate within the larger school culture?
3. How do Academies High School Latina/o students with high educational aspirations develop college-going and college-navigating identities?

This chapter reveals examples of caring educators situated within institutional instability that presented obstacles to improve college-going efforts. In addition, multiple climates in the school served to counter college-going efforts and resulted in the stratification between 4-year college preparation and tracking into vocational programs of aspiring community college students. Finally, this chapter presents a college-going and navigation identity development process to exemplify how students' racial, gender, class, and immigration status influenced the established high aspirations of Latina/o students and the determination to meet educational goals despite foreseeable obstacles.

Overall, this study reveals how institutional processes can both create and close the gap between high aspirations to attend college and the educational outcomes of Latinas/os. In addition, I discuss why researchers who conduct future studies should use a critical framework to reveal systemic injustices experienced by students of color.

THEORETICAL FRAMEWORK AND REVIEW OF THE LITERATURE

Although my goal in using a qualitative case study was to develop a theoretical understanding of a topic, a case study design alone was insufficient to build theory (Diaz Andrade, 2009). Therefore, I included a strong theoretical foundation to build theory from findings (Yin, 2013) and I applied critical race theory in education (CRTE).

Critical Race Theory in Education

Critical race theory (CRT) began in the legal field during the 1970s. However, education scholars began to utilize CRT as a research tool during the 1990s (Solorzano, 1998). Solorzano (1998) defines critical race theory in education as a framework, which "challenges the dominant discourse on race and racism as they relate to education by examining how educational theory, policy, and practice are used to subordinate certain racial and ethnic groups" (p. 122). Solorzano (1998) identifies five principal tenets of CRTE after drawing from several fields, including ethnic studies, history, law, psychology, sociology, and education. The tenets call for scholars to (1) centralize race and racism, (2) challenge the dominant perspective, (3) commit to social justice, (4) value experiential knowledge, and (5) conduct interdisciplinary research. In this study, I examined the concepts of race and racism as they intersected with other forms of subordination, such as gender and class. Since I aimed to understand how Latina/o students experienced college-going efforts I conducted multiple interviews with Latina/o students and educators of color, which revealed the deficit ideologies that students overcame.

In addition, because I focused on Latinas/os, I also used LatCrit—a branch of critical race theory—to guide the study. LatCrit enables researchers to understand, analyze, and articulate the specific experiences of Latinas/os through a closer examination of the unique forms of oppression that Latinas/os encounter (Solorzano & Delgado Bernal, 2001). The framework acknowledges the particular needs of Latina/o communities, such as issues of immigration status, language, and culture. In particular, the integration of LatCrit facilitated the analysis of students who experienced educational inequities due to an undocumented immigration status. Finally, the implementation of LatCrit and CRTE frameworks challenges contemporary deficit thinking in educational research as defined by Valencia and Solorzano (1997).

School Culture

The concept of school culture also informed this study to examine the college-going efforts at AHS. Because a relationship exists between school culture and climate (Miner, 1995), I merged the conceptualization of Schein (1985, 1996), Steele and Jenks (1977), and Rodríguez and Brown (2009) to define school culture as a set of actions informed by the intersections of school structures, climates, and individual agency. I defined school structures to include school history and policies. School climate entailed the prevailing standards, attitudes, and practices enacted by administrators and teachers within spaces in the school and classrooms. Therefore, I used the term *college-going climate,* as opposed to *college-going culture,* which is used widely in education research. Finally, I defined individual agency to include the ideologies, perceptions, experiences, and actions of students, teachers, and administrators.

College-Choice Organizational *Habitus*

To bridge the school- and student-level processes, college-choice organizational *habitus* also informed this study. McDonough (1997) expands on Bourdieu's (1979) concept of *habitus* to develop college-choice organizational *habitus.* First,

McDonough (1997) accounts for the role of institutions shaping individual agency and established organizational *habitus*, which she defines as the "impact of a cultural group or social class on an individual's behavior, through an intermediate organization" (p. 107). Although McDonough (1997) categorizes "groups" through social class, the concept of organizational *habitus* allows for race to serve as a critical dimension in how "dispositions, perceptions, and appreciations" are organized (Diamond, Randolph, & Spillane, 2004, p. 76). Second, McDonough (1997) establishes a college-choice organizational *habitus* to refer to the "patterns of college-choices and behaviors that are manifested in schools with similar socioeconomic status environments" (p. 108). She finds that college-choice organizational *habitus* influences how individual students understand the available postsecondary options. Therefore, I centralized college-choice organizational *habitus* to understand the role of school processes in reproducing and challenging social inequalities through college choice.

College-Going Culture

College-going culture in high schools represents a form of college-choice organizational *habitus*. McClafferty, McDonough, and Nuñez (2002) contend that students who have families with limited college knowledge or resources often resort to school to (1) understand the value of college, (2) receive advice on appropriate classes, and (3) obtain assistance with college choice. Since the number of counselors in schools is limited, studies argue that all school staff should establish a college culture (Corwin & Tierney, 2007; McClafferty et al., 2002; Pathways to College Network, 2006). McClafferty and her colleagues (2002) establish that a college-going culture entails a school environment where all students are prepared to make informed postsecondary decisions by receiving structural, motivational, and experiential college preparatory opportunities. While studies argue for the need to develop a college-going culture to assist students during the college choice process, more research is needed to examine how this process occurs (McClafferty et al., 2002; Tierney et al., 2003). In particular, this study examined a dearth in the literature by addressing the implications of college-going culture on the college choices and transitions to postsecondary education for Latinas/os.

THE CASE STUDY PROCESS

By using a qualitative case study design, I aimed to expand upon existing theoretical propositions in the areas of college-going culture, college choice, and college transitions. To do so, I collected data from one high school in northern California—Academies High School (AHS).[1] Since the majority of Latina/o students attend highly segregated and under-resourced high schools (Orfield & Lee, 2007; Rogers, Bertrand, Freelon, & Fanelli, 2011), AHS could provide an in-depth understanding of such contexts.

In 2012, AHS served more than 1,600 students, with 83% identifying as Latina/o and 73% of students qualifying for free/reduced lunch. In 2009, about 22% of AHS seniors took the SAT exam but only 8% enrolled in a California State University (CSU) (Rogers et al., 2011). However, in 2012, 39% of those graduating from AHS completed the A-G college admission required curriculum, compared to the state average of 37%. Moreover, in alignment with the increase in urban schools participating in career academies, the selected school site was organized into five Linked Learning career academies.[2]

On Oral History Interviews

I conducted oral history interviews with 57 student participants during two points in time. The first round was collected during their senior year in high school, and the second round occurred during the first semester in college. Of the 57 students, 47 were Latina/o. The remaining 10 participants reflected the racial composition of 12th-grade students, including five Black or African American, four Asian American or Pacific Islander, and one White. Since the majority of Latinas/os have parents who did not graduate from college and are low-income (Alon & Tienda, 2005; Zarate & Gallimore, 2005), every student participant selected for interviews had parents who did not graduate from a 4-year college in the United States, lived in a low-income household, and aspired to earn a college degree.

The graduating GPA of the students ranged from .824 to 4.06, with 17 students earning below a 2.0, 19 earning between a 2.0 and 3.0, and the remaining earning above a 3.0 GPA. For the second interview, I contacted only the Latina/o student participants to gain insight about their transition to college. I called participants, sent a text message, and/or sent an email message to select a date and time for the interview. Although 40 students responded, I was able to interview only 37 due to a limitation of time. Of the 37 Latina/o students in the follow-up oral history interviews, 23 were female and 14 were male. During the second interview, 20 had enrolled in (or planned to enroll in) a 2-year college, six in a University of California UC campus, six in a California State University (CSU) campus, and three a private for-profit vocational college. In addition, two males stopped attending the local community college and another two were completing a final semester of high school but applied to the local community college.

Oral history interviews allowed me to analyze college choice and transition to college. In addition, oral history interviews enabled this study to make meaning of how the participants' personal and educational histories impacted their educational aspirations. During the first interview, participants elaborated on previous schooling experiences, college aspirations, access to college information, and how they were selecting a college. The second interview reviewed points from the first interview but emphasized how the students chose a college and experienced the transition and integration into college.

I also conducted semi-structured interviews with 17 practitioners and administrators, including three college advisers, seven teachers who supported college-going efforts, three support staff, and one full-time counselor. I interviewed three administrators, including the principal and two vice-principals. I conducted informal follow-up interviews with participants to address issues that surfaced during observations. Interview questions aimed to understand the ideologies underlying college-going policies and practices.

Finally, I observed college-going activities at AHS, at least once per week during the school year, to understand how teachers, college advisers, and other educators developed a college-going climate. Observations included school-wide events, classroom workshops, and individual meetings with college advisers. During observations, I used handwritten fieldnotes and/or audio recordings, and after the event, I would write memos. My goal was to observe the workshop facilitator, not the students. However, the workshop facilitators were college advisers at AHS whom I had interviewed.

The Process of Uncovering the Findings

This study was guided by grounded theory and critical race grounded theory, or CRGT (Malagon, Perez Huber, & Velez, 2009). Therefore, I utilized an inductive data analysis process but I also considered how larger structural phenomena shaped the data (Malagon et al., 2009). This occurred while utilizing the three stages of coding used in grounded theory: open coding, axial coding, and selective coding (Strauss & Corbin, 1990). The first round of coding occurred prior to collecting the student interviews, the second occurred after collecting the student interviews, and the third occurred upon collecting all interviews. In the third round, I also compared findings with relevant theories, such as Anzaldúa's (2002) concept of *conocimiento*. Considering that the college-choice process has proven to be a rather complex topic, I found it essential to use multiple methods and to triangulate the data (Cohen & Manion, 1986).

MULTIPLE CLIMATES WITHIN SCHOOL CULTURE

The first finding addresses research question one: What is the structure and culture of Academies High School? The culture of AHS was of one change, instability, and marginalization, which resulted from inequitable funding policies and the organizational structure. AHS culture entailed at least four climates: high aspirations, college-going, low expectations, and surveillance and control. The climates intersected with one another and students experienced multiple climates at once, depending on space and time. After explaining the climates of high aspirations and low expectations, I elaborate how I applied a CRTE lens to examine, analyze, and critique the climate of surveillance and control.

Several teachers created climates of high aspirations. In these climates, the teachers aspired for students to succeed in college and integrated college-going activities, which resulted in college-going climates (discussed in the second finding). Teachers who created climates of high aspirations worked to align course standards with college and were willing to invest additional time and resources to support students. The teachers attributed their focus on a strength-based approach to sharing similar backgrounds as the AHS students.

However, teachers and administrator participants also created climates of low expectations, rooted in deficit ideologies about academics and a lack of role models. During his interview, I asked Mr. Olson, a teacher, to discuss the biggest obstacles he experienced when attempting to create a college-going classroom environment. He explained:

> The biggest detriment to college is mindset—generational poverty. Kids that have not seen anything but poverty. . . . Changing that mindset, getting them to think outside of "gangland," and out of the mindset of street culture is the hardest thing to do because you have to have an incredible amount of credibility with the student before they will take you seriously and that is hard to gain.

Mr. Olson spoke about generational poverty and emphasized a deficit ideology when framing students and their families as the greatest limitation to increasing college-going rates. He framed students as individuals who did not care about school because they lived in impoverished situations and did not understand the value of school. Similar to Mr. Olson, two other teachers emphasized students as the "problem" when attempting to implement college-going efforts.

However, students experienced overlapping and multiple climates. Two AHS teachers, Ms. Noguera and Mr. Rivas, argued that all educators needed to nurture a climate of high aspirations. The teachers recalled an incident when a counselor disturbed the climate of high aspirations they had established in the classroom:

> One of our kids came in with the counselor and the counselor was like, "I heard that this kid is trying to apply to college? I don't know what's going on, what are you telling the students?" In front of the whole class! I stepped outside and he was like, "I don't understand why you think this student has the potential." He had like a 2.7 GPA, he was qualified to go to a state college—that was his goal. He had an IEP, so if he carries the IEP through college, he can get help there. We made sure everybody could apply; we didn't just have anybody apply. But you have to have some belief in these kids. His approach was "They are going to mess up." My approach was "Let's be optimistic, at least we can try." I think these kids have that fight or flight, they don't flight. They have a lot of perseverance, they can adapt to any situation, that's something that most of these kids

develop growing up in the city. . . .That's why I have faith that they can be successful. Some people don't see it that way, but I do, maybe that's why we help the kids go to college.

During this incident, students encountered a climate of low expectations intersecting with the high aspiration climate established in the classroom.

Mr. Rivas elaborated on his high aspiration ideologies and argued that students possessed strengths and skills that supported postsecondary perseverance and success. Mr. Rivas created a climate of high aspirations that focused on providing students with an opportunity to pursue a college education. On the other hand, the counselor perceived students with a deficit ideology and as academically unprepared to complete a 4-year college degree. This particular exemplar provides insight into how climates can trespass spaces and that individuals help create climates.

In alignment with the low-expectations climate, educators also developed a climate of surveillance and control, with high levels of security and regulations that aimed to maintain student safety by controlling student behavior. Administrator and teachers argued that incidents of violence on school grounds led to an increasing presence of surveillance and policing that took the form of security measures, enacted through funding, disciplinary regulations, and allocation of space. The surveillance climate was primarily a result of the five measures of security— rooted in paternalistic policies, structures, and practices. For example, as depicted in Figure 3.1, upon entering the school building, students were welcomed with a jail-like fence, which was closed during most of the day.

Figure 3.1. AHS Students Eating Lunch Against the Black Gate

Ultimately, the students argued that the climate of surveillance and control restricted their abilities to navigate college independently. Juan Pablo, who maintained a 2.25 GPA, described the experience of being an AHS student as aligning with feelings of being in jail and also articulated how this climate would hinder him in college:

> Here at Academies, it feels like a jail, they have us locked in here. . . .I feel trapped. . . .[F]or a long time I thought this was a jail before it was a high school. There's always structure here and if there is no structure, they think it's not going to work. In college they give you more freedom so that's going to be a tough transition. Here they tell you, "You have to do this, you have to do that," and they give you all these type of rules. The guards they tell you, "Do this, do that" and you have to do it, there's not much else you can do 'cause they have the authority.

Students elucidated that a climate of surveillance and control in AHS did not support college aspirations. Instead, the climate pushed some students out of college in the future by not equipping them with the appropriate skills required to navigate such an independent space.

In addition, the principal knew that some teachers maintained low expectations and he emphasized the urgency to view all students from a strength-based approach. Given the four climates within AHS, it is important to note that the personal ideologies from administrators, teachers, and staff determined the climates. As seen in the low expectations and surveillance climates, cultural deficit perceptions framed how educators viewed AHS students. On the other hand, centering the strengths of students allowed educators to establish climates of high aspirations and college-going in order to support students. Mr. Fernandez, the principal of AHS, expressed the significance of teachers having low expectations. He argued the urgent need to replace low expectations with high expectations:

> You have to believe it. They [teachers] have to believe that the kids can do it— that's what we don't have sometimes. We still have some teachers who don't believe in our kids, *porque uno es de diferente color* [because we are a different color] we cannot achieve. We might have an accent but that doesn't mean I cannot build a bridge. I think that's one of the hardest things to do, changing the meaning system of the teachers. . . .The new teachers we can mold our way. . . .I want people who come from the community, people who see a Juan and they believe that the kid can learn. . . .[T]he key issue is people believing.

Mr. Fernandez argued that teachers had to believe in students' abilities to achieve and succeed in college. However, he acknowledged that some teachers did not have high expectations for AHS students—some teachers did not believe in the students' ability to succeed academically.

Mr. Fernandez highlighted the issues of race, racism, and language abilities as possible reasons for teachers having deficit notions of students. He explained that changing a teacher's ideologies was the most difficult issue for him to address. As a result, he hoped to replace the deficit teachers with new teachers to mold an ideology of high expectations. As principal of AHS, Mr. Fernandez hoped to equip his school with teachers who saw strengths in students, had high expectations, and believed in students. His aim was that teachers would support students by bridging high aspirations with high expectations. Ultimately, Mr. Fernandez revealed that personal ideologies shaped how educators perceived students and the actions taken to support or hinder students' educational journeys.

Generally, students reinforced the notions expressed by administrators and teachers. One student explained that teachers "want us all to succeed." Moreover, students differentiated between some teachers "not caring" and other teachers having high aspirations for students to attend college. Most students argued that teacher aspirations and expectations "depend on the student." Finally, students believed that their English teachers hoped they would succeed in college.

During the second round of interviews, students reinforced Mr. Fernandez's argument that teacher ideologies informed practices, which could prepare or hinder student abilities to navigate college. For example, during the follow-up interview, after completing her first quarter in community college, Anaís clarified how the restrictive climate of surveillance and control limited the possibility of success in college for students:

> In Academies High School, it's like they want us to grow up but we have to ask permission to go to the bathroom. . . .The first 2 years, we didn't have the gates but then we had no freedom, we didn't really have a say in anything. They controlled us and they wanted us to do certain things. Then we graduate and have freedom and now it's hard. In high school, you have to ask permission for everything. Then, when you graduate, you have to do things for yourself. If we had done things differently, I would be more independent and know how to do things by myself. It's harder now. I don't know how to explain it.

Much like the other students who attended AHS since 9th grade, Anaís explained that the school implemented tougher security measures throughout her high school years. Anaís contrasted the child-like experience of having to ask permission to use the restroom with the expectation of being an adult in college. She compared the constant control that she and other students experienced while at AHS with the complete freedom that a community college provided. Anaís could not articulate why the restrictive policies and practices of AHS limited her ability to navigate college successfully. However, she blamed the restrictive AHS policies and practices for her lack of the skills necessary to succeed as an independent college student and argued that the experiences hindered her college transition.

CRTE ANALYSIS OF THE COLLEGE-GOING CLIMATE

The second finding addressed the research question: How do AHS educators utilize policies, resources, and practices to develop a college-going climate within the larger school culture? The college-going climate included several elements, such as the college center, collaborative efforts with college outreach programs, community college outreach, college-going teachers, college visits, engaging with students' identities, and internships. The college-going climate was composed of two sub-climates: 4-year college-going and vocational college-going efforts.

The 4-year climate focused on supporting students who were eligible to attend a 4-year college to take the required college admission exams. The climate also focused on eligible students applying to and enrolling in 4-year colleges. The 4-year college-going sub-climate was developed by several educators; it was uncoordinated and not a streamlined process. Ms. Jacobs, the director of the college and career center, explained, "My job is dictated by the different deadlines throughout the year. The big focus is always to make sure the students that are eligible to apply to 4-year schools are prepared to apply to 4-year schools." Ms. Jacobs explained that as the director of the college and career center, she focused on working with students who met eligibility requirements for admission to 4-year colleges. As opposed to 4-year colleges, community colleges did not have application or admission deadlines, which contributed to the 4-year college sector being a priority throughout the year.

On the other hand, the career academy structure facilitated a vocational pathway for the students who planned to attend a community college—regardless of aspirations to transfer from a 2-year college to a 4-year college. Nick, the outreach counselor for the local community college, supported students with the enrollment process for the 2-year college but focused on vocational programs.[3] Nick explained that the local community college recruited AHS students into vocational college pathways:

> There was an organization called Career (Pathways); they wanted to help link, high school academies to related community college programs. . . .We can query all (vocational law) students, we can target those students, send them info about that program, look at students who want to do culinary arts and send them info. . . .As far as transfer goes, we will have a couple of years to go over that. We will re-establish the transfer center . . . it was eliminated about 5 years ago so we are going to re-establish it.

Nick explained the connection between the high school program and a nonprofit organization, funded by several national foundations, which established career pathways into vocational programs. For example, the AHS students in the Law Academy could easily transition into the law vocational program, which offered a certificate. Students could earn certificates, such as "Security Specialist," or continue to earn an associate's degree, which facilitates transfer admission into a

CSU campus. Although Nick acknowledged that "a lot of students want to transfer," the institutional mechanisms in place do not prepare incoming community college students for the transfer pathway.

LATINA/O COLLEGE CHOICE AND NAVIGATION

To address the third question—how do AHS Latina/o students with high educational aspirations develop college-going and college-navigating identities?—I applied and adapted Anzaldúa's (2002) path to *conocimiento*.[4] *Conocimiento* is an identity development process that entails self-reflection and outward-directed action that results in a social justice epistemology (Anzaldúa, 2002). Based on the student experiences, I established a theory of college choice and navigation, which I called *conocimiento colegial*. I defined *conocimiento colegial* as a reflective collegial consciousness where Latinas/os use their ethnic/racial identity and social positionalities in an empowering college identity. This process engaged with the seven stages of *conocimiento* as they pertain to the process of (1) preparing for college, (2) searching for colleges, (3) choosing a college, (4) transitioning into college, and (5) navigating college. The process of *conocimiento colegial* is nonlinear and complex. Finally, data revealed that a college-going climate could foster a *conocimiento colegial* identity but was not designed to prepare students for postsecondary pathways.

CRTE AND THE DEBUNKING
OF DEFICIT IDEOLOGIES

Using CRTE, I challenged the deficit notions within the study by centralizing race, racism, and other forms of subjugation when analyzing the data. First, I acknowledged the positive climates of high aspirations and college-going developed by educators. However, I argued against the ongoing notion that urban students of color need police and other measures of control. Similar to the perceptions of students, a previous study found that students perceive the policing measures to be unnecessary and restrictive (Bracy, 2011). The student perspectives reinforced an urgent need for administrators to consider how measures of surveillance impact the day-to-day schooling experiences of students.

Furthermore, the AHS physical environment contributed to the feeling of being in prison. Alexander (2010) established the concept of the New Jim Crow (NJC), which argues that mass incarceration serves to maintain a racial caste system. Given my application of CRTE, the NJC is an essential point to consider. Alexander (2010) alluded to the education system serving a role in the NJC through unequal educational opportunities alongside police surveillance (Sokolower, 2012). Alexander (2010) aligned the lack of educational opportunities coupled with police surveillance as a contribution to the NJC. A climate of surveillance and control exemplifies the NJC within the educational system. Essentially, the AHS methods of surveillance and control served to maintain a panopticon (Foucault, 1977) and prepare students for other controlled environments, not the freedom of college.

Second, CRTE calls for social justice–oriented work. Thus, I examined the college-going processes developed in an under-resourced high school but called attention to the postsecondary tracking functions for future community college students. By combining the nonexistence of transfer preparation with the push for vocational short-term programs, students who aspired to transfer into 4-year colleges were not prepared well. The bridge between the AHS career academies and the local community college served as a future vocational workforce. Since AHS enrolled a majority of students of color and low-income students, it served as an acceptable space to prepare students for vocational careers as "short-term goals" and contributed to social reproduction.

Although previous research found that career academies support high school graduation rates (Conchas, 2006; Stern, Dayton, & Raby, 2010), this study showed that AHS students were steered toward vocational degrees and, as a result, not one of the 27 students who aspired to transfer was aware of concrete resources for transfer to a 4-year college. This coincides with the Kemple and Willner (2008) study, where higher percentages of academy students were earning certificates and associate degrees instead of bachelor degrees. The data suggest the need to examine more in-depth how career academies facilitate a new form of tracking students into vocational pathways. Given the goals of Latina/o students to transfer into a 4-year college (Nuñez & Elizondo, 2013), educators need to provide more emphasis on transfer information beginning in high school, as opposed to tracking students into vocational postsecondary programs.

Third, a CRTE lens supports researchers in expanding current theories that do not address the experiences of students of color. Traditional theoretical frameworks of college choice and college integration are limiting due to the lack of applicability to nontraditional and underrepresented students. Furthermore, as the following section will explain, by utilizing CRGT, I applied my cultural intuition in the research process, and understood the need for a theory that bridges college choice with college integration.

RECOMMENDATIONS FOR QUALITATIVE CASE STUDY DESIGNS

This study includes three key recommendations for future case studies that examine the educational contexts of students of color. First, I highlight the need to use critical theoretical frameworks and methods to activate our *facultad* (Anzaldúa, 2002) as researchers in communities of color. *La facultad* allows researchers to see beneath the surface and reveal continued systemic injustices based on issues of race, class, gender, immigration status, and other forms of subjugation. To support the process of *la facultad*, education researchers who conduct future studies should use a critical framework that allows the data to reveal the systemic injustices experienced by students of color.

Second, this study emphasizes the significance of using interdisciplinary concepts to produce findings that address educational issues for students of color. By using CRTE and CRGT, I used my cultural intuition to understand how the data aligned with various Chicana feminist theoretical frameworks. Thus, I was able to gain a clear understanding of the nonlinearity and continuous questioning present in the college choice and college navigation process of Latina/o students.

Finally, this study calls for scholars who research students of color to consider the importance of reciprocity with participants of color. As a Chicana researcher, I identified with the students and entered the research site with *buena voluntad* (good will). Figueroa and Sanchez (2008) explain that "*buena voluntad* embodies the enactment of being mindfully courteous at all times to those around you to demonstrate your persona and intentions" (p. 23). In this process, I was guided by tenets three and four of CRTE and I used my cultural intuition of professional experiences as a college adviser by providing student participants with college advising sessions to redirect any previous misadvising that occurred in previous interactions with college guidance. In doing so, I hoped to provide guidance, resources, and/or bridge the high educational aspirations with expectations.

In the college advising session, I provided concrete information about possible pathways and outcomes, as well as resources to support students in their educational quests. Similar to Espinoza's (2011) pivotal moments framework, my goal was to support students to learn how to navigate higher education systems. I went beyond entering a research site to gather information and leave. If a researcher cares about the well-being of the communities she studies, she should enact *buena voluntad* to potentially have a positive impact.

CONCLUSION

This study revealed that individual educators in the under-resourced high school site care about students succeeding in college but that a lack of institutional sustainability and stability presented obstacles to improving college-going efforts. In addition, multiple climates in the school revealed how a climate of surveillance and control countered the college-going efforts. When examining the college-going efforts within the school, the stratification between 4-year college and the tracking into vocational programs of aspiring community college students was evident. Finally, the interdisciplinary analysis of individual college-going and navigation identity development exemplified how students' racial, gender, class, and immigration status influenced the established high aspirations of Latina/o students and the determination to meet educational goals despite foreseeable obstacles. Overall, despite various obstacles and a lack of institutional resources, students maintained high aspirations and continued to strive for completing a college degree. It is our responsibility as educators, educational leaders, researchers, and scholars to foster the high aspirations of students to ensure the success and completion of postsecondary goals.

NOTES

1. Academies High School and the other names used in this chapter are all pseudonyms used to maintain the anonymity of the participants. Although I had worked with other local schools, I did not have any previous connection to AHS. However, the principal, the director of the college and career center, and several teachers were supportive of my study once I explained the aim and intention of the study.

2. Stern, Dayton, and Raby (1992) define *career academy* as a school-within-a-school or a small learning community.

3. Although in this study the career academies model facilitated the vocationalization process, previous studies find that the career academy models integrate a college-readiness approach (Stern, Dayton, & Raby, 2010), provide coursework to prepare for college by centering around a specific career-related theme (Stern et al., 2010), and benefit student graduation rates, for males in particular (Conchas, 2006; Kemple, 2008; Moore & Oppenheim, 2010; Stern et al., 2010).

4. Anzaldúa (2002) defines the *conocimiento* theory of development: "Skeptical of reason and rationality, *conocimiento* questions conventional knowledge's current categories, classifications, and contents. . . . *Conocimiento* comes from opening all your senses, consciously inhabiting your body and decoding its symptoms. . . . *Conocimientos* challenge official and conventional ways of the world, ways set up by those benefiting from such constructions" (pp. 541–542).

REFERENCES

Alexander, M. (2010). *The new Jim Crow: Mass incarceration in the age of colorblindness*. New York, NY: The New Press.

Alon, S., & Tienda, M. (2005). Assessing the "mismatch" hypothesis: Differences in college graduation rates by institutional selectivity. *Sociology of Education, 78*(4), 294–315.

Anzaldúa, G. (2002). Now let us shift . . . the path of *conocimiento* . . . inner work, public acts. In G. Anzaldúa & A. Keating (Eds.), *This bridge we call home: Radical visions for transformation* (pp. 540–578). New York, NY: Routledge.

Bourdieu, P. (1979) *Algeria1960: The disenchantment of the world, the sense of honour, the Kabyle house or the world reversed*. Cambridge, England: Cambridge University Press.

Bracy, N. L. (2011). Student perceptions of high-security school environments. *Youth and Society, 43*(1), 365–395.

California Department of Education. (2013). *Statewide enrollment by ethnicity, 2012–13*. Sacramento, CA: Author. Retrieved from http://dq.cde.ca.gov/dataquest/EnrollEthState.asp?Level = State&TheYear = 201213&cChoice = EnrollEth1&p = 2

Cohen, L., & Manion, L. (1986). *Research methods in education*. London, England: Croom Helm.

Conchas, G. Q. (2006). *The color of success: Race and high-achieving urban youth*. New York, NY: Teachers College Press.

Corwin, Z. B., & Tierney, W. G. (2007). *Getting there—and beyond: Building a culture of college-going in high schools*. Los Angeles, CA: USC Center for Higher Education Policy Analysis.

Diamond, J., Randolph, A., & Spillane, J. (2004). Teachers' expectations and sense of responsibility for student learning: The importance of race, class, and organizational habitus. *Anthropology & Education Quarterly, 35*(1),75–98.

Diaz Andrade, A. (2009) Interpretive research aiming at theory building: Adopting and adapting the case study design. *The Qualitative Report, 14*(1), 42–60.

Espinoza, R. (2011). *Pivotal moments: How educators can put all students on the path to college.* Cambridge, MA: Harvard Education Press.

Figueroa, J. L., & Sánchez, P. (2008). Technique, art, or cultural practice? Ethnic epistemology in Latina/o qualitative studies. In T. P. Fong (Ed.), *Ethnic studies research: Approaches and perspectives* (pp. 143–177). Lanham, MD: AltaMira.

Foucault, M. (1977). *Discipline and punish. The birth of the prison.* London, England: Allen Lane.

Fry, R. (2004). *Latina/o youth finishing college: The role of selective pathways.* Washington, DC: Pew Hispanic Center.

Kemple, J. J. (2008). *Career academies: Long-term impacts on labor market outcomes, educational attainment, and transitions to adulthood.* New York, NY: MDRC.

Kemple, J. J., & Willner, C. (2008). *Career Academies: Long-term impacts on labor market outcomes, educational attainment, and transitions to adulthood.* New York, NY: MDRC.

Kimura-Walsh, E., Yamamura, E. K., Griffin, K. A., & Allen, W. R. (2008). Achieving the college dream? Examining disparities in access to college information among high achieving and non-high achieving Latina students. *Journal of Hispanic Higher Education, 8,* 298–315.

Malagon, M., Perez Huber, L., & Velez, V. (2009). Our experiences, our methods: Using grounded theory to inform a critical race theory methodology. *Seattle Journal for Social Justice, 8*(1). Retrieved from digitalcommons.law.seattleu.edu/sjsj/vol8/iss1/10

McClafferty, K., McDonough, P., & Nuñez, A.M. (2002). What is a college culture? Facilitating college preparation through organizational change. Paper presented at the annual meeting of the American Education Research Association.

McDonough, P. (1997). *Choosing colleges. How social class and schools structure opportunity.* Albany, NY: State University of New York Press.

Miner, J. B. (1995). *Administration and management theory.* Brookfield, VT: Ashgate.

Moore, E., & Oppenheim, E. (2010). *Learning in context: Preparing Latina/o workers for careers and continuing education.* Washington, DC: National Council of La Raza.

National Women's Law Center & Mexican American Legal Defense and Educational Fund (NWLC & MALDEF).(2009). *Listening to Latinas: Barriers to high school graduation.* Retrieved from https://www.maldef.org/assets/pdf/ListeningtoLatinas.pdf

Nuñez, A., M., & Elizondo, D. (2013). *Closing the Latina/o/a transfer gap: Creating pathways to the baccalaureate.* Perspectivas Issues in Higher Education Practice and Policy. Retrieved from http://www.aahhe.org/_resources/pdf/Perspectivas-Vol2.pdf

Orfield, G., & Lee, C. (2007). *Historic reversals, accelerating resegregation, and the need for new integration strategies.* Los Angeles, CA: Civil Rights Project/Proyecto Derechos Civiles, UCLA.

Pathways to College Network. (2006). *A shared agenda: A leadership challenge to improve college access and success.* Boston, MA: The Education Resources Institute.

Pew Hispanic Center. (2005). *Hispanics: A people in motion.* Washington, DC: Pew Hispanic Center.

Roderick, M., Nagaoka, J., & Allensworth, E. (2006). *From high school to the future: A first look at Chicago graduates' college enrollment, college preparation, and graduation from four-year colleges.* Chicago, IL: Consortium on Chicago School Research at the University of Chicago.

Rodríguez, L. F., & Brown, T. M. (2009). From voice to agency: Guiding principles for participatory action research with youth. *New Directions for Youth Development, 123,* 19–34.

Rogers, J., Bertrand, M., Freelon, R., & Fanelli, S. (2011). *Free fall: Educational opportunities in 2011.* California Educational Opportunity Report UCLA's Institute for Democracy, Education, and Access; UC All Campus Consortium on Research for Diversity.

Rogers, J., Fanelli, S., Freelon, R., Medina, D., Bertrand, M., & Del Razo, M. (2010). *Educational opportunities in hard times: The impact of the economic crisis on public schools and working families.* California Educational Opportunity Report UCLA's Institute for Democracy, Education, and Access UC All Campus Consortium on Research for Diversity.

Schein, E. H. (1985). *Organizational culture and leadership.* San Francisco, CA: Jossey-Bass.

Schein, E. H. (1996) Culture: The missing concept in organization studies. *Administrative Science Quarterly, 41,* 229–240.

Sokolower, J. (2012). Schools and the new Jim Crow: An interview with Michelle Alexander. *Rethinking Schools.* Retrieved from http://www.rethinkingschools.org//cmshandler. asp?archive/26_02/26_02_sokolower.shtml

Solorzano, D. (1998) Critical race theory, racial and gender microaggressions, and the experiences of Chicana and Chicano Scholars. *International Journal of Qualitative Studies, 11,* 121–136.

Solorzano, D., & Delgado Bernal, D. (2001). Critical race theory, transformational resistance and social justice: Chicana and Chicano students in an urban context. *Urban Education, 36,* 308–342.

Solorzano, D., Villalpando, O., & Oseguera, L. (2005). Educational inequities and Latina/o undergraduate students in the United States: A critical race analysis of their educational progress. *Journal of Hispanic Higher Education, 4,* 272–294.

Steele, F. I., & Jenks, S. (1977). *The feel of the work place.* Reading, MA: Addison-Wesley.

Stern, D., Dayton, C., & Raby, M. (1992). *Career academies: Partnerships for reconstructing American high schools.* San Francisco, CA: Jossey-Bass.

Stern, D., Dayton, C., & Raby, M. (2010, February 25). *Career academies: A proven strategy to prepare high school students for college and careers.* UC Berkeley Career Academy Support Network Working Paper.

Strauss, A., & Corbin, J. (1990). *Basics of qualitative research: Grounded theory procedures and techniques.* Newbury Park, CA: Sage Publications, Inc.

Tierney, W., Corwin, Z., & Colyar, J. (2003). *Preparing for college.* Los Angeles, CA: Center for Higher Education Policy Analysis.

U.S. Census Bureau. (2012). *Statistical abstract of the United States: 2012* (Table 279). Washington, DC: U.S. Government Printing Office.

Valencia, R., & Solorzano, D. (1997). Contemporary deficit thinking. In R. Valencia (Ed.), *The evolution of deficit thinking in educational thought and practice* (pp.160–210). New York, NY: Falmer.

Venezia, V., Kirst, M. W., & Antonio, A. L. (2003). *Betraying the college dream: How disconnected K–12 and postsecondary education systems undermine student aspirations.* Palo Alto, CA: Stanford Institute for Higher Education Research.

Yin, R. K. (2013) *Case study research: Design and methods* (5th ed.). London, England: Sage Publications.

Zarate, M. E., & Gallimore, R. G. (2005). *Gender differences in factors leading to college enrollment: A longitudinal analysis of Latina and Latina/o students.* Cambridge, MA: Harvard Educational Review.

CHAPTER 4

Race, Brotherhood, and Educational Engagement in the Urban Context

A Case Study of Structured Peer Bonding Among Boys of Color

Irene I. Vega, Leticia Oseguera, & Gilberto Q. Conchas

The Palmview Male Cooperative (PMC) is an out-of-school-time program that involves students of color from varied achievement levels in a "brotherhood" focused on personal excellence, group accountability, and mutual support. This case study shows how participating in this organization impacts Black and Latina/o student engagement. Results indicate that achieving students, those who entered with a grade point average above 2.5, understand this organization as a way to maintain their school involvement and academic performance while serving as role models for others. Aspiring students, those with an entering grade point average below 2.5, increased their academic efforts and reported a heightened sense of belonging in the school community. Overall, we argue that framing this organization as a Black and Latina/o "brotherhood" effectively promotes peer bonding, which builds attachment to the larger school community.

On a national scale, Black[1] and Latino males have the highest dropout rates (Kaufman, Alt, & Chapman, 2004), are least likely to attain postsecondary credentials (King, 2006), and suffer from disproportionate rates of incarceration (Kupchik, 2009, Leiber, 2002). Districts around the country are developing positive innovations in response to these disturbing trends (Conchas, 2001; Conchas & Rodriguez, 2008; Noguera, 2008). The Male Cooperative is one example of such promising practices in a large urban city in southern California. The program's mission is to decrease high school dropout rates among minority males and increase their awareness of postsecondary and career options.

While the goals of this innovation are relatively common, the implementation strategy is quite novel. Instead of focusing on tutoring or other academic skill development activities, the program targets students' socio-emotional well-being and social integration to achieve improved educational outcomes. In fact, the innovative program is presented as a peer-led "brotherhood" focused on personal excellence, group accountability, and mutual support for African American and Latino males. There is one teacher who serves as the "sponsor," but his role is to facilitate rather than lead the organization. Perhaps the most unique aspect of the program is that while participation is voluntary, the organization successfully recruits both highly engaged minority males, as well as their most marginalized counterparts; we make this distinction by referring to achieving (engaged) and aspiring (marginalized) students, respectively.

Drawing on Finn's (1989) participation-identification framework, survey data, in-depth interviews, and participant observation conducted over a 12-month period, this chapter examines how participating in this "brotherhood" at Palmview High School[2] influences students' engagement. We argue that the following three features of the organization are particularly consequential in recruiting students with different achievement levels and ensuring that the program met their diverse needs: (1) race-conscious recruitment, (2) discourse of "brotherhood," and (3) peer-run structure. Through these features, we elucidate how the process of increased engagement with school comes about, especially for the most marginalized students. Our work disrupts the homogeneous image of racialized males as disengaged students and demonstrates that "school engagement" is a dynamic construct that may look different based on the population being studied.

A BLEAK CYCLE FOR BLACK AND LATINO MALES

Although student engagement is often discussed as a unidimensional student-level construct, it is actually a multifaceted construct that is shaped by schools' sociocultural milieu and students' background characteristics (Johnson, Crosnoe, & Elder, 2001). The interplay between individual factors and institutional context is critical to our work with Black and Latino males because research documents that school cultures can be alienating for minority males, especially those with working-class backgrounds. Indeed, the compounded effects of schools favoring the cultural capital of the middle class (Bourdieu, 1986; Carter, 2005), a misalignment between the student role and gender roles for males (Entwisle, Alexander, & Olson, 2007), and being a member of a racially subordinated group results in pernicious interactions between school personnel and minority males. Specifically, societal stereotypes that associate Black and Latino boys with criminality lead to constant patrolling and harsher disciplinary patterns in schools, which effectively compound the marginalization of this already vulnerable population (Cammarota, 2004; Fergus & Noguera, 2009; Lopez, 2003).

For instance, Noguera (2003, 2008) argued that Latino and Black boys are so overrepresented among those with discipline referrals that their underachievement has become normalized. He contended that schools' zero-tolerance policies may be creating a pipeline into the criminal justice system for males of color. Rios's (2006, 2009) ethnographic study also showed how Latino and Black male criminalization disrupts their ability to develop a healthy masculine identity. He described a process by which public consensus about the meaning and physical representations of "deviance" are eventually legitimized within social institutions such as schools, community centers, and even family units.

According to existing research, Black and Latino males' criminalization leads to marginalization in school and eventually, disengagement from school. This work sets the context in which Black and Latino male schooling takes place, but it also presents a bleak cycle: Broad structural forces intersect with school-based sociocultural processes to reproduce minority males' marginal social position. In contrast, this case study presents a different perspective by showing that schools can actually intervene in the disengagement process and set students on a more advantageous path.

TURNING SCHOOL FAILURE ON ITS HEAD

The participation-identification model (Finn, 1989) differentiates between behavioral and psychological aspects of students' schooling experiences; participation refers to school-related behaviors whereas identification is students' attitudes toward school. (See Table 4.1 for theory-derived operationalization of constructs.) In this model, school participation and identification are linked to measurable academic achievement (such as grade point average), but the basic premise is that " participation in school activities is essential for positive outcomes, including the students' sense of belonging and valuing school related goals, to be realized" (p. 129).

Table 4.1. Finn's (1989) Participation-Identification Model Concepts

Participation	Identification
Level 1: Basic classroom engagement	Sense of belonging
Level 2: Increased effort in classroom	Valuing school-related goals
Level 3: Extracurricular involvement	
Level 4: School governance	

*Note: We added college awareness to the framework as a participation measure.

Finn (1989) distinguished four levels of participation. At level 1, students fulfill the minimum requirements, such as attending school regularly, paying attention in class, following teachers' directions and answering their questions, and submitting completed homework regularly. Level 2 represents increased effort toward classroom activities, such as initiating questions and spending more time working than is minimally required. Level 3 refers to involvement in extracurricular activities in school as well as leadership and cooperativeness skills, whereas level 4 is participation in school governance. Given the PMC's dual goal of reduced dropout rates and increased awareness of postsecondary options, we extend Finn's model to include college awareness levels 3 and 4. College awareness level 3 includes talking with friends about college and level 4 is a student's preparedness for college, including making college visits and receiving guidance about college.

The other major component of this model is identification, a two-part construct that includes (1) "sense of belonging," a congruence between students' sense of self and the school community, and (2) "valuing school-related goals," a correspondence between participants' personal goals and the purpose of schooling. In this study we focused on the goals of the PMC, school graduation, and awareness of a variety of postsecondary options, as the purpose of schooling. Finn (1989) hypothesized that school identification emerges from participation, but both are mutually reinforcing.

This mixed-method case study used Finn's participation-identification model to examine how participating in the PMC influences African American and Latino males' school engagement. More specifically, we drew on survey data to examine whether involvement with this program influences students' behavioral participation and attitudinal identification with school. Also through surveys, we asked whether the program differently impacts aspiring (engaged) and achieving (marginalized) students. Finally, we turned to semi-structured interviews with students to examine the process through which changes in participation and identification occurred.

Palmview High School

Palmview High School (PHS) is located in a large urban city in southern California. The city's racial composition is 41% Latino, 30% White, 14% Black, 13% Asian, and 2% other, and the median household income is $52,711 (Census 2010). The ethnic/racial composition of the school during the 2008–2009 school year approximated the city demographics. Together, Latino and African American students constituted 54% of the school population, 41% and 13%, respectively. Whites constituted 31% and Asians 10% of the student population. Forty-eight percent of PHS students qualified for free or reduced lunch, with Black and Latino students overrepresented among this group.

PHS is located in an urban community that draws from affluent as well as low-income areas of the city. This results in an economically and ethnically diverse student body with varying academic preparation levels. Nevertheless, it is one of four Sandy Unified School District (SUSD) high schools that received a national award for the number of students who are enrolled in advanced placement (AP) courses and has been selected as a California Distinguished School on several occasions. Despite this overall academic success, the distribution of success is not experienced similarly by all groups on campus. In particular, Black and Latino males are underrepresented in AP courses and are most likely to leave school before graduating.

Palmview Male Cooperative

Coach, a veteran Spanish teacher and former varsity basketball coach, is the "club sponsor." His role is to plan at least two events per month (such as community service, leadership activities, and college awareness presentations) in addition to monthly meetings. The monthly meetings, which take place in Coach's classroom during 7th period, center on student-led discussion on topics such as "Creating Positive Labels," "Hope Is Not a Plan," and "Holding Ourselves Accountable to the Group." Student presenters, who have either volunteered or were invited by Coach or peer leaders to present, have between 2 and 4 weeks to prepare their discussion points.

The Students

This chapter is based on a sample of 25 (out of 44) PMC members. The sample included 15 Black and 10 Latino students[3] (see Table 4.2). While the PMC includes 10th- through 12th-grade students, we focused on juniors and seniors since they can evaluate their experiences at Palmview before and after the PMC.

The PMC's novel recruitment strategy is important to note because it resulted in a diverse group of members with distinct school performance profiles. The first 10 members of the organization were identified by teachers and counselors as either (1) a student who could provide leadership and have a positive influence on peers, or (2) a student who was not living up to his potential. These "leaders," as they were subsequently referred to, were asked to recruit other boys for the inaugural cohort of this club. Unlike other school organizations, no eligibility requirements were established. Most of the leaders recruited from their friendship networks whereas others approached students randomly on campus.

As a result of the recruitment strategy, some members of the organization had solid academic records and were involved in multiple extracurricular activities at Palmview; others had weak grade point averages and had never participated in a school organization. To illustrate, during the 2008–2009 school year, members of the PMC included the president and vice president of the Associated Student Government at PHS, star athletes and campus leaders, as well as students who were on academic probation, one student who served time in a juvenile detention center for a gang-related shooting, and one senior who was transitioning back into PHS after having dropped out his sophomore year. According to school administrators, the PMC reflects the diversity of minority males at PHS.

Table 4.2. Sample by Race/Ethnicity, Grade Level, and Grade Point Average in 2008-2009

Pseudonym	Race/Ethnicity	Grade	Total GPA
Teddy[†]	Black	11	0.23
RayBon	Black	11	0.91
Michael	Black	11	1.2
Bay	Black	11	1.5
Gilbert	Latino	11	1.6
Kory*	Black	11	1.74
Oso	Latino	11	1.84
John Brown	Black	11	1.84
Brian	Black	11	2.09
Cyrus*	Black	12	2.1
MJ	Black	11	2.22
Marquis	Black	11	2.31
Dion*	Black	11	2.37
Dell	Black	11	2.4
David	Latino	12	2.4
Jesse*	Latino	12	2.4
Clay	Latino	11	2.43
AJ	Latino	11	2.62
Thomas*	Black	12	2.84
C-Rod*	Latino	11	2.95
Esteban*	Latino	12	2.95
Alexander*	Latino	12	2.98
Dre	Black	11	3.43
Mitchell*	Black	12	3.79
Conner	Latino	11	3.9

Notes:
[†]Spring 2009 GPA data not available for this student.
*Identified as a PMC Leader
Students identified their own pseudonyms.
Total GPA—Includes elective course grades and prerequisite
    courses for UC/CSU admission (A–G Courses)

The Proof

Survey of high school experiences. The survey was adapted from a larger study of the PMC administered at the beginning of the fall semester and again at the end of the spring semester. The survey evaluated students' goals, values, self-ratings, aspirations, and within- and out-of-school behaviors pre- and postpro-gram involvement. Only survey items reflecting Finn's (1989) participation-identification framework were included in this case study. Since participation is related to observable behavioral markers, we measured this using the survey data. School identification refers to a sense of belonging and feeling of attachment to others, so we drew primarily on qualitative data for this component. However, we also presented some survey findings on identification; see Tables 4.3 and 4.4.

Under participation, we included items reflecting Finn's (1989) four levels, which ranged from how often students completed homework (level 1 participa-tion) to whether students had held a leadership position in school (level 4 partic-ipation). Under identification, we included students' reports of the importance of graduating from high school (i.e., valuing school-related goals) and whether students developed close friendships with others (i.e., sense of belonging). See Tables 4.3 and 4.4 for a complete list of items organized within the conceptual framework.

Semi-structured interviews: Interviews were conducted at the end of the spring term during the first year of the program's implementation. The interviews lasted between 45 and 60 minutes, and were audio-recorded and transcribed verbatim. The interview protocol consisted of five major sections: (1) general background about student life; (2) opinions on success and failure; (3) race, class, culture, and gender; (4) aspirations; and (5) experiences in the PMC.

Observations: Researchers attended meetings and other events throughout the 2008–2009 school year and took ethnographic fieldnotes (Emerson, Fretz, & Shaw, 1995) that focused on observed actions and scenes. These fieldnotes guid-ed the development of lengthier descriptive accounts of the observation session. These observations allowed us to document specific elements of program imple-mentation and changes in student behaviors over time. We also collected artifacts such as newspaper articles about the PMC, meeting agendas, and materials that were distributed at meetings.

How We Interpreted the Proof

Descriptive statistical analyses. Analyses of the survey of high school expe-riences are organized according to Finn's (1989) framework. To address research question 1, whether the PMC influences students' participation in and identifica-tion with school, we utilized a series of descriptive analyses, including paired t-test comparisons, to determine changes in student attitudes and behaviors pre- and post-program involvement. To address research question 2, regarding differences between aspiring and achieving students in the effect of the PMC, we split the file by grade point average (those with a GPA above 2.5 are achieving students and those with a GPA below 2.5 are aspiring students) and applied independent sample t-tests. Since the goal of research question 3 is to document the process through which a change occurred (if at all), we drew on the strength of interview and observation data to answer it.

Inductive and theory-driven qualitative analyses. Interview data were analyzed in two phases. During the first phase, transcripts were reviewed line by line with the goal of identifying recurrent words, phrases, expressions, and significant events or aspects of informants' experiences. Memos written during this phase reflected emerging conceptual categories. The second phase consisted of focused coding using Finn's (1989) participation-identification model and the themes that emerged from the first phase. This deductive process consisted of coding excerpts where students referred specifically to their involvement with the PMC and if/how it influenced their (1) school-related behaviors (participation), and (2) attitudes about school (identification).

DIFFERENCES BETWEEN ASPIRING
AND ACHIEVING STUDENTS

Our survey showed that all students reported speaking more in class, improving their public-speaking abilities, and increasing preparation for college. However, a more nuanced pattern emerged when we examined the data across achievement level. Much of the change was among the aspiring members, those with beginning grade point averages below 2.5. We saw significant increases in participation levels 2 through 4 for these students. Specifically, they reported speaking up in class (level 2), improving their public-speaking abilities (level 3), and rating the importance of becoming a community leader high (level 4) after 1 year of being in the program. Notably, we did not see statistically significant changes (increases or decreases) at the basic level 1 of participation (skipping class or turning in course assignments late).

In interviews, however, aspiring students did report changes in these basic levels of participation. In particular, they reported making increased effort toward their studies and avoiding behaviors that were detrimental to school success. We also found greater gains among aspiring students in their perceptions of college awareness, which we added to Finn's model given the goals of the PMC. In particular, we saw a significant increase in aspiring students' rating becoming a community leader as essential (level 4) and an increase in students' college preparedness (level 4). Under the identification variables, both aspiring and achieving members reported more confidence in their understanding of college after their first year of the PMC.

Table 4.3. T-tests Paired Sample Results by Achievement Level

	ALL STUDENTS (N = 25)		ACHIEVING (N = 10)		ASPIRING (N = 15)	
	Before PMC	After PMC	Before PMC	After PMC	Before PMC	After PMC
PARTICIPATION VARIABLES (COLLEGE AWARENESS VARIABLES)						
Level 1: Basic Classroom Engagement						
Often complete homework[a]	3.40	3.12	3.70	3.70	3.20	2.73
Hours studying/doing homework[b]	3.12*	2.20*	4.40**	2.30**	2.27	2.13
Skip class[a]	1.88	1.68	1.30	1.50	2.27	1.80
Turn course assignment in late[a]	2.60	2.64	2.50	2.30	2.67	2.87
Level 2: Increased Classroom Effort						
Speak up in class factor[a]	2.97**	3.40**	3.37	3.67	2.71*	3.22*
Receive tutoring[a]	2.12	2.04	2.50	2.20	1.87	1.93
Take honors courses[a]	2.50	2.50	2.90	3.00	1.64	1.64
Level 3: Extracurricular Involvement						
Hours participating in school clubs/groups[b]	3.20	2.40	3.90	2.50	2.73	2.33
Public speaking ability/oral communication[c]	3.24**	4.12**	3.30	3.80	3.20**	4.33**
Leadership and cooperativeness factor[c]	4.13	4.19	3.99	4.17	4.23	4.20
Talk with friends about college[a]	3.04	3.20	3.70	3.50	2.60	3.00
Level 4: School Governance						
Held leadership position[a]	2.40*	2.96*	2.60	3.00	2.27	2.93
Becoming a community leader[d]	2.72+	3.04+	3.50	3.40	2.20**	2.80**

(continued)

Table 4.3. (continued)

College preparedness factor[a]	2.94*	3.46*	3.33	3.67	2.68*	3.30*
Visit colleges[a]	2.60	2.80	2.90	2.90	2.40	2.73
On track for college[e]	3.12	3.44	3.40	3.70	2.93	3.27
IDENTIFICATION VARIABLES						
Valuing School-Related Goals						
Importance of graduating from high school[d]	4.00	3.93	4.00	4.00	4.00	3.82
Importance of going to college[d]	3.47	3.67	3.80	3.80	3.27	3.40
That going to school matters[a]	3.12*	3.64*	3.30	3.60	2.45	3.67
Motivated to work harder[a]	3.24	3.36	3.80	3.60	2.89	3.20
Often meet teachers' expectations[f]	2.28	2.72	2.30*	1.80*	2.67	2.67
Understanding of college[e]	2.80***	3.68***	3.30+	3.80+	2.47**	3.60**
Sense of Belonging						
Intimidated by teachers[a]	1.40	1.52	1.30	1.50	1.47	1.53
Receive emotional support from teacher[a]	2.44	2.44	2.50	2.30	2.40	2.53
School staff meet individual needs[a]	3.40	3.24	3.90	3.50	3.07	3.07
Develop close friendships with students[g]	2.60	2.80	2.40	2.70	2.73	2.87
Resources are available if I have trouble[a]	3.00	3.17	3.40	3.60	3.07	3.13

Note: Items in italics reflect college preparation variables at the respective participation or identification level.

a 1 = not at all to 4 = frequently; b 0 = none to 7 = over 20 hours; c 1 = lowest 10% to 5 = highest 10%; d 1 = not important to 4 = essential;
 e 1 = not confident to 4 = very confident; f 1 = always to 5 = rarely; g 1 = unsuccessful to 3 = completely successful
See the appendix at the end of this chapter for factor items, scaling, and alphas.
***p < .001, **p < .01, *p < .05, +p < .10

63

Table 4.4. T-tests Independent Sample Results by Achievement Level

	BEFORE PMC (N = 25)		AFTER PMC (N = 25)	
	Achieving	Aspiring	Achieving	Aspiring
PARTICIPATION VARIABLES (COLLEGE AWARENESS)				
Level 1: Basic Classroom Engagement				
Often complete homework[a]	3.70*	3.20*	3.70***	2.73***
Hours studying/doing homework[b]	4.40*	2.27*	2.30	2.13
Skip class[a]	1.30**	2.27**	1.50	1.80
Turn course assignment in late[a]	2.50	2.67	2.30	2.87
Level 2: Increased Classroom Effort				
Speak up in class factor[a]	3.37*	2.71*	3.67*	3.22*
Receive tutoring[a]	2.50	1.87	2.20	1.93
Take honors courses[a]	2.90**	1.64**	3.00**	1.64**
Level 3: Extracurricular Involvement				
Hours participating in school clubs/groups[b]	3.90	2.73	2.50	2.33
Public speaking ability/oral communication[c]	3.30	3.20	3.80	4.33
Leadership and cooperativeness factor[c]	3.99	4.23	4.17	4.20
Talk with friends about college[a]	3.70**	2.60**	3.50+	3.00+
Level 4: School Governance				
Active in leadership role[a] (fall survey only)	3.00	2.45		
Held leadership position[a]	2.60	2.27	3.00	2.93
Becoming a community leader[d]	3.50**	2.20**	3.40+	2.80+
College preparedness factor[a]	3.33*	2.68*	3.67	3.30

(continued)

Table 4.4 (continued)

Visit colleges[a]	2.90	2.40	2.90	2.73
On track for college[e]	3.40+	3.07+	3.60+	3.13+
IDENTIFICATION VARIABLES				
Valuing School-Related Goals				
Importance of graduating from high school[d]	4.00	4.00	4.00	3.82
Importance of going to college[d]	3.80	3.27	3.80	3.40
That going to school matters[a]	3.30	3.30	3.60	3.67
Motivated to work harder[a]	3.80**	2.89**	3.60+	3.20+
Often meet teachers' expectations[f]	2.30+	2.67+	1.80*	2.67*
Understanding of college[e]	3.30*	2.47*	3.80	3.60
Sense of Belonging				
Intimidated by teachers[a]	1.30	1.47	1.50	1.53
Receive emotional support from teacher[a]	2.50	2.40	2.30	2.53
School staff meet individual needs[a]	3.90**	3.07**	3.50	3.07
Develop close friendships with students[g]	2.40	2.73	2.70	2.87
Resources are available if I have trouble[a]	3.40+	3.07+	3.60+	3.13+

Note: items in italics reflect college preparation variables at the respective participation or identification level.

a) 1 = not at all to 4 = frequently; b) 0 = none to 7 = over 20 hours; c) 1 = lowest 10% to 5 = highest 10%; d) 1 = not important to 4 = essential; e) 1 = not confident to 4 = very confident; f 1 = always to 5 = rarely; g 1 = unsuccessful to 3 = completely successful

See Appendix 4.1 at the end of this chapter for factor items, scaling, and alphas.

***p < .001, **p < .01, *p < .05, +p < .10

Research question 2 required that we compare the changes separately by pre- and postsurveys and by achievement level. In doing so, we saw larger differences on the participation and identification indicators between achieving and aspiring members. However, a glaring fact is that the participation level 3 and 4 differences between the achieving members and the aspiring members were reduced or eliminated by the end of the year. Specifically, prior to any exposure to the PMC, achieving members were significantly more likely to rate the importance of becoming a community leader high, to report talking to their friends about college, and to report confidence in their college preparedness, but after 1 year of the program, the differences between them and the aspiring members disappeared.

In evaluating the earlier levels of participation, three of the four variables under level 1 of this construct were higher for the achieving students prior to program exposure. After program exposure, however, only one of the participation variables (how often a student reports completing homework) was significantly different between the achieving and aspiring members. At level 2 of participation, we saw less change between pre- and postsurvey behavior among the aspiring and achieving members. Specifically, achieving members reported higher means before and after program exposure relative to their aspiring counterparts. See Table 4.4 for the independent sample t-test results.

Our survey analyses demonstrated that the PMC had the largest effect in increasing effort toward school activities, including extracurricular involvement and leadership and cooperation skills; this is at levels 2–4 of participation in our theoretical model. Students, regardless of entering achievement profile, reported increased confidence in their ability to speak up in class and to speak in public, as well as an increased commitment to becoming a community leader. Notably, however, the aspiring students experienced the greatest increases. One explanation for different effects is that although the PMC involves students of varying achievement levels, much of the emphasis was on raising aspiring students' status. Therefore, it may not be surprising that in terms of traditional participation, we saw greater gains for those students who were mostly disengaged. A second explanation is a statistical ceiling effect where achievers already exhibited high participation levels in school prior to their involvement with the PMC. Indeed, based on their academic records, achieving students were already participating at levels 1 and 2: attending school regularly, following teachers' directions, completing homework, and exerting enough effort toward these activities to earn average to above-average grades. Most of them were also participating in extracurricular activities (such as sports teams and school clubs) aside from the PMC—this indicates that level 3 participation in school existed among these students prior to their involvement with the PMC. In fact, several achieving students were even participating in school governance, which is the highest level indicated by Finn.

Although the PMC mostly maintains participation and is understood as another extracurricular activity by achieving students, they do recognize something unique about this organization. According to interview data, they understand that their achievement level qualifies them as a leader and peer mentor for their aspiring counterparts. This is not surprising given that, according to Coach, students who were "maxing out their ability" before their involvement in the PMC are expected to provide leadership and mentorship for those who are struggling academically and/or socially at school.

In contrast, aspiring students, those with a GPA below 2.5, reported that the PMC positively influenced their behaviors in school at the basic participation levels. Aspiring members reported that they avoid behaviors that are considered counterproductive to school-related goals, such as ditching classes, being late to school, and sleeping during class. Furthermore, examination of the official academic records of the aspiring members showed a reduction of absences and tardiness from the beginning of the program to the end of the first year. John Brown was one example; he earned a 0.50 GPA the year prior to joining the PMC and had never participated in a school organization:

> Last year I was the type of student that I walked into class like "'ok, you can go ahead and teach teacher. I'm gonna go to sleep." That was in all my classes last year. This year it's more like, I'm gonna stay up, I go to bed on time, I try to get as much sleep to where I'm not falling asleep in class. I pay attention. I'm actually able to learn something rather than just sitting there to be sitting there.

In contrast to their achieving counterparts who understood the PMC as a leadership opportunity, John Brown and other aspiring students reported an increase primarily in levels 1 and 2 of participation. Aspiring students who were ditching school, sleeping in class, and ignoring homework began to reverse the pattern of disengagement that leads to school dropout. According to Finn (1989), if these students continue participating at these basic levels and experience social or intrinsic rewards from doing so, they will also become identified with school and dropout can be averted. Surely, this is an encouraging prospect. But rather than endorsing Finn's model, our analyses led us to ask an obvious but challenging question: How can schools get students who are disengaged to start participating even at these most basic levels? After all, John Brown had never participated in a school organization before and it was not for lack of options. What made him and others like him want to participate in the PMC in the first place?

RACE, BROTHERHOOD, AND ACCOUNTABILITY
TO EXPLAIN IDENTIFICATION

In this section we draw on interview and observation data to answer our third research question, which seeks to document the process that preceded students' increased participation. Since aspiring students were most alienated prior to their involvement with the PMC, their change provided the most vivid illustration of Finn's (1989) model in action.

Although Finn's model purported that identification emerges from participation, we found that the opposite is true. In order to get Black and Latino boys to participate (especially aspiring students), the PMC had to signal that it was different from the array of student organizations on the Palmview campus; it had to get them to identify with the organization before they even became members. In this section we elaborate the process through which aspiring students became more engaged in school by presenting the three organizational features that attracted and retained them: (1) race-conscious recruitment, (2) discourse of "brotherhood," and (3) peer-run structure.

Our analysis showed that including high-achieving Black and Latino males in the same organization with those who are struggling had a positive influence on both. For those who had solid academic records and were otherwise participating in school, the PMC was an involvement opportunity where they were seen as leaders who were helping others. For those who were disengaged, the fact that the PMC is an all-male, Black and Latino school club demystified academic achievement and school involvement as activities reserved for White students. These findings support other research showing that having access to "same race models" or high-achieving minority students increases minority students' school engagement (Johnson, Crosnoe, & Elder, 2001).

The salience of race abounded as both aspiring and achieving students described the PMC as a much-needed alternative to the rest of the (White) involvement opportunities on campus. This was true of members who did not participate in any school organization, as well as those who were highly involved on campus. For example, Esteban, a highly involved senior, expressed discontent over this imbalance when the interviewer asked him if he considers himself part of the school community:

> Sometimes I feel like I'm part of it but sometimes I feel like I'm out of it cuz it's mostly run by Whites. I mean, I don't want to be racial or anything but it's mostly the truth. Most of the Whites control everything like student council and there's nothing we can do, we can just try but we still can't. It's racial discrimination.

This quote illustrates that even if school organizations are not overtly exclusive, the perception (based on students' actual experiences) that clubs are for White students may keep students from these productive social networks. This is reinforced by AJ as he describes the PMC:

> We're all together on it, so we're not just in our little groups . . . you know how some people have White clubs? I'm pretty sure a Mexican doesn't want to get in a White club, so a brotherhood is basically everybody. You know? Getting together not caring about who they are.

Indeed, even though Black and Latino students make up 54% of the PHS student body, students reported that White students dominate the majority of involvement opportunities. While race keeps students out of other school organizations, once embedded in the PMC members express a sense of pride and unity that is tied to their shared experience as minorities in the broader racial context. Clay, a Latino aspiring student, said that what he enjoys most about the PMC is "it's freeing because it's people that are like me—that are in the same situation. It's not like somebody (pause) like a White person that is doing better." It is not clear how White people "are doing better" than Clay, but it is important to note that he makes no distinction between Black and Latino members, suggesting that a shared racial experience in comparison to the White majority is what unifies them within the PMC.

While students spoke openly about the salience of race in their decision to participate in the PMC, they did not demonstrate as much awareness about the fact that it was an all-male organization. This supports what Cammarota (2004) found in his ethnographic study of the schooling orientations of Latino youth. Since gender is a privileged identity for males, they tend not to be as aware of it as they are of race. However, we suggest that gendered perceptions may have been enveloped within the discourse of brotherhood, and this is something that students discussed at length.

Framing the PMC as a brotherhood is actually one of its most consequential features, especially in attracting aspiring students; they had an especially strong affinity toward their membership in a Black and Latino brotherhood and a nuanced understanding of what this meant. Aspiring students explained with great consistency that being part of the PMC influenced their attitudes and behaviors in school because they felt accountable to a group. However, this accountability was not motivated by anxiety that their peers or school personnel would reprimand them for doing something wrong. Rather, this sense of group accountability was motivated by what we call "affective sanctions"—the prospect of disappointing Coach or, especially, a PMC brother was enough to deter behaviors that are detrimental to student success. In Brian's words, "knowing that people are there showing me that they care. . . . I really appreciate it so I'm not just going to turn my back to 'em."

The idea of turning one's back on a PMC brother is something that students want to prevent at all costs. However, "turning one's back" or disappointing a brother does not require that students literally direct a negative action toward that person. Students can disappoint a brother by engaging in behaviors that are detrimental to themselves and, more specifically, detrimental to their academic goals. This is so because while there are social aspects to the PMC, students understand that school success is a primary purpose of the organization. Therefore, being a "good brother" is directly tied to being a good student—in this way, the PMC connects students' sense of self and their commitment to one another with school-related goals.

Indeed, this finding resonates with research on school friendship networks, which shows that academically oriented friendships can serve a protective function against school problems (Crosnoe, Cavanagh, & Elder, 2003). This suggests that including both aspiring and achieving students in the same organization is a promising practice for schools that are interested in this type of intervention because "friendships with students who are more centrally located in the social structure of the school may foster a stronger sense of belonging" (Johnson, Crosnoe, & Elder, 2001, p. 336). Ream and Rumberger's (2008) analysis of friendship networks also suggested that students who are involved in school tend to avoid behaviors that jeopardize their educational success. The authors recommended that schools should facilitate "resource-rich, school-oriented friendship networks" (p. 125) to foster a sense of attachment among marginalized students. These school-based relationships serve as nonfamilial forms of social capital that are critical to student outcomes (Conchas, 2001) and, in the case of the PMC, are especially consequential to aspiring members' school engagement.

The salience of affective sanctions within the PMC peer network is also illustrated through students' level of awareness of the broader school context. Before PMC membership, students felt a sense of anonymity, or as Dell put it, "I was just another face in the crowd." However, they reported becoming aware that their actions and inactions have repercussions for themselves and the entire group as a result of their involvement with this organization. As Oso illustrates, PMC members have to represent the brotherhood positively at PHS:

> I do feel like I'm part of Palmview community because we're basically representing Palmview. Let's say I do something real bad like I'm ditching class or I'm slipping or I'm just putting PMC in a bad name, then the PMC gets blamed and I don't want to put a bad word on it so I put a positive word. I get recognized by teachers saying that I'm doing a great job, you know? So they'll say, "I heard this organization is great."

Similarly to Oso, Gilbert acquired a sense of belonging within the broader school context as a result of his membership in the PMC. He also considered himself a representative of this organization and felt the responsibility to "show that this is a good thing." Furthermore, he reiterated that his effort in school is partly a result of the prospect of affective sanctions—he did not want to disappoint those who care about him and his academic success:

> I felt it helped me have a better focus in school because I'm a part of this school; a part of this thing in school. I want to represent this and I want to show that this is a good thing. And you know these people actually care about me. I don't want to let them down.

Students who were already involved in other organizations or were high academic achievers did not articulate these same ideas. As mentioned previously, achieving students understood the PMC as a way to build their resumé for college, increase their leadership abilities, and help others. They did not express the same degree of attachment to the organization and did not consider it as consequential to their high school career as aspiring students. One reason may be that they were already embedded in other school networks that aspiring students were lacking—they were not isolated from the school.

That the discourse of brotherhood resonates most with aspiring students is encouraging because this means that with institutional initiative to create supportive learning environments and facilitate productive social networks, even the most marginalized students can achieve success in high school. Other research has also found that with the support of institutional agents, boys of color are able to resist negative societal labels and achieve educational success (Conchas & Noguera, 2004). Conchas (2001, 2006) also found that schools can foster cultures of success among racial minority and low-income students by facilitating caring and beneficial relationships with peers and teachers in small learning communities.

CONCLUSION

This case study has shown that framing the Palmview Male Cooperative as a Black and Latino "brotherhood" effectively promotes peer bonding, which builds attachment to the larger school community. Specific organizational features of the PMC disrupt the process of school dropout among the most disengaged African American and Latino boys, while simultaneously maintaining engagement among high-achieving boys of color. The organizational features we flag as attracting and retaining students with different school profiles are (1) race-conscious recruitment, (2) discourse of "brotherhood," and (3) peer-run structure.

The discourse of brotherhood is particularly significant because it engenders shared goals and bonds among students, which results in increased school identification among aspiring students. In this case, identification by way of brotherhood leads to participation for those students who were most alienated from their school as evidenced by their grade point average, as well as their own self-reported disaffection. Simultaneously, the discourse of brotherhood engenders a sense of responsibility among the achieving members. Their position as role models and leaders within the organization hinges upon their continued academic performance and involvement in other organizations that maintains participation in school. However, given the salience of race in their schooling, they come to understand their role as specific to helping ensure the academic success of more men of color.

Therefore, brotherhood as a rhetorical device does what "club" or "program" cannot do—it implies a relationship that goes beyond the confines of organizational membership. Yes, it implies friendship, but it also implies family, intimacy, integration, unconditional support, and other powerful sentiments that, when internalized by students, transform their individual academic trajectory into a collective struggle. These are the ingredients for increased school identification, which subsequently reinforces the importance of meaningful participation.

Our findings are nuanced in that we find distinct patterns based on students' entering school profile. Achieving students, those who entered with a grade point average above 2.5, understand this organization as a way to maintain their school involvement and their academic performance, while helping other men of color succeed in school. This suggests a higher level of participation, levels 3 and 4, which is expected given their incoming profiles and the leadership role they were expected to play. Among aspiring students, those with an entering grade point average below 2.5, we see an increase in the basic levels of participation (e.g., avoiding behaviors that are detrimental to school success, such as sleeping in class or ditching classes) and a notable positive change in their attitude toward school.

An explanation for the modest participation (behavioral) changes is derived from our observations of member meetings and activities. That is, while students discussed the importance of developing more effective academic study habits and behaviors, there was no actual intervention to teach study skills or time management. One suggestion for improvement is to integrate workshops and sessions on study skill development in addition to motivational speeches and other efforts to promote college awareness. Also, our continued observations throughout the school year confirm that as the program grows in size, the implementation strategy will also have to evolve. School personnel have responded to the increase in student members by assigning each student a mentor teacher who is responsible for monitoring and encouraging student success. It remains to be seen if and how this aspect will change the organization's dynamics since an important aspect of its success is the mutual accountability established through the peer-run format. Furthermore, it is important to note that we expected that PMC members would acquire distinct benefits from the organization given the diversity of students' entering profiles. In fact, we find the inclusion of students with distinct school performance profiles to be one of the most important, and perhaps effective, aspects of this organization.

In addition to the practical implications for school programming, our findings have theoretical implications for how scholars think about student engagement. While Finn (1989) asserted that dropout interventions should target students' participation levels, he left the method of doing so unspecified. That is, how do schools get students who are already disengaged and not participating to reverse this alarming pattern? In this study, we argue that increasing identification is a way to get even the most disenfranchised students to begin to participate. An obvious question may ask how we can purport to get aspiring students identified without their participation in the organization in the first place. Our findings suggest that certain structural features and cultural elements of the PMC effectively generated student interest in this organization; namely, its race-conscious recruitment and peer-run structure that are enveloped in the discourse of "brotherhood."

Appendix 4.1: Factor Items, Alpha, and Loadings

	Factor Loadings	
Items	Before PMC	After PMC
LEADERSHIP AND COOPERATIVENESS FACTOR		
Self-ratings[a]:		
Communication skills	.815	.565
Understanding of others	.740	.501
Popularity	.720	.373
Creativity	.700	.335
Cooperativeness	.548	.716
Leadership ability	.529	.431
Ability to work with others	.409	.717
Alpha =	*.848*	*.810*
SPEAKS UP IN CLASS FACTOR		
How often student[a]:		
Asks questions in class	.844	.899
Speaks up in class	.734	.987
Asks a teacher for help	.664	.363
Alpha =	*.797*	*.736*
COLLEGE PREPAREDNESS FACTOR		
Frequency with which student[a]:		
Receives guidance about college from high school personnel	.816	.823
Feels that high school is preparing you for college	.711	.522
Has heard presentations about how to go to college	.682	.339
Alpha =	*.730*	*.550*

[a]1 = not at all to 4 = frequently

NOTES

1. We use *Black* and *African American* interchangeably.

2. All identifiers are pseudonyms.

3. At least four students in the subsample identify as "mixed"; three are Black/Pacific Islander and one is Mexican/Puerto Rican. Others may also be biracial, but did not identify as such in the interview.

REFERENCES

Bourdieu, P. (1986). The forms of capital. In J. Richardson (Ed.), *Handbook of theory and research for the sociology of education* (pp. 241–258). New York, NY: Greenwood.

Cammarota, J. (2004). The gendered and racialized pathways of Latina and Latina/o youth: Different struggles, different resistances in the urban context. *Anthropology and Education Quarterly, 35*(1), 53–74.

Carter, P. (2005). *Keeping it real: School success beyond Black and White.* New York, NY: Oxford University Press.

Conchas, G. Q. (2001). Structuring failure and success: Understanding the variability in Latina/o school engagement. *Harvard Educational Review, 70*, 475–504.

Conchas, G. (2006). *The color of success: Race and high-achieving urban youth.* New York, NY: Teachers College Press.

Conchas, G. Q., & Noguera, P. (2004). Understanding the exceptions: How small schools support the achievement of academically successful Black boys. In N. Way & J. Y. Chu (Eds.), *Adolescent boys: Exploring diverse cultures of boyhood* (pp. 59–77). New York, NY & London, England: New York University Press.

Conchas, G. Q. & Rodriguez, L. F. (2008). *Small schools and urban youth: Using the power of school culture to engage students.* Thousand Oaks, CA: Corwin Press.

Crosnoe, R., Cavanagh, S., & Elder, G. H. (2003). Adolescent friendship as academic resources: The intersection of friendship, race, and school disadvantage. *Sociological Perspectives, 46*(3), 331–352.

Emerson, R. M., Fretz, R. I., & Shaw, L. L. (1995). *Writing ethnographic field notes.* Chicago, IL: The University of Chicago Press.

Entwisle, D. R., Alexander, K. L., & Olson, L. S. (2007). Early schooling: The handicap of being poor and male. *Sociology of Education, 80* (April), 114–138.

Fergus, E., & Noguera, P. (2009). *Latina/o males, masculinity, and marginalization: A summary report on a research and policy forum.* Metropolitan Center for Urban Education: NYU Steinhardt School of Culture, Education, and Human Development.

Finn, J. D. (1989). Withdrawing from school. *Review of Educational Research, 59*(2), 117–142.

Johnson, M. K, Crosnoe, R., & Elder, G. H. (2001). Students' attachment and academic engagement: The role of race and ethnicity. *Sociology of Education, 74*, 318–340.

Kaufman, P., Alt, M. N., & Chapman, C. (2004). *Dropout rates in the United States: 2001* (NCES 2005-046). Washington, DC: National Center for Education Statistics, Institute of Education Sciences, U.S. Department of Education.

King, J. E. (2006). *Gender equity in higher education: 2006.* Washington, DC: American Council on Education.

Kupchik, A. (2009). Things are tough all over: Race, ethnicity, class, and school discipline. *Punishment and Society, 11*(3), 291–317.

Leiber, M. J. (2002). Disproportionate minority confinement (DMC) of youth: An analysis of state and federal efforts to address the issue. *Crime & Delinquency, 48*(1), 3–45.

Lopez, N. (2003). *Hopeful girls, troubled boys: Race and gender disparity in urban education.* New York, NY: Routledge.

Noguera, P. A. (2003). Schools, prisons, and social implications of punishment: Rethinking disciplinary practices. *Theory Into Practice, 42*(4), 341–350.

Noguera, P. A. (2008). *The trouble with Black boys and other reflections on race, equity, and the future of public education.* San Francisco, CA: Jossey- Bass.

Ream, R. K., & Rumberger, R. W. (2008). Student engagement, peer social capital and school dropout among Mexican American and non-Latina/o White students. *Sociology of Education, 81,* 109–139.

Rios, V. M. (2006). The hyper-criminalization of Black and Latino male youth in the era of mass incarceration. *Souls, 8*(2), 40–54.

Rios, V. M. (2009). The consequences of the criminal justice pipeline on Black and Latina/o masculinity. *The Annals of the American Academy of Political and Social Science, 623,* 150–162.

PART II

CRITICAL CASE STUDIES DOCUMENTING FAMILY, CULTURAL RESOURCES, AND COMMUNITY STRENGTHS

CHAPTER 5

"Listen to Us"

Using Participatory Action Research to Engage Latina/o High School Intellectuals in Transforming Race and School Inequality

Louie F. Rodriguez

The Participatory Research Advocating for Excellence in Schools (PRAXIS) Project is a school-based, university-affiliated research collaborative aimed at recognizing and responding to the dropout crisis facing the United States. In response to educational challenges, the PRAXIS Project carried out two innovative research-based initiatives. The first involved an in-depth analysis of school culture through the voices, experiences, and research projects led by groups of students over 2 academic school years. The second level of research findings involved surveys and interviews of students across the school that centralized student voices. Through the lens of institutional culture, the PRAXIS Project has contributed to a series of process- and outcome-oriented efforts resulting in policy and practical changes.

Every year approximately a thousand students start their freshman year at Martinez High School (this is a pseudonym). However, 4 years later, only about 450 students will graduate. This graduation/dropout crisis facing Martinez is a snapshot of what is happening in high schools across the United States, particularly those serving students who are low-income, racialized students of color, English learners, and immigrant students. At Martinez High, over 85% of the students are Latina/o, as is the case in the region, and in most areas facing housing and school segregation across America.

The dropout/push-out problem facing Martinez and similar high schools across the country needs less research describing the crisis and more progressive efforts that attempt to respond to the crisis. Rather than attempting to tell a story describing the problem, this chapter aims to tell the story of the PRAXIS Project. However, as the story unfolds, it should become increasingly apparent that this story is more about student engagement than it is about dropouts. Thus, this chapter is wrapped around a few key questions: What happens when students' voices and experiences are used to understand what is happening on the ground level? What are the possibilities for practical and policy change when students educate the educators about ways to keep them engaged with school? These are the key questions driving the work associated with the PRAXIS Project.

This chapter tells the story of the PRAXIS Project. Two research-based initiatives are described. The first involved an in-depth analysis of school culture through the voices, experiences, and research projects led by groups of students over 2 academic school years. In preparation for this research, students were engaged in four pedagogical experiences. The second level of research findings involved surveys and interviews of students across the school that centralizes student voices. The findings from both research approaches shaped a series of research and policy initiatives such as the 10-Point Plan. The PRAXIS Project has contributed to a series of process- and outcome-oriented efforts resulting in policy and practical changes.

THE PRAXIS PROJECT IN COMMUNITY CONTEXT

In December 2009, the principal of Martinez High School (MHS) expressed interest in a collaborative effort to help improve the overall quality of education for all students at Martinez High. I was born and raised in the community, and so the work at Martinez would not only be a professional endeavor for me as an educational researcher, but a personal journey and a unique opportunity to give back to my community. Prior to working at MHS, I engaged in a series of school-based, university-affiliated research projects addressing issues of student engagement, school culture, school dropout, and educational policy analysis as related to students' achievement and their experiences in school. These projects span over 15 years of work in three major urban centers across the United States (Rodriguez, 2014).

Central to this work has been the power placed on the voices and experiences of low-income students, particularly African American and Latina/o youth. It is well documented in the educational research that these students are among the most neglected and voiceless when it comes to educational reform. Our project finds this reality to be counterintuitive and counterproductive to educational equity and excellence, especially because the people most directly affected by the theories, policies, and practices in education—the students—have been the least consulted constituency in determining, examining, and evaluating educational policy and the effectiveness of reform efforts. Thus, the PRAXIS Project aimed to fill this void, not just as a contribution to research, but also to help inform school, district, and state policy formation, pedagogical decisionmaking, and school and classroom practice. In sum, this work sought to contest race and inequality in the schoolyard.

Several goals drove the project. The first goal was to learn and highlight the voices and experiences of students. In most schools and communities across the

United States, particularly in low-income communities of color, students' voices and experiences often go overlooked or ignored. Yet inequality is rampant. The second goal was to engage in collaborative, productive, and outcome-oriented efforts that could respond to the 50% dropout rate facing the community. The third goal was to build momentum among a diverse group of community stakeholders, both within and outside of the field of education, for the purposes of developing advocacy efforts for these students who have historically been left behind. Finally, the last goal was to build, challenge, and confirm some of my previous research carried out in two demographically similar yet geographically distant regions across the country.

As the leader of the PRAXIS Project, I assembled a team of six research assistants from the community and who were currently enrolled as undergraduate and graduate students at local colleges and universities. The research team also included the teacher-on-record and the entire group of student researchers (see below). With the support of school leadership and our partner teacher, we entered one classroom twice per week during year 1 and concentrated our research efforts on two multicultural issues courses involving a total of 76 students. During year 2, we partnered with a new group of students (34) and concentrated our efforts on just one class due to scheduling and accessibility.

THEORETICAL FOUNDATIONS OF THE PRAXIS PROJECT

The work of the PRAXIS Project was inspired, in part, by Paulo Freire's work, particularly his ideas on liberatory pedagogy. According to Freire, an exciting, engaging, and relevant education encourages students and teachers to use problem-posing methods that encourage learners to capitalize on knowledge from their own lives by connecting real-life issues with academic content. Students are encouraged to ask critical questions, create and own knowledge, and work to realize democratic processes in classrooms and in society. The goal is to create spaces where students (and teachers) learn by "recreat[ing] the way we see ourselves, our education and our society" (Shor, 1993, p. 26).

We drew upon other critical frameworks such as Critical Race Praxis. We committed to prioritizing (1) an examination of race, class, gender, language, and other critical social categories; (2) the questioning of long-standing explanations of the achievement and underachievement of historically marginalized groups; (3) a commitment to positive, transformative change; and (4) a commitment to incorporating the knowledge of students and teachers. For example, students' counter-narratives were used as a source of legitimate knowledge—a source that has been historically devalued, overlooked, or altogether silenced. These principles also informed the ways in which students were engaged. For example, there was a spectrum of voices in the room by race, generational status, language, gender, class, and sexual orientation. We challenged dominant ideologies, particularly through the curriculum, by introducing more culturally, contextually, and historically relevant stories to students at Martinez High School. Our curriculum not only disrupted traditional constructions of history and knowledge, but also included pedagogical activities that were committed to positive change.

For example, during one of the opening exercises that launched the project, we asked students, "Why do students drop out of school?" This open-ended discussion had multiple goals. Because we prioritized the voices and experiences of students, we had to prove it. In other words, it could not just be lip service. So, the purpose of this opening dialogue was to begin to build a classroom culture committed to listening to students. As students began to chime in about the reasons why students drop out of school, we had to note their responses and monitor the process of the conversation. This initial dialogue generated over 30 reasons why students drop out of school. This carefully constructed exercise began to plant the seeds of "proof" that was necessary to demonstrate that we were committed to hearing what they had to say, particularly on a topic with which they have much expertise yet little opportunity to engage: why some students fail and why some succeed. One of the major structural elements needed was time in the context of a regular classroom subject area: a course focused on multicultural issues in society. The necessary cultural ingredients were the political will to engage in such a dialogue and a pedagogical commitment to monitoring and understanding group process dynamics, particularly among youth of color who have historically been silenced by traditional teaching and learning approaches, policies, and other system-wide practices.

RESEARCH DESIGN AND THEORY OF ACTION

A two-level methodological process drove the PRAXIS Project. The first level revolved around our interest in understanding the process of student engagement and achievement from the perspectives, voices, and experiences of students. The students were evenly split between males and females, and over a majority were Latina/o (90%+), with a handful of Black/African American and White students. The Latina/o student population was mostly U.S.-born, but there were a growing number of immigrant students, particularly from Mexico and Central America. These demographics reflected the overall student demographics at the school and region. The second level of research, on the other hand, was more novel and involved participatory action research (PAR) methodologies and pedagogies. Both approaches are described below.

Level 1 Research Approach

Upon entry into Martinez High, students were made aware of the two primary objectives of the research project: (1) to engage high school students in research opportunities that give them a voice to address student engagement issues in school, and (2) to allow researchers to understand how participation in these processes will impact student engagement and achievement. Parent consent and student assent were acquired. The objective of the project was to expand understanding of the role of meaningful student engagement to contest racial inequality, mediate against student failure, and produce critical, high-performing, college-bound students. Through qualitative methods, this research sought to identify specific practices that engage and alienate students from school and offer insights into how high school students meaningfully engage with school. This project was driven by the following three overarching research questions:

1. What are the root causes of student (dis)engagement across two classrooms of high school students in a large public high school?
2. In what ways can these students best be re(engaged) to mediate dropout and promote student success (i.e., boost graduate and college-going rates)?
3. To what degree can the lessons learned from this project be utilized to guide our understanding and prevention of student dropout at the school, district, and national levels?

At this level, the research team took a rigorous approach to data collection. We captured the students' voices and experiences by conducting traditional semi-structured interviews, making critical ethnographic observations in the school and classrooms, and examining the impact and promises of national-, state-, district-, and school-level policies on students' opportunities in school. At this level of research, the research team led the design, data collection, and data analysis. Most simply, we were interested in "how students experience and make sense of school."

Level 2: Participatory Action Research (PAR) Approach

PAR is a methodological and pedagogical approach rooted in engaging historically marginalized communities in research, knowledge-creation, and advocacy to positively impact school and community change. Its roots exist in both Europe and Latin America. Our approach is rooted in the "Southern" tradition that recognizes the indigenous, cultural, linguistic, and historical contributions of scholars, thinkers, and researchers from Latin America, the Caribbean, and the American South who have helped define and shape the origins of PAR as a research methodology (see Ayala et al., in press).

PAR with youth in the classroom aims to engage students in research and advocacy efforts to positively transform school-level practices and policies. Whereas traditional research (Level 1) privileges the researchers throughout the process, the PAR process values, seeks, and capitalizes on the students as researchers. Students develop research topics, research methodologies, collect data, analyze data, and present their findings to relevant stakeholders. Much like graduate students are trained in doctoral programs, the research team taught students various types of data collection techniques. Students then decided which approaches were most relevant to their research inquiry. With regard to the research topic(s), we used dialogical pedagogies by posing critical questions to students such as *Can you identify one empowering or disempowering experience in school?* Or, *Why do some students graduate and why do some drop out?* These questions generated rich discussions and became the basis for the topics of the group research projects led by the students.

This research methodology was driven by four core principles: (1) using context-relevant and inquiry-driven curriculum, (2) participatory engagement, (3) liberatory pedagogy, and (4) a commitment to individual, school, and community transformation. For example, through problem-posing dialogues, we triggered participatory engagement with students. We sought to work *with* students, not over them or on their behalf, and recognized students as intellectuals and builders of knowledge. The goal was to facilitate the opportunity for students to reposition themselves as owners of their education and the schooling process.

Limitations

Like any research initiative, there were several limitations to our study. Due to time constraints, we were not able to measure progress over time, and there was limited access to certain types of data such as real college-going rates of exiting high school seniors. We also focused our analysis on school life from the student perspective. We had to consider many other stakeholders such as parents. Although we found their perspectives important, we were also cognizant of the real challenges facing students and their families—a struggling economy, a high unemployment rate, and transient living situations. Families struggle with healthcare, childcare, and transportation. While all of these factors are critical, we wanted to argue that despite these conditions of structural inequality, schools matter. Finally, we did not engage in an in-depth study of teachers and their perspectives and experiences. Although we value teachers and recognize the tremendous pressure they are under to help schools meet local, state, and national achievement targets, we know many teachers persist and excel, even in high-poverty, high-minority high schools. Our primary purpose was to listen to students, our school system's main priority.

A PEDAGOGY OF THE PRAXIS PROJECT—BECOMING ORGANIC INTELLECTUALS THROUGH A CRITICAL PEDAGOGICAL APPROACH

Because PAR is an action-oriented process, the research team strategically selected several core elements to drive the pedagogical and curricular experience. The ultimate goal was to provide students with the opportunity to recognize themselves as true organic intellectuals—something that all students are capable of but are rarely given the opportunity to realize within the traditional classroom/school context. Thus, we arranged our approach around four key experiences we find to be critical to the development of critical, reflective, and action-oriented student-researchers: (1) educational journeys, (2) the history of educational inequality, (3) powerful ideas in education, and (4) the group research project. Below is a brief description of each approach.

Educational Journeys

The educational journey exercise is a pedagogical and curricular tool that reflects the values, beliefs, and principles that drive the PRAXIS Project. The idea was inspired by a similar project led by my colleague, Dr. Tara Brown, at the University of Maryland, College Park. This approach was an attempt to realize one of Freire and Faundez's most vital stances on education: "the starting point for a political-pedagogical process must be precisely at the level of the people's aspirations and dreams, their understanding of reality and their forms of action and struggle" (p. 27). In recognition of this, the educational journeys provided students with the opportunity to identify both positive and negative experiences. Some students wrote poems, some constructed Microsoft PowerPoint presentations, and some created musical lyrics. To initiate the process, members of research team shared their journeys as a gesture to open up, build community, and position ourselves in a vulnerable role by presenting very personal experiences to a room of complete strangers. Often the educational scars that students have endured within the school system are shared as well as moments of triumph and success. We began to see patterns of empowerment and disempowerment that is caused, perpetuated, or challenged by possibilities or limitations provided by the schooling experience. We then engaged in dialogue about root causes and posed a series of questions based on their experiences.

History of Educational Inequality

By and large, the history of people of color and their role as builders of knowledge and their contributions to the development of our democracy are largely excluded from the curriculum and pedagogical practices in the K–12 school system. Therefore, we provided opportunities for students to explore relevant moments, court cases, and key figures and movements that have helped shape the path to educational equality and equity in U.S. schools and society. We covered the following topics: *Plessy v. Ferguson* (1896), the Great Debate between Booker T. Washington and W. E. B. Du Bois, Native American education, women in education, *Lopez v. Secommbe* (1943), *Mendez v. Westminster* (1948), *Brown v. Board of Education* (1954), *Plyler v., Doe* (1981), Chicano walkouts of 1968, and the Boston desegregation/busing incident in 1972.

In addition to reading and discussing the cases, students were assembled into groups and "acted out" their specific case. They were given creative license to communicate the core elements of the case in a 3-minute skit, mini-play, or a method of choice. This effort aimed to create a deeper understanding of the cases, and students were able to use their creative energy to communicate the case to the entire class.

Powerful Ideas in Education

Another pedagogical approach to our work was to engage students in perspectives about education, schools, and society that are likely to have been overlooked or excluded from traditional curriculum. By engaging with critical texts of American society and culture, students were encouraged to discuss, analyze, and connect these ideas with their own schooling experiences. These theoretical foundations served as the basis by which they begin to connect their educational journeys, theory and research, and their current schooling experiences to shape a research topic for the group project.

Group Research Projects

The group research project was a core feature of the PRAXIS Project at Martinez High. Before assembling themselves into groups, students identified critical issues at their particular school. Then, based on a topic of interest, students selected a group and committed to engaging in a long-term (2–3 months) research effort on that topic. Students shaped the research questions, identified participants, selected data collection tools and data analysis techniques, and identified implications of their work. All students were required to present their findings to the class and were given the option to present their research to the school, school board, and community stakeholders.

WHAT STUDENTS FOUND IN THEIR RESEARCH

Based on the student-driven research concerning their experiences, perspectives, and ideas about what works and does not work in school, they narrowed their topics to a handful of key issues. Many of these issues were directly or indirectly concerned with school culture. Table 5.1 shows an overview of selected topics explored, research questions, methods used, key findings, and implications/recommendations for policy and practice.

Once students summarized their findings, developed presentations, and created a set of recommendations for stakeholders, the PRAXIS Project created opportunities for students to present their findings. The stakeholders were identified by students and organized by leaders of the PRAXIS Project. Later in this chapter a description of presentations that were delivered to key stakeholders is provided.

STUDENTS SPEAK OUT ON TEACHER QUALITY

A recurring theme of our intensive 2-year project revolved around the importance of teacher quality. Coincidentally, as the country discusses significant policy changes associated with teacher quality, student-researchers felt the need to address the

Table 5.1. Student Research Topics and Outcomes for 2009–2010 School Year

Research Topic	Findings	Implications
School Image	Overall cleanliness matters	School image/cleanliness shape school pride
Tardy Policy	Most students believe policy doesn't work; transportation issues; contributes to student absence	Longer passing periods; mark students late but keep them in class
Overall Quality of Education	English teachers received highest ratings; math received lowest	Math teachers should focus on creating a "comfortable" learning environment
Dropout Issue	Limited number of motivating teachers; student laziness is not the major reason; student motivation related to individual goals	Boost communication with students; more opportunities to participate in school activities; need for a student-led support group
Teacher Effectiveness	78% of teachers rated "good"; top 3 teacher qualities—energy, patience, knowledge; 40% of teachers "care" about them; AP teachers rated highest	Teachers need to go "beyond the call of duty"

issues as well, albeit from an entirely different perspective. That is, while policymakers, interest groups, and other stakeholders typically take a detached or superficial perspective toward teacher quality (i.e., measuring teacher quality by student test scores), students took a more on-the-ground perspective by reflecting on the degree to which they teach, inspire, and motivate them in the classroom. Further, while many of the students acknowledged poverty, struggling families, academic struggle, and self-motivation as important variables affecting student achievement, almost every student identified the significance of quality teachers in their lives and their role in diminishing the effects of any life challenge. After conducting a series of interviews, we defined representative perspectives that capture the essence of quality teachers from the perspectives and experiences of students.

By far, good teachers not only provide students with input in the classroom but they engage in instruction driven by creativity. Melissa, a senior, shared her perspective:

A quality teacher is someone who listens to their students and is actually concerned with what they have to say. They also teach the class, they just don't pass out worksheets. They also take the time to go through the curriculum and teach it to the best of their ability. I think a quality teacher is Mr. D because he takes the time to come up with creative things for students to do, for the students can learn better.

Felipe, a senior, concurred and added that quality teachers ensure that students are understanding the material:

A quality teacher is someone who knows how to teach and knows what they are doing in the field of that they are trained in. They understand students' needs. A good example of that is Mr. B. He actually teaches students. He makes people understand various concepts of the subject areas.

In addition to instructional approaches, another set of characteristics revolved around the notion of caring as demonstrated by a teacher's willingness to provide access to resources and learning opportunities. Adriana, a senior, stated:

A quality teacher is someone who honestly cares about the students and takes their time to make sure the students understand what they are learning. For example, if it's a math teacher, they make sure they don't move on to the next subject until the student has an understanding and takes the time to do it for all of them [students]. A good example of a quality teacher is Ms. L. The course is pretty rigorous and you have to be quick and analyze. She really goes out of her way to try to help. She gives us reference books and does a really good job at teaching. Mr. S's class is more of a discussion class and tries to get everyone interested and involved. Ms. B is a really great teacher. She takes the time to give several examples of whatever she is teaching. She doesn't stop explaining until everyone understands it. Even after that she will stay after school.

Relationships were also vital to the description of quality teachers as defined by students. Relationships help bridge teaching and learning but they also humanize the schooling experiences, especially when the teacher "knows where they [students] are from." Juan, a senior, stated:

A quality teacher is someone who has a relationship with the student, more than just teaching but they actually interact with the student. They are on a good standing basis with them. They know where they are from. They teach what they are supposed to teach and they actually help them. They actually teach the work instead of just giving it to them. Mr. S is one. He interacts with us. He does more than just teaching. He knows where students are from and what's going on with us.

A final characteristic of a quality teacher was the presence of student voice in the classroom. Allowing students to share their voices and opinions seemed vital to their engagement in the classroom. Jeff, a senior, stated:

A quality teacher is someone who can relate to the students and someone who is good at expressing their ideas and they let the students have a say when they are learning. Mr. S is a good-quality teacher because we have a voice, he lets us think of new ideas. . . .We talk a lot. Most classes are "just do your work." But [in his class], there is more voice and expressions of opinions.

Through students' voices, experiences, and perspectives, they affirmed what most decisionmakers and other adults believe to be a quality teacher—one who can effectively teach their content areas. However, students also believed that creativity in the classroom, caring teachers, teachers who go out of their way, teachers who give second chances, and teachers who allow students to have a voice in the classroom matter tremendously. The district and community should learn from and celebrate teachers who use a relational approach to student engagement as models of quality teachers.

MAKING OUR WORK "PUBLIC"—TWO STEPS TOWARD COMMUNITY ENGAGEMENT

In addition to conducting research and collecting data, the PRAXIS Project prioritized publicly sharing our results. Below is a description of both experiences.

A Challenge and an Opportunity

At the end of year 1, the student-researchers presented their findings to the entire MHS staff, including administrators, teachers, staff, and specialists (such as instructional coaches and teachers on assignment). With an invitation from the school principal, the entire research team was thoroughly prepared to discuss dropouts, teaching quality, teacher pedagogy, and the impact of the budget cuts on student engagement. While we anticipated a warm reception, the crowd focused their energies on the more critical findings. For instance, many students mentioned difficulty with finding teachers who supported or inspired them. At the same time, there was a significant cadre of supportive teachers who recognized and appreciated the rigorous work carried out by the students and noted their passion and interest for the subject matter. They emphasized and appreciate the power of student voice.

This proved to be a pivotal moment for the PRAXIS Project and for the entire research team. In fact, this moment encouraged us to be more deliberate about identifying examples that facilitate student success and inspired the next presentation.

Two Steps Forward—A Community's Embrace

After year 2 of the project, we presented our findings to a more inclusive group of people—the school *and* the larger community. With the support of school and district leadership, we invited everyone—faculty and staff, students, parents, grandparents, school alumni, and various stakeholders across the community.

There were several goals for the community event: (1) to have students present their research findings, (2) to recognize three exemplary MHS teachers, (3) to dialogue about engaging alumni and community stakeholders, (4) to create networking opportunities for students, and (5) to provide a space for community members to share testimonies about ways to improve MHS.

Our experiences at this event were starkly different from our presentation the prior year. Parents, grandparents, siblings, alumni, and other community stakeholders were explicitly supportive of this work. Students presented their work and felt affirmed, recognized, and respected. Parents were in tears, and two different families approached members of the research team who were excited about their son's or daughter's engagement, interest, and leadership within the project. One parent stated, "I've never seen my son so excited about something in school. This is really great. Thank you." Another parent said, "I didn't know my son was capable of speaking in public. I'm very proud of him."

Students also recognized three exemplary educators: The Most Caring Teacher, The Most Committed Teacher, and The Most Creative Teacher. The three teachers graciously and emotionally accepted the recognition, and many students showed tears of appreciation.

To close the evening, an open-mic opportunity for community members to dialogue was created. We learned that MHS alumni were represented in the audience from every decade going back to the 1940s. This experience showed the community's love, recognition, and hope.

HOW THE PRAXIS PROJECT SHAPES PRACTICE AND POLICY

The need to be "public" about what is happening in public schools through the voices and experiences of Latina/o and other marginalized youth is vital to improving and shaping 21st-century public education in the United States. Below are five significant outcomes of our work.

Outcome 1: Eliminating Counterproductive School Policy

After 8 years of implementation, the school's tardy policy was eliminated as of August 2011. Our research, and the students' experiences specifically, demonstrated the negative impact of the policy and highlighted key challenges facing students such as transportation issues.

Outcome 2: Raising Graduation Rates

After 2 years of work in the school, the school reported the highest graduation rate in the school's history. Although we cannot take sole credit for this increase in graduation rates, we believe that putting emphasis on dropouts and graduation rates may have raised awareness and encouraged deliberate action to more vigorously promote on-time graduation. The two major school/community "town hall" events certainly contributed to this effort. Not only were these town hall meetings organized in the context of the dropout crisis, but the student-researchers also explicitly addressed this topic in their research and presented their findings to the community. In attendance were school educators and leaders, parents and grandparents, community leaders and policymakers, and nonprofit leaders. In addition, when the focus on our work shifted from understanding and responding to the student dropout crisis to one of excellence, students were driven by identifying educators who facilitate student success through creativity in the classroom, caring, and commitment to students. At an evening event, the students honored three teachers who exemplified these practices in the classroom. In addition to these town halls, the students presented to the principal and district superintendent. The students received endless accolades for their research and commitment to improving their school. This multipronged series of actions contributed to creating a school and community-wide culture that recognized the dropout crisis. We learned that this shift resulted in 100 more students who graduated compared to the previous year.

Outcome 3: Engaging Alumni and the Community

The third outcome is our ability to mobilize community members around key issues impacting the school and community. This is important to acknowledge given that such an emphasis was absent before our arrival. While there were notable efforts by community stakeholders such as raising scholarship money for students, there were no previous efforts that explicitly sought to help improve the schooling conditions for students, especially with an emphasis on the voices and experiences of students. One concrete step forward was triggering a series of dialogues that led to the creation of tangible programs and experiences (e.g., summer programs and internships) for students.

Outcome 4: Recognizing and Celebrating the Work of Teachers

We firmly support and believe in the work of teachers at MHS and across the region and country. Our research demonstrates that teachers are and continue to be one of the most significant school-level factors that shape students' experiences, outcomes, and opportunities in school and in life. By recognizing and celebrating caring, committed, and engaging teachers at MHS, we hope we ignited a movement that recognizes, celebrates, and learns from teachers doing the work every day.

Outcome 5: Impact on Students

Our final outcome revolves around the PRAXIS Project's impact on students. For many students, their engagement with the project was the first time they had the opportunity to shape the parameters of their learning experience. For others, it was the first time they spoke in front of a classroom or a public forum. Still, for others, it was the first time when they "felt like my thoughts and ideas mattered to the community." Many of our students were enlightened by local history or other important historical moments that have been excluded from the traditional curriculum. We believe our impact has been academic, social, and cultural. Below are some of the voices and perspectives of students who participated in the PRAXIS Project:

- "It made me feel like my thoughts and ideas mattered to the community."
- "It's always refreshing to see other educators show a genuine interest in the well-being of students."
- "Made me feel like my voice counts and I have a say and can make a difference."
- "It is important because we are making a step forward for change."
- "I think this is important so that our voices as students can be heard through our communities and to make change."
- "I think it is important because we get to do something new and exciting and we also get to show ourselves what we are capable of in class."

Not only did we provide an opportunity for students to share their voices, experiences, and perspectives, but the learning processes simultaneously allowed students to build academic skills and raise their consciousness about themselves and their communities.

THE PRAXIS PROJECT'S 10-POINT PLAN

While one of the PRAXIS Project's goals was to delve deeply into the student experience, particularly among low-income students of color, we were also interested in responding to the dropout crisis by devising a plan and set of criteria to drive policy and practice, not only as a project, but as a community through a collaborative effort. Thus, this chapter will end with an emphasis on implications for policy and school practice framed as a 10-Point Plan. Like many schools across the country, particularly those serving Latina/o students, MHS is large and faces a student achievement crisis, which results in an inacceptable number of students denied from graduating. The community also struggles politically, economically, and historically, which has an impact on what happens inside schools. Yet many students who attend such schools and who live in these same communities typically rely on public schools to create a pathway toward opportunity and possibility. The work of the PRAXIS Project and the students' voices and experiences specifically have taught us a series of lessons learned, not just for MHS, but for schools nationally. Below is a set of practical, pedagogical, and policy recommendations drawn from our 10-Point Plan (see Rodriguez, 2014) that teachers, schools, districts, policymakers, and other education advocates across the country should discuss, analyze, and implement to create more equitable opportunities for student success.

1. *We need to focus on relationships:* Student–teacher relationships facilitate academic achievement, promote opportunities, and contribute to the overall well-being of students.

2. *We need to dialogue about critical issues:* A school culture that promotes dialoguing about critical issues requires persistence, support, and courage. It is never easy but it is vitally necessary.

3. *We should promote student voice:* Listening to and learning from students should inform leadership and school staff about policies and practices that work or do not work.

4. *We should respect students as public intellectuals:* Leadership and educators need to provide opportunities for students to become the teachers and demonstrate their wealth (Yosso, 2005).

5. *We should recognize that our students matter:* Recognition through relationships, curriculum, pedagogy, context, and realization of the transformative possibilities of education is vital (see Rodriguez, 2012).

6. *We should centralize the experiences of marginalized students:* Students who are marginalized or silenced by policies, practices, and processes in school tend to be the most insightful about ways to improve schools and serve as a tool to promote student engagement.

7. *We should develop community-relevant curricula:* Students who are exposed to community-relevant events, key figures, and places tend to engage and inspire students. These opportunities typically promote student voice and can spark interest in other community-related topics.

8. *We must realize that community matters:* Most schools are surrounded by a pool of interested adults who are committed to student success. We should use these resources to create mentoring, internships, and scholarship development.

9. *We should celebrate excellence in schools and communities:* While everyone believes in excellence, it is a vitally underused pedagogical opportunity. Excellence has shown to be a powerful tool for community engagement and promoting a shift in institutional culture.

10. *We should make public schools "public":* Thriving public schools, particularly those serving low-income students of color, need to publicly promote the practices, processes, and policies that facilitate their success.

CONCLUSION

After several years of engaging in this work directly in school and with stake-holders, our work suggests that any response to the host of challenges will require collective, collaborative, and intentional efforts. This work largely suggests that although a series of historical, policy, and practical challenges affects students and the people who serve them, responses must be addressed while necessary laws, policies, and processes are created, implemented, and monitored. In other words, until progressive, deliberate, and expedient laws and policies are created (see Orfield, 2014), this work argues that school culture matters tremendously and will require thoughtful, relevant, and courageous action in classrooms, schools, and communities—from the schoolhouse to the statehouse.

This work also suggests that those responsible for responding to the needs of Latina/o students, and other students of color for that matter, must be willing to learn from their voices, experiences, and perspectives. This approach to the work is not only necessary but also political. Why? It is political because not every-one believes that we need to hear or learn from students. Not everyone believes they have a voice or perspective. And not everyone is used to taking the position of learner and being willing to listen, learn, reflect, and act differently. Students' voices are also critical because they are an essential form of systemic and cultural accountability. If the people we intend on serving are dissatisfied, disengaged, or disrespected by the very system that purports to serve them, our leadership and policymakers must be willing to make an abrupt turn in the ways in which they are serving their students. Similarly, if students are thriving, we also need to be equally intentional and courageous in recognizing and learning from models of excellence. Teachers and leaders who seek out and learn from the voices of stu-dents must be the ambassadors and leaders of this work. The latter is a cultural shift that is paradigmatic in proportion.

Finally, this case study is an example of praxis in action. This work emanates from the field and systematically assesses key challenges and possibilities. While we went into the work interested in dropout prevention, we came out focusing on in-stitutional culture as a mechanism to prevent dropouts and also capitalize on the strengths and possibilities that exist in every classroom and school that struggles to serve Latina/o students. In other words, we collected data while simultaneously framing our work in the field. We then used the voices and experiences of the peo-ple within schools and communities to shape the conclusions, solutions, and rec-ommendations to the necessary stakeholders responsible for the well-being of our students. Our findings became a set of solutions via the 10-Point Plan along with a set of tangible outcomes, like increasing the number of high school graduates. We have learned that confronting historic race and educational inequality will require intentional action, driven by the realities on the ground level, and for the purpose of our work, driven by the voices and experiences of low-income youth of color who have historically been excluded no more. They are silent no more. But are we ready to listen?

REFERENCES

Ayala, J., Cammarota, J., Rivera, M., Rodriguez, L., Berta-Avila, M., & Torre, M. (in press). *PAR entremundos: A pedagogy of las Americas.*

Friere, P.. & Faundez, A. (1989). *Learning to question; a pedagogy of liberation.* New York: Continuum.

Orfield, G. (2014). Tenth annual *Brown* lecture in education research. A new civil rights agenda for American education. *Educational Researcher, 43,* 273–292.

Rodríguez, L. F. (2012). "Everybody grieves, but still nobody sees": Toward a theory of recognition for students of color in U.S. education. *Teachers College Record, 114,* 1–31.

Rodríguez, L. F. (2014). *The time is now: Understanding and responding to the Black and Latina/o dropout crisis.* New York, NY: Peter Lang Publishing.

Shor, I. (1993). Education is politics: Paulo Freire's critical pedagogy. In P. McLaren & P. Leonard (Eds.), *Paulo Freire: A critical encounter* (pp. 25–35). London, England: Routledge.

Yosso, T. J. (2005). Whose culture has capital? A critical race discussion of community cultural wealth. *Race Ethnicity and Education, 8*(1), 69–81.

CHAPTER 6

Contesting Racism, Marginalization, and Mexican Immigrant Youth Failure

Examining the Elusive Path Toward Earning a Diploma from a Nontraditional High School

Eduardo Mosqueda & Kip Téllez

Latina/o students have among the highest school push-out and lowest GED-passing rates among all racial/ethnic groups in the United States. Within this group, Mexican-origin students are even more likely to leave school without a diploma. In this chapter we investigate the experiences of Mexican American youth from a low-income agricultural community who are enrolled in a dropout prevention program in a nontraditional high school. Our findings show that despite the odds stacked against them, individual and school-level factors are tied to persistence. In addition to student commitment to education, the combination of academic and social supports from family ties, peer groups, and institutional agents was critical to their engagement and persistence in school. We apply a social capital framework to examine the approach taken by "institutional agents" who facilitated access to resources that increase school persistence.

Latina/o immigrant students have among the highest dropout/push-out and lowest GED-passing rates among all racial/ethnic groups in the United States (Fry, 2010), and Mexican-origin students are even more vulnerable to being pushed out of school (Valencia, 2002). In the most distressed school contexts, Latina/o student dropout/push-out rates range between 30% and 70%. The majority of estimates place the Latina/o push-out rate at about half of all students (Orfield, 2004; Rumberger, 2004, 2008). The precise figure is unknown because students expelled from one school may enroll in another whereas others may simply move their residence. Unless students and their parents alert the school, most states mandate that the students be placed on the dropout/push-out list. Nonetheless, we know very little about student experiences in these programs.

This chapter examines immigrant Mexican youth enrolled in a dropout prevention program in a nontraditional high school. We investigate individual characteristics of persistence. We also apply a social capital framework to examine how school personnel or "institutional agents" (Stanton-Salazar, 2001, 2011) in a nontraditional high school are able to facilitate access to resources primarily in the form of both social and academic support that positively influences educational outcomes. We also draw attention to the influence of "peer" networks that provide achievement-oriented pro-diploma supports that counteract the lure of disengaged street-socialized peers. However, we depart from traditional conceptualizations that emphasize the social capital of middle- and upper-class students, and instead focus on the types of social capital available to support the social mobility of marginalized youth in low-income communities (Conchas, 2001, 2006; Conchas & Vigil, 2012; Oseguera, Conchas, & Mosqueda, 2010; Stanton-Salazar, 2001, 2011; Yosso, 2005).

Conchas and Vigil (2012) describe the unique challenges to the process of facilitating access to social capital to marginalized youth in low-income schools and communities:

> Institutions within enduring pockets of poverty build functional social structures based on networks and relationships, which may lead to various forms of social capital. On the one hand, some networks may be advantageous (i.e., teachers and other supportive adults), but on the other hand, some networks may promote negative consequences (adults socialized in the criminal justice system or other adults who follow a street lifestyle). (p. 4)

Our case study explores marginalized students' experiences and interactions with institutional agents and their peers as they work toward the diploma in an alternative school context. As Barrat and Berliner (2013) point out, little is known about the effectiveness of nontraditional secondary schools, in spite of the recent growth in enrollments.

As a step in understanding the role that nontraditional schools play in advancing the social capital of underperforming students and how such schools may reduce the push-out rate, we completed a case study of the educational experiences of 16 Mexican American students enrolled at La Costa High School (a pseudonym), a community day school in central California. Using semi-structured interviews, we invited La Costa students to share thoughts on their immigrant status, peer support, school engagement, and gang participation. Our study was guided by the following broad research questions:

- Why do Mexican-origin students who are enrolled in a continuation high school persist in school, while others leave without a diploma?
- How do adults and peers at the continuation school forge meaningful and supportive relationships that foster the social capital necessary to attain a high school diploma?

NONTRADITIONAL SCHOOL CONTEXTS

A wide range of educators (e.g., Sizer, 2004) have suggested that the structure and pedagogy found in large public high schools in the United States fail to meet the educational needs of even average students. For those students whose circumstances place them at risk of being pushed out, most high schools lack even the minimal funding and staff to overcome their challenges. Consequently, many marginalized students are pushed out of school, a costly failure for both students and society (Rumberger, 2004).

In California alone, the economic losses to society owing to high school dropouts/ push-outs are estimated in the billions of dollars. High school noncompleters earn significantly lower salaries (or are perhaps unemployed for extended periods), which results in diminished salaries, in turn yielding much lower tax revenues (Murnane, Willett, & Boudett, 1999). In addition, high school push-outs and their families tend to rely heavily on social service institutions such as welfare and state-subsidized health care. More concerning is the increased likelihood that push-outs will find themselves involved with the criminal justice system (Belfield & Levin, 2007).

In response to high push-out rate, the state of California has developed two types of nontraditional secondary schools: the continuation school and community day school.[1] These alternatives to traditional high schools have become the cornerstones in the state's dropout push-out prevention strategy; in fact, these schools are legally bound by California state policy to provide students with the opportunity to complete the required academic courses of instruction to graduate from high school (Ruiz de Velasco, Austin, Dixon, Johnson, McLaughlin, & Perez, 2008). Although both types of schools often enroll similar students, their specific charges differ. Continuation schools are designed to serve students who are 16 years of age and older who have not yet completed high school, who are at risk of being pushed out, and who are not yet exempt from compulsory school attendance (see http://www.cde.ca.gov/sp/eo/ce/ for a full description). By contrast, community day schools were developed specifically to serve youth whose previous schooling experiences include expulsion, probation, chronic truancy, or some combination of these factors. These schools are mandated to provide challenging academic curriculum and to develop students' prosocial skills and resiliency (see http://www. cde.ca.gov/sp/eo/cd/ for a full description). A review of nontraditional schools in California (Barrat & Berliner, 2013) reported that there are over 770 continuation and community day schools statewide, enrolling approximately 22,000 students.[2]

Several recent reports have indicated that the number of students who leave comprehensive high schools and attend alternative, nontraditional, or GED programs has grown significantly (see Goldin & Katz, 2003, for a review of nontraditional schools in the United States). Such nontraditional schools settings are largely viewed as dropout prevention programs (Foley & Pang, 2006; Ruiz de Velasco et al., 2008; Rumberger, 2004, 2008). However, generalizations about schools serving marginalized youth are unwarranted because we found great variability in the structure and quality of continuation programs. Some continuation programs may function as "dumping grounds" for disruptive students and ineffective educators, whereas others offer innovative settings leading students to higher education, work, or a return to the comprehensive school (Kennedy, 2011; Ruiz de Velasco et al., 2008).

STREET-SOCIALIZED YOUTH AND SCHOOL PERSISTENCE

Even if we are unsure regarding the effectiveness of nontraditional secondary schools, we have a clearer picture of the students they serve: Most are left unsupervised by adults, and, as a consequence, become deeply embedded in peer networks where identification with peer groups is dominated by a set of expectations and approvals that are learned outside of adult-supervised settings. This street socialization often results in gang membership owing to "multiple marginality" (Vigil, 1988, 1997). Lacking meaningful relationships with adults in schools (Brown & Rodriguez, 2008; Fine, 1991; Flores-Gonzales, 2002), street-socialized youth are often further marginalized in large schools, becoming increasingly disenfranchised (Vigil, 2002, 2004)—often leading to gang participation.

Understanding gang involvement and affiliation for street-socialized youth differs across parts of California, especially in the central part of the state. In this geographical area, gang membership is established not by neighborhoods but rather by two large gangs known as the *Sureños* and the *Norteños*. Although the precise origins of these gangs is disputed, most researchers agree that in about 1960, incarcerated Chicanos from southern California formed a protection gang that eventually became known as the *Sureños* (Moore & Garcia, 1978). Another gang composed of members from the northern part of the state formed soon thereafter and became known as the *Norteños*. Each gang seeks the control of specific regions, including the drug traffic in specific parts of their city. Consequently, members from both gangs have access to a wide array of weapons, and the inevitable violence and multiple retaliatory acts of violence tend to consume their activities.

As we know from both the research literature (Vigil, 1988) and testimonials (Rios, 2011), breaking this cycle of violence is very challenging, and it is not clear if schools can play a role. Once members, youth find it difficult to leave the gang. However, Téllez and Estep (1997) found that Latina/o youth gang members who wanted to leave the gang believed that earning a GED or diploma would "signal" to the gang that they were making a new life and therefore be allowed to leave the gang on agreed-upon terms. This option was considered far superior than either getting "jumped out" of the gang (i.e., getting severely beaten up by the gang) or remaining on the periphery, knowing that one could be called upon to commit a crime on behalf of the gang at any moment. As Vigil (1988) suggested, "for a small but considerable portion of barrio youth with problematic backgrounds, the street gang has arisen as a competitor of other institutions, such as family and schools, to guide and direct self-identification."

SOCIAL CAPITAL AND MITIGATING DROPOUT/PUSH-OUT

Having access (or lack thereof) to social capital has become a popular term for explaining educational outcomes, including dropping out of school. Several studies have applied a social capital framework to educational outcomes and have expanded on Coleman's (1988) conceptualization. According to Coleman (1988), social capital facilitates the creation of human capital through access to resources or support through closely knit ties. An important aspect of Coleman's conceptualization of social capital includes the notion of social or intergenerational closure—whether parents know the parents of their children's friends—which is one of the ways that social capital influences the educational outcomes of children (Dika & Singh, 2002; Oseguera, Conchas, & Mosqueda, 2010). In a study that examined the potential social capital that teachers can provide students to diminish dropout/push-out rates, Croninger and Lee (2001) found that although teachers' support and guidance benefited all students, disadvantaged students with weak academic records benefited much more from such teacher-based social capital.

A small number of studies has focused on the relationship between dropout and access to social capital specifically for low-income Mexican-origin youth. Stanton-Salazar (2001, 2011) documented how access to social capital from school adults, or "institutional agents," along with pro-school-oriented peer supports, helped some Mexican-origin working-class youth navigate social networks that promoted school persistence and also fostered empowering forms of resiliency (Stanton–Salazar, 2001).

A recent study focused on Mexican-origin students' access to "peer" social capital and dropping out relative to forms of social capital available to White students. Rumberger and Ream (2008) found that school engagement and school-oriented friendship networks helped foster school completion. However, Mexican-origin youth were found to be less engaged in academic endeavors and extracurricular activities than their White peers, and Mexican-origin youth were also more involved with academically disengaged peers who tended to expose students to street orientations. Research on Mexican-origin youth that examines the link between access to social capital and dropout highlights both the importance of connections to institutional agents and also peer supports that provide encouragement and a pro-school orientation. Portes (1998), however, argued that not all forms of social capital are positive and asserted that social capital can also have negative consequences.[3]

Lastly, Briggs (1998) expanded the notion of social capital to account for the "amount and quality of resources" that are accessed through social relationships by drawing a distinction between two forms of social capital. Briggs (1998) distinguished between *social support* as social capital that helps one "get by" or cope, and *social leverage*, which is defined as a form of social capital that helps one "get ahead" or change one's opportunity (e.g., access to job information, or a recommendation for a scholarship). In this study, we drew attention to individual drives of persistence, school-oriented supports, as well as potential sources of negative social capital or what has been termed "marginal" social capital from street-socialized peers (Conchas & Vigil, 2012).

THE RESEARCH SITE AND THE PEOPLE

La Costa is located in a city that is largely Latina/o (about 70%) in which agri-business attracts a consistent job market for undocumented workers. Thus, many of the families moving into the area experience the dislocation common to immigrant families worldwide. Combine the general shock of a new culture with enduring poverty, and the result can create a wide gulf between the cultural understandings of immigrant parents and those of their children.

La Costa Community Day School began in 1992 with a mission to serve non-traditional youth who had been expelled from the traditional high schools in a medium-sized school district. But, as we will explain shortly, the history and ongoing educational purpose of La Costa School cannot be understood without a brief history of Latina/o gangs in northern California.

In the late 1980s, gang activity in the city surrounding La Costa High School grew at an alarming rate and several highly motivated and energetic educators embarked on creating La Costa, a school that would "unite" the community and help to stop the *Sureño/Norteño* violence. Over its 21-year history, La Costa has enrolled approximately 75 students per year, nearly half of them seniors. Virtually all of La Costa's students are Latina/o, and most of Mexican origin. Three-quarters qualify for free or reduced-price lunches, although it is likely that nearly all would qualify if the remaining one-quarter chose to return the necessary forms to the school. About half the students are considered English learners. The current staff includes a principal, four teachers, a counselor, and an office staff. Although the principal and teachers at the school are all White, several Latina/o teachers have taught at the school during its history. Class size is typically around 10 students.

We used case study methodology to investigate a contemporary phenomenon within a real-life context (Yin, 2014). We collected qualitative data with a focus on the context that included interviews and observations of the study participants within the school—14 students (8 female and 6 male). We conducted interviews during the school day in a private office space. Most interviews took place on Fridays when students had more free time in their schedules. All but two interviews were conducted in English, but Spanish was used throughout all the interviews, especially when students did not know a term in English or if the interviewer was asked to clarify a question.

THE COMPLEXITY OF EXPERIENCES AT THE
SCHOOL AND COMMUNITY CONTEXTS

Students attending La Costa High School were there for several interrelated reasons (e.g., truancy or fighting), so it is difficult to point to distinct explanations for why students were removed from the mainstream high school and referred to La Costa. For example, Nadia stated:

> I ended up coming here because . . . my credits were really low. I had problems of like going to [comprehensive] school. Like with the teachers, they really wouldn't like focus 'cause there were a lot of students, like 35 students in one class, and I really wouldn't understand the teacher. Like, if I would ask him over and over again, he would get mad. He would get impatient with us . . . . They're really strict so like then I stopped going to school and I would always ditch, or like get into trouble, or I don't know. Um, I started hanging out with people I wasn't supposed to and that's how I ended up here.

Nonetheless, we found four themes that clearly emerged from our data and help explain why students in La Costa worked hard to earn a high school diploma despite their economic hardships and social challenges. These themes are (1) students' commitment to getting a high school diploma, (2) family ties, (3) peer-group influence, and (4) institutional agents as sources of academic and social support. These themes represent both school- and community-level factors, and the last three themes specifically embrace a social capital framework.

Commitment Toward Diploma

The data revealed that the primary reason why Latina/o students were motivated to stay in school was because of their belief that a diploma was the key to finding a meaningful and well-paying job. The students were also well aware that La Costa was their final opportunity to earn the right to return to the comprehensive high school or, if they remained at La Costa, their avenue to a high school diploma.

All of the participants in this study affirmed that they were committed to attaining a high school diploma. This finding challenges the deficit perspectives and debunks the myths and stereotypes about Mexican-origin youth not caring about their education (Gándara & Contreras, 2009; Valencia, 2002; Valenzuela, 1999)—even among the most vulnerable to school failure. Also clearly evident in the participants' responses was that the diploma was not an end in and of itself, but a means that students believed would help them improve their occupational attainment prospects.

Specifically, students revealed that earning a diploma would allow them to either continue their education in the local community college to enhance their career opportunities or to directly get a "better job" than what is available to them without a diploma. As Nadia noted:

> Because that represents the education, not only education, but that you did it. That you put yourself into a goal and you went far. And that you should be really proud about yourself. It's really important for going to college or any job.

Similarly, Francisco expressed the desire to graduate to enhance not only his own career opportunities but also set a positive example for his son. He stated:

> Because I want to have better, I want to give a better life to my kid . . . like work in a good job and get whatever I can to give to my kid . . . 'cause I don't know like I just want to go school, so he could see that when he grows up that I am not a failure or I am not all like that I am like a good person, so that he would want to graduate and go to college or have a good career probably he will be motivated to graduate.

When asked about what motivates her to stay in school, Alejandra responded, "My parents, and I [also] want to graduate and need to go to college." Similarly, Brenda shared, "I want to become like one of those nurses that work at [the women's clinic]." These responses reflect students' investment in the high school diploma in order facilitate their transition to a technical career program at the local community college.

Other students were motivated by their belief that attaining a high school diploma would help them find a job that was "better" compared to what their parents did for a living. In this community, most of the parents work in agricultural fields. Luz noted, "Because I don't want to be like, like my parents right now, they're working in the fields and I don't want that for myself." The study participants were committed to attaining a diploma from the continuation school to improve their opportunity to find a better-paying job or to continue on to community college to pursue a vocational training program.

We now turn to the findings on social capital—family ties, peer connections, and institutional agents—that influence nontraditional student progress toward the diploma. These, in turn, help explain students' increased commitment toward attaining a diploma.

Family Ties

Family ties provided an important external source of intangible support in the form of encouragement to earn a diploma. In the context of La Costa, social capital from family members provided *social support* to help students "get by" as they progressed toward a diploma.

Our interview with Pedro revealed that he was very conscious of support from his mother, along with a school counselor, in trying to get him to stay in school. Pedro noted, "Mostly my mom and my counselor. They've been there trying to get me in school." Similarly, Lidia explained the ways in which her older sister provided her with advice and encouragement to stay in school. She noted:

> Like when I was having problems in my house last year. Yeah, but I talked to my sister, she's 23 now and she's like my mom 'cause I tell her everything. . . .

> She graduated from a school like this. She just tells me not to leave school, to go back to regular [comprehensive] school 'cause like right now she's a nurse, but she told me if you graduate from a normal school you can like do something way better and get paid more.

The importance of kin ties has been shown to increase school persistence.

However, in marginalized communities such as La Costa, where low-paying agricultural jobs are by far are the most common sources of employment, breaking the cycle of poverty seems to leave students and families susceptible to street socialization. In a limited number of instances where street socialization spilled into a family's home life, relationships between parents and their children were strained. Often a result of tension from stressed relationships with their parents, some students did not experience positive pro-school supports from family members.

Lisa, for example, described that she felt her father had low expectations for her and she often felt put down. Lisa explained:

> Like my dad, he doesn't believe in me. He's always telling me you're dumb and you're never going to graduate. He's always trying to make me feel bad, but I don't listen to him. I'm going to do my work and, well, do something for myself and, just watch me.

Similarly, Nadia described the tense relationship she had with her mother and how she sometimes turned to drugs to help her deal with their intense arguments. Nadia's father was in jail for drug distribution and use, so when her mother would confront Nadia about using drugs and warned her to avoid the same fate as her father, arguments with her mother would turn emotionally charged and dysfunctional. Nadia noted:

> I would get mad and I know she's my mom but I would start screaming at her back and cursing, and I started turning into a person that I didn't even know myself. I completely lost myself. And that's when I started getting involved with drugs and she would tell me don't turn like your dad, 'cause my dad he's in jail right now because of selling drugs and drug dealing, and because he used drugs.

In situations where parents were unable to buffer their children from street socialization because parents themselves were impacted by such dynamics, family ties did not always result in positive support. While some students received encouragement and support at home from family members, others students received negative messages about their potential to succeed in school. In Nadia's case, because her father was in jail and she found it difficult to relate to her mother, positive support from her family was missing. For youth in Nadia's circumstances, schools can intensify supports and attempt to buffer from the impact of street socialization spilling into the home life.

Peer Group Influence

Similar to the findings on family ties, the influence of peers at La Costa High was positive for some students but negative for others. As the research has shown, peer influences have a powerful influence on individual students' school engagement (Gibson, Gándara, & Koyama, 2004). For some students, having consistent sources of pro-diploma-oriented peers provided an important source of support that contributed to their persistence in school. In contrast, some students were provoked by street-oriented peers to cut classes and hang out, whereas other students felt threatened by street-oriented gang members who would come around after school to look for trouble.

Luz, for instance, discusses how at first she did not care about school or her future. However, as a result of having friends who often discussed their goals and educational aspirations, Luz changed her study habits. She stated:

> Oh yeah, because now like since I came to La Costa like now everything is different, like I see friends, like different friends, that they want to succeed and I was like, I just thought about by myself, like they want to succeed and I just don't care about my life and then I don't know I just started to think about it like more . . . and then I decided that I wanted to study too.

Similarly, Maria's peer group was focused on attending community college. She notes how her friends have their sights set on completing high school to transfer to college:

> Well, what are you going to do when you get out of here? And then some of them are going to graduate from here. But like most of us are going to transfer out. Well, they all want to go to college and one of my friends, Maria, wants to be a soccer player and go to a university. We all have different goals.

Roberto and his male friends described how they often discussed their post–high school goals. While Roberto was interested in entering the military, most of his peers expressed an interest in pursuing a vocational trade in a community college. Roberto said:

> We would talk about what we were going to do when we were out of high school. Like what if we were going to go to college or, I mean, what computer technician, or mechanic, or just something . . . . Like I always say Navy Seals . . . something like that.

Students with access to pro-diploma-oriented peers received support to remain engaged in school. While many students were encouraged by their peers to think about their post–high school goals, Lourdes described how her friends consistently reminded her to stay in school to improve opportunities for herself and her child. Lourdes stated, "Well, they tell me to think about my baby, to get an education."

Another student mentioned the positive academic support and encouragement she received from her peers to complete her schoolwork. Alejandra explained, "By coming and sitting with me [while I am] doing my work, we help each other out." Another student, Roberto, mentioned that he also received support from his peers who provided encouragement to consistently attend school and held him accountable for attendance. Roberto stated, "If I don't come to school, they will call me [and say], 'Hey why didn't you come to school? Get your ass to school!'"

Not all students received positive support from peer ties. Others reported that their street-oriented peers often provoked them to cut classes, engage in deviant behavior, or to get involved with gangs. In a joint interview, Luz and Lidia described to the interviewer how they were influenced by their peers to cut class:

> *Luz:* Because I didn't go for 6 months.
> *Int:* So why did you stop going to school?
> *Luz:* Because I didn't have much time to be with my friends after school and that was like my only time to be with my friends. So I didn't go to class and [I would] go with my friends.
> *Lidia:* Well, I was cutting a lot too. The second semester there was this girl who was my friend . . . so she would like get me to cut and stuff, but I would never do that and like she got me to like cutting and stuff and I wouldn't go to class, so, yeah.

Without sharing specific details, Francisco described the pressure he felt from peers to become involved in illicit activities that could potentially lead to his arrest if he was caught and thereby jeopardize his opportunity to complete high school. He noted:

> My friends . . . because they keep on telling me, oh do this and that, and whenever if I do listen to them, um, I will end up in prison or jail for a really long time, and get myself to ruin my life, like not graduating.

The lure of involvement with street-socialized peers often led to youth being provoked into gang activity.

Thus, it becomes evident that peer ties become essential—students with friendship networks that are school-oriented can be critical for low-income youth to achieve institutional goals such as attaining a high school diploma.

Institutional Agents as Sources of Academic and Social Support

Students not only felt a higher sense of academic support at La Costa than at the traditional school, they also felt that teachers better explained material they were struggling to learn. As one student noted:

Well, just the teachers [at La Costa] make it really easy. 'Cause like in the other schools, they'll just hand you out the assignment and like the papers they have to do. They don't explain it. And right here they explain everything . . . and you have to do your homework. (Lidia)

Students seemed to appreciate their perceived greater attention to instruction at La Costa relative to what they received at their former school. Perhaps the smaller class setting at La Costa created a greater sense of both instructional support on the part of teachers, and also fostered a sense that teachers were more caring with regard to students' personal lives and challenges. For example, Ramon described his experience:

It's kind of the environment and the teachers. Like they didn't really pay that much attention, like they do here . . . they pay more attention to like your life, school work, and everything.

Most of the students we interviewed described how much more positive their experiences were in terms of the academic support they received from adults at La Costa relative to their perceptions of teachers that did not really "pay attention to them" at their former comprehensive school.

Students also spoke of the importance of social support. Students perceived school adults as supportive and critical to their persistence in school. Relative to students' experiences with "uncaring" adults at their former comprehensive schools, school adults at La Costa were considered to be highly caring of students above and beyond the academic supports they required to succeed in school.

In addition to the administrative function of the school leader, the principal played the role of a caring adult at La Costa. A student described her relationship with the principal in contrast to the less responsive comprehensive school adult leadership she experienced in the following way:

There was nobody to help you at [the comprehensive school]. And [at La Costa] we could tell our problems to the principal. An over there it wasn't the same . . . because he understands and he's nicer to you. (Nicole)

Counselors at La Costa also provided much appreciated emotional support that fostered caring and supportive relationships with students. As a student notes:

Um, because my adviser has helped me a lot, and she is always there for me when I need her. And she talks to me, and teachers are nicer here; they help you a lot. They're really nice. (Yolanda)

Students at La Costa reported that counselors extended their emotional support in ways they didn't experience at their former comprehensive schools.

Then another support is the counseling. Like they get really into your emotions when you're feeling sad you know, the emotions you are feeling for that day. They get really into it and they don't really do that at other high schools. (Julie)

Adults at La Costa structured very rigid behavioral expectations for students and the students had to adhere to the behavior expectations set forth in the intake contract. The contractual policies were strictly enforced and led to being expelled from the school if the rules were not followed. Thus, the provision of both academic and social/emotional support for students—in relation to the limited sense of support they experienced in the former comprehensive schools—became an important source of motivation to stay in school.

WHAT DOES ALL THIS MEAN?

Latina/o students enrolled in La Costa's nontraditional program were heavily invested and committed to earning a diploma, which they believed was the key to finding a meaningful and well-paying job. The students were also well aware that La Costa was their final opportunity to return to the comprehensive high school or, if they remained at La Costa, their avenue to a high school diploma.

The school culture at La Costa appears to be largely responsible for the students' dedication. Defined by a balance of small size, behavioral control, and caring adults, La Costa did not have the typical surveillance and monitoring often found in schools serving similar students (Noguera, 2003). There are no metal detectors at the main school entrance, police officers and security guards do not routinely patrol the grounds (although students could be demanded, at any time, to undergo a urine test for the presence of drugs or alcohol), and the principal was viewed as one of the teaching staff who demanded that "gang affiliation stays at the door while on school grounds."

Furthermore, a signed contract—a condition for school enrollment—forced students to promise that their gang affiliation would not interfere with their schooling. Requiring students to refrain from gang activity, rather than asking them to renounce their gang affiliation altogether, was a practical decision.

Nevertheless, the process of getting La Costa students to agree to renounce their gang ties and to sustain a "gang-neutral" school environment was no easy task given the strong influence and lure of street-socialized youth in the surrounding community. This mechanism, however, was important for buffering students from street-oriented youth and helped students maintain a pro-diploma orientation.

By establishing a diploma-oriented culture, La Costa was able to create a safe and "gang-neutral" space in which the institutional agents played a critical role in school success. At La Costa, peers and family were most often seen as social support while the school provided the social leverage to attain a diploma. Thus, hiring caring institutional agents is critical in developing a diploma-oriented school culture.

Consequently, we believe that state credential agencies must develop specific licenses for teachers who choose to work in alternative settings such as La Costa. At present, continuation and community day school teachers are prepared in routine comprehensive middle or high schools. Specialized credentials would require new teachers in these schools to have significant experiences in such school and community settings and recruit only those teachers who genuinely want to work in alternative schools. That career choice ought to be clear at the outset.

It has become clear that nontraditional schools can potentially provide more "leverage supports" to further capitalize on students' commitment to attain a high school diploma. Students' dedication toward a diploma is only a means to an end and not an end in and of itself. In other words, their goal is to get a high school diploma because they believe it will help improve their job prospects and opportunities. Future research should focus on whether or not it may be useful for nontraditional programs to provide institutional agents that can provide social and academic supports and also serve as a bridge to work opportunities by facilitating access to students who earn a diploma to either continue their education (e.g., community college enrollment), or to serve as "leverage ties" by connecting students with concrete employment opportunities via internships or job placement in local businesses. This is the point at which social capital may transform into material capital for students growing up in low-income communities such as La Costa's—this conveyance cannot be ignored.

NOTES

1. Continuation and community day schools are not typically charter schools, although some charter schools are created to meet the needs of students who might normally attend a nontraditional school.

2. The figures do not include nontraditional secondary schools designed specifically for students requiring special education (n = 103 schools statewide) or juvenile hall schools (n = 56).

3. See Portes (1998) for an elaboration of the negative consequences of social capital, which include exclusion of outsiders, excess claims on group members, and restrictions on individual freedoms.

REFERENCES

Barrat, V. X., & Berliner, B. (2013). *The invisible achievement gap: Educational outcomes of students in foster care in California's public schools.* San Francisco, CA: WestEd.

Belfield, C. R., & Levin, H. M. (2007). *The economic losses from high school dropouts in California.* Santa Barbara, CA: California Dropout Research Project.

Briggs, X. S. (1998). Brown kids in white suburbs: Housing mobility and the many faces of social capital. *Housing Policy Debate, 9*(1), 177–221.

Brown, T., & Rodriguez, L. F. (2008). School and the co-construction of dropout. *International Journal of Qualitative Studies in Education, 1*, 1–21.

Coleman, J. S. (1988). Social capital in the creation of human capital: The ambiguous position of private schools. *American Journal of Sociology, 94*, 95–120.

Conchas, G. Q. (2001). Structuring failure and success: Understanding the variability in Latina/o school engagement. *Harvard Educational Review, 70*, 475–504.

Conchas, G. Q. (2006). *The color of success: Race and high-achieving urban youth.* New York, NY: Teachers College Press.

Conchas, G. Q., & Vigil, J. D. (2012). *Streetsmart schoolsmart: Urban poverty and the education of adolescent boys.* New York, NY: Teachers College Press.

Croninger, R. G., & Lee, V. E. (2001). Social capital and dropping out of high school: Benefits to at-risk students of teachers' support and guidance. *Teachers College Record, 103*(4), 548–581.

Dika, S. S., & Singh, K. (2002). Applications of social capital in educational literature: A critical synthesis. *Review of Educational Research, 72*(1), 31–60.

Fine, M. (1991). *Framing dropouts: Notes on the politics of an urban public high school.* Albany, NY: State University of New York Press.

Flores-Gonzalez, N. (2002) *School kids, street kids: Identity development in Latina/o students.* New York, NY: Teachers College Press.

Foley, R. M., & Pang, L. S. (2006). Alternative education programs. *The High School Journal, 89*, 10–21.

Fry, R. (2010). *Hispanics, high school dropouts and the GED.* Washington, DC: Pew Hispanic Center.

Gándara, P., & Contreras, F. (2009). *The Latina/o education crisis: The consequences of failed social policies.* Cambridge, MA: Harvard University Press.

Gibson, M. A., Gándara, P., & Koyama, J. P. (2004). *School connections: U.S. Mexican youth, peers, and school achievement.* New York, NY: Teachers College Press.

Goldin, C., & Katz, L. (2003). *Mass secondary schooling and the state: The role of state compulsion in the high school movement.* Cambridge, MA: National Bureau of Economic Research.

Kennedy, B. L. (2011). The importance of student and teacher interactions for disaffected middle school students: A grounded theory study of community day schools. *Urban Education, 46*(1), 4–33.

Moore, J. W., & Garcia, R. (1978). *Homeboys: Gangs, drugs, and prison in the barrios of Los Angeles.* Philadelphia, PA: Temple University Press.

Murnane, R. J., Willett, J. B., & Boudett, K. P. (1999). Do male dropouts benefit from obtaining a GED, postsecondary education, and training? *Evaluation Review, 23*(5), 475–502.

Noguera, P. A. (2003). *City schools and the American dream: Reclaiming the promise of public education.* New York, NY: Teachers College Press.

Orfield, G. (2004). *Dropouts in America: Confronting the graduation rate crisis.* Cambridge, MA: Harvard Education Press.

Oseguera, L., Conchas, G. Q., & Mosqueda, E. (2010). Beyond family and ethnic culture: Understanding the preconditions for the potential realization of social capital. *Youth & Society, 43*(3), 1136–1166.

Portes, A. (1998). Social capital: Its origins and applications in modern sociology. *Annual Review of Sociology, 24*, 1–24.

Rios, V. M. (2011). *Street life: Poverty, gangs, and a Ph.D.* Published by CreateSpace, a division of Amazon.

Ruiz de Velasco, J., Austin, G., Dixon, D., Johnson, J., McLaughlin, M., & Perez, L. (2008). *Alternative education options: A descriptive study of California continuation high schools.* Palo Alto, CA: John W. Gardner Center, Stanford University.

Rumberger, R. W. (2004). Why students drop out of school. In G. Orfield (Ed.), *Dropout in America: Confronting the graduation rate crisis* (pp. 131–155). Cambridge, MA: Harvard Education Press.

Rumberger, R. W. (2008). *Solving California's dropout crisis.* Sacramento, CA: California Research Project Policy Committee Report.

Rumberger, R. W. & Ream, R. (2008). Student engagement, peer social capital, and school dropout among Mexican American and non-Latina/o White students. *Sociology of Education, 81,* 109–139.

Sizer, T. (2004). *Horace's compromise: The dilemma of the American high school.* New York, NY: Houghton Mifflin Company.

Stanton-Salazar, R. D. (2001). *Manufacturing hope and despair: The school and kin support networks of U.S. Mexican youth.* New York, NY: Teachers College Press.

Stanton-Salazar, R. D. (2011). A social capital framework for the study of institutional agents and their role in empowerment of low-status students and youth. *Youth & Society, 43*(3), 1066–1109.

Téllez, K., & Estep, M. (1997). Latina/o youth gangs and the meaning of school. *The High School Journal, 81*(2), pp. 69–81.

Valencia, R. R. (2002). "Mexican Americans don't value education!" On the basis of the myth, mythmaking, and debunking. *Journal of Latina/os and Education, 1*(2), 81–103.

Valenzuela, A. (1999). *Subtractive schooling: U.S. Mexican youth and the politics of caring.* Albany, NY: State University of New York Press.

Vigil, J. D. (1988). *Barrio gangs.* Austin, TX: University of Texas Press.

Vigil, J. D. (1997). *Personas Mexicanas: Chicano highschoolers in a changing Los Angeles.* Dallas, TX: Harcourt Brace.

Vigil, J. D. (2002). *A rainbow of gangs: Street cultures in the mega-city.* Austin, TX: University of Texas Press.

Vigil, J. D. (2004). Gangs and group membership: Implications for schooling. In M. Gibson, P. Gándara, & J. Koyama (Eds.), *School connections: U.S. Mexican youth, peers, and school achievement* (pp. 87–105). New York, NY: Teachers College Press.

Yin, R. K. (2014). *Case study research design and methods* (5th ed.). Thousand Oaks, CA: Sage.

Yosso, T. J. (2005). Whose culture has capital? A critical race theory discussion of community cultural wealth. *Race Ethnicity and Education, 8*(1), 69–91.

CHAPTER 7

"YES, We Care!"

Understanding the Role of Community-Based Organizations and Latina/o Parent Cultural Wealth in a Large Urban City

Alejandra S. Albarran & Gilberto Q. Conchas

Disparities in academic achievement, often along racial and economic lines, begin in early childhood, before children step foot into a classroom. Children who are well prepared at entry are able to take full advantage of school, whereas children who enter less prepared spend more time trying to catch up. Using organizational interviews and observations of services by two community-based organizations (CBOs), this study uncovers how CBOs promote school readiness through parent education services to inform early childhood educational reform by providing insight into the impacts CBOs are having on families and children. Findings demonstrate that CBOs help parents to become educational advocates on behalf of their children and point to an advantage out-of-school processes have for in-school change.

It is a perfect fall day—crisp from the morning chill but you can feel the sun beaming down. Today is the day of the Latina/o Family Education Fair hosted by a southern California university, the local Spanish radio station, and countless other community-based organizations (CBOs). The event opens at 10:00 A.M. but by 9:00 A.M. Latina/o families are already trickling in, asking where the workshops are held. The day is expected to exceed last year's number of attendees, over 10,000.

The event is organized into four distinct areas: classrooms for workshops, a courtyard for a book fair, a field of activities, and the gym with various informational booths. Parent Education Institute (PEI)—a local CBO—has a booth to answer questions and invite parents to learn more about their services. Booth workers call out to the highly engaged participating parents, "*Tenemos talleres*" (We have workshops); "*Enseñar a los padres como apoyar a sus hijos*" (We show parents how to support their children); *"Escríbanse!"* (Sign up!). Families stop to learn more.

Near their booth, PEI has tables covered in butcher paper. The director of PEI states that it is easier to visualize your goals when you see them on paper, so the workers tell people passing, *"Escriban sus huellas!"* (Write your goals!). Children hesitate, but eventually trace their hands and write their dreams; "teacher," "police officer," and "doctor" are among the most popular. Parents' faces beam as they read, for the first time, about their children's lifelong goals. You can see the pride radiate from their faces, possibly envisioning their children in their future careers. Little Raul, maybe about 5 years old, writes, "I don't know yet." Alina, a young teenager, writes, "I hope to one day help mi RAZA (sic) in passing policies and laws." Parents are also encouraged to write their dreams and goals because "it is never too late to dream." One mother writes, "My dream is to be able to get my three children to university! Nestar, Luna, & Antonio for you guys. Your Mom."

As parents leave PEI's booth, they join the line that forms the length of the gym where 10 tables are covered with free education and fiction books for all ages. Boxes are provided for parents to take as many books as they would like. Some walk away with so many books they need a cart. It takes an hour before parents and children are able to select their books.

We start this chapter with the details of the Latina/o Family Education Fair because Latina/o parents have received a bad reputation within the educational system (Conchas, 2001; Delgado-Gaitan, 1992). Some teachers believe that Latina/o parents are lazy, do not care about education, or would rather work than engage in their children's schooling. If this is true, then how does one explain the interest and desires of the thousands of parents who participated in the Latina/o Parent Education Fair? How do we explain the parents who waited to get their children free books that they could not afford otherwise? How do we explain the fact that these parents want the best for their children, that they are doing their best for their children's educational mobility, and that they are seeking resources to help them navigate the school system despite their potentially limited knowledge of the U.S. education system? This chapter takes us one step closer to ascertaining the factors that enable Latina/o parents to attain the resources necessary to support their children's educational trajectories.

Negative perceptions of Latina/o parents have caused schools to ignore or disengage Latina/o parents from the education process. Despite some schools' active efforts to push parents out, Latina/o parents are finding informational avenues in the community that assist in pushing back in. This chapter focuses on parent education programs offered by two CBOs that help Latina/o parents to regain access to the education system. CBOs were selected as a source due to their unique positioning in the community—situated directly in the neighborhood and run by members of the community. Drawing from interviews and observations at two CBOs' parent education workshop series, we examine how CBOs reinforce Latina/o parents' strengths and assets while championing them to engage their children's schooling through active parent involvement in education. This chapter finds extensive evidence that Latina/o parents, in fact, co-create spaces to engage in their children's education.

FROM EDUCATION DISCONNECT TO EDUCATIONAL SUPPORT

Research has found that many parents care about education and want their children to do well (Lareau, 2000; Valdés, 1996; Villenas & Foley, 2002). However, parental value of education does always match their "participation" in schooling (Lareau, 2000). These differences occur for many reasons, often associated with class and race. In a study of parent involvement, Lareau (2000) found that schools "draw unevenly on the social and cultural resources in the society," unintentionally supporting the high socioeconomic status (SES) communities. In addition, working-class families have strong ties to family and weak ties to educators, whereas in upper-middle-class families the opposite is true. These relationships help upper-middle-class parents and, therefore, their children.

Parent–school engagement began gaining recognition in the 1960s, with the creation of Head Start (Boger, Kuipers, & Beery, 1969; Bronfenbrenner, 1974), which ignited the push for home-school partnerships. This originated as a push to assist parents how to parent but has shifted to a team role where both perspectives are valued. The partnership model aimed to work with parents so that they were both informed of educational options and had input in their children's education. Although this model sounded great in theory, in practice there were a lot of challenges.

Caring About Education and Participation

Many Latina/o parents, in particular foreign-born, have high respect for teachers and believe that teachers have more expertise teaching than they, as parents, do (Trumbull, Greenfield, Quiroz, & Rothstein-Fisch, 1996). Such parents have such complete trust in teachers and adults of authority that they do not question their educational practices. This stands in contrast to many of their White peers or U.S.-born Latina/os, who are less afraid to speak up in opposition to authority figures. Additionally, many immigrant families lack knowledge of how the school system works, given that they were educated outside the United States. This lack of knowledge appears to feed into the stereotype that Latina/o parents do not want to engage in their children's schooling. However, it is not that Latina/o parents do not want to engage, but rather that their approach to engaging is not seen as engagement. That is why a third party, who understands the Latina/o families' perspective, becomes important. With a respect and understanding of the Latina/o culture and U.S. educational know-how, CBOs are the perfect link between parents and schools through their role as institutional agents.

CBOs as Key Institutional Agents

Formal schooling reproduces class differences (Bourdieu, 1977) but also has the power to change class status, specifically through social capital: "relationships and networks that transmit vital forms of resources and institutional support that enable young people to become effective participants within mainstream institutional spheres, particularly the school system" (Stanton-Salazar & Dornbusch, 1995, p. 20). Social capital could come in the form of tips, referrals, or advice that occur through word of mouth, or increased examples (Conchas, 2006; Conchas & Vigil, 2012). These resources differ from tangible resources, such as books, in that you cannot solely provide more tangible resources and assume that children will find their own way. The tools gained through social capital expose knowledge that is necessary to succeed academically but may otherwise be hidden, such as the "A-G" requirements or the value of having extracurricular activities. Without such social knowledge, competing for a position at a university might not even be possible.

Researchers have studied school personnel, specifically teachers and counselors, as vital sources of social capital for lower-class and diverse students (Conchas, 2006; Valenzuela, 1999). They propose that, while teachers have the obvious obligation to teach, they also hold the power to provide students with social capital. This occurs through regular interactions between students that are based on trust and positive rapport. Typically, lower-class students and ethnic minorities do not have equal access to those institutional agents that are vital to their academic success. Students, however, are not the only people who can benefit from this increased educational knowledge. Parents, especially those from lower-class and immigrant homes, often lack the knowledge to support their own academic success, let alone their children's academic success.

In addition to the typical school setting, communities hold sources of social capital that parents could and should tap into (Woolcock & Narayan, 2000). Portes and Sensenbrenner (1993) argue that this is especially true for recent immigrants, who must rely on the resources in the community to help them navigate their new environments. Because parents, especially during the early years, are called on to make decisions for their children's educational careers, these early years are especially crucial. Similar to students' relationships with teachers, parents can connect with community members to help promote their children's educational opportunities. This could become vital given that, even in early childhood, parents who felt less competent in helping their children held lower expectations for their children, thus limiting their academic and career potentials.

It is suggested that education-based CBOs are well poised to support Latina/o parents' educational quest through their more familial approach to engage families, making Latina/o families feel more comfortable to continue their participation. These third parties are key because they expand Latina/o parents' networks to include educational agents. We suggest that Latina/o parents care about their children's education and can be seen as an educational resource for their children with the support of educational CBOs. CBOs connect with parents in a unique and supportive way to expose the nuances of the education system, in an inclusive and respectful manner to develop advocacy and pride and ultimately build relationships with parents founded on trust.

SPEAKING TO PEOPLE IN THE COMMUNITY

The current study took place at two CBOs in the larger Los Angeles area. California has one of the highest percentages of high-poverty schools in the nation (National Center for Education Statistics, 2010), many of which are located in Los Angeles. Every year, more than 65% of Los Angeles County's students receive free or reduced lunch—a national marker of poverty—and more than 28,000 children drop out of high school (California Department of Education, 2011). The bulk of these children are of Latina/o descent, the fastest-growing population in area and in the nation. These statistics point to a clear need for attention in these communities. Many studies investigate the in-school factors contributing to these statistics, but few are looking out of schools factors, specifically CBOs that are working to help minimize these damaging statistics. This case study draws from 2 months of observations, surveys, and interviews at parent education workshops at two CBOs—PEI and Amigos.

The Process of Doing Fieldwork

The two study CBOs were randomly selected from a collection of eight parent-focused CBOs that had previously participated in a broader study with the researchers. Directors of the organization were contacted and informed that the study was aimed at understanding (1) how the structure and organization of their workshops help Latina/o parents in their efforts to better support their children, and (2) how Latina/o parents perceived their own participation in the workshops. They were told that the researcher would serve as a participant observer during one series of workshops, and that at the end of the observations the researcher would ask parents to voluntarily complete a questionnaire regarding their experience. Both directors immediately agreed to participate in the study. PEI's "Parent Education Night Workshops" and Amigos' "New Moms' Group" were selected for participation.

During the workshops, we provided unstructured notes, including objectives, topics, facilitators' behavior toward parents, and parents' reactions to assignments, and we actively participated with the parents. Although our roles as participant-observers were identical at each workshop, the workshops themselves varied.

Who We Spoke With

PEI Parents. Both mothers and fathers attended PEI, but they were predominantly female (80%) and immigrants from a Latin American country (90%). All parents at the Latina/o Parent Education Night were over the age of 18 and had at least one child of elementary age or older. Fifteen of the 22 parents at PEI completed the survey. PEI restricted additional demographic information.

Amigos Moms. Amigos' participants were all female. Amigos had 11 consistent participants, 6 of whom were above the age of 18 and were included in the present study. Mothers ranged in age from 18 to 23 years old, with an average age of 20.5 years old. The level of education ranged from completing 8th grade to completion of a technical program. Most mothers had completed high school. Amigos mothers had been participating in the workshops 9 months to 5 years (the average participation was 2 years and 9 months). Demographic information is available in Table 7.1.

How We Interpreted the Voices in the Field

The qualitative analysis used a grounded theory, constant comparative method, which began with the careful coding of hundreds of pages of interview, observation, and survey data, broken down analytically. The data were reviewed line by

Table 7.1. Demographic Information of Participants

	PEI Parent Education Night n = 16	Amigos New Mom Group n = 6
Gender		
Female	12 (80%)	6 (100%)
Male	3 (20%)	0
Ethnicity		
Latina/o	14 (93%)	6 (100%)
Did not report	1 (7%)	
Schooling (range)	Not available	8th grade– technical program
Years Attending (range, average)	Not available	9 months–5 years 2 years & 9 months
Age (range, average)	Not available	18–23, 20.5 years
Immigration status (immigrant)	18 (90%)*	1 (16%)

Note: The asterisk (*) indicates the total of participants who were immigrants from the total regular attendee population. It is not known how many who completed the surveys were immigrants.

line with the goal of identifying recurrent words, phrases, expressions, and significant events or aspects of informants' perceptions. A laundry list of codes was created, and then re-coded and grouped into thematic clusters, which enabled the construction of meaningful micro- and macro-categories. These thematic codes or categories, in turn, were applied to new chunks of data. Throughout this process, we kept an open mind to new codes and new data-derived formulations. At this stage, relationships among categories were examined and explained using theoretical memos. This co-constructed process for understanding adults' perspectives helped clarify and organize relationships among categories.

A CRITICAL LINK BETWEEN PARENTS AND SCHOOLS IN TWO CBOS

Parent Education Institute

> PEI's mission is to connect families, schools, and the community as partners
> to advance the education of every child through parent engagement.
>
> —PEI

Organizationally, PEI is a well-oiled machine, with a clear mission, vision, philosophy, and outcomes written on every document they provide. These serve as reminders or checks and balances to ensure that their focus remains on supporting children through supporting parents. Each aspect of their mission, vision, and philosophy articulates the respect they have for parents. Excerpts like these emphasize their true respect of parents and vision of parents as advocates for their children's education: "All parents love their children and want a better future for them," and "PEI is working to create a community in which parents and educators collaborate to transform each child's educational environment." The power of parents' ability to change educational environments is articulated over and over again.

Over their 25 years of service, originating in southern California, PEI has expanded to all major cities in California and five additional states. Within California, PEI has built standing relationships with additional programs and organizations, most notably the California State University (CSU) system. Children of parents who complete the program will receive an additional credit during admissions to their local CSU university—one credit for each of the four (early childhood, elementary, middle school, and high school) series of workshops attended. This is an important benefit designed to assist children in pursuing higher education and is an additional incentive for parents to attend and complete the workshops.

Latina/o Parent Education Night: The Latina/o Parent Education Night is PEI's elementary school workshop. It is an 8-week structured program, held in Spanish, from 5 P.M. to 7 P.M. one night a week. The first night is an informational session during which parents discuss topics they would like to learn more about, and the following six nights follow a structured educational curriculum. Although the topics are preset, the facilitator draws from the first night to emphasize parents' concerns and to make connections. The final night is a graduation ceremony, during which the principal and parents engage in a conversation based on their new understanding of the education system. A ceremony is held where every parent receives a certificate of completion. This structure sandwiches parents at both ends of their workshops, highlighting concerns before proceeding and addressing new questions as a product of their new knowledge. This ensures that parents feel respected as members of the organization from day 1 and leave feeling empowered.

Amigos

> Amigos' mission is to foster strong, self-sufficient families, joyful, resilient children, and vibrant communities by providing respectful, *responsive family support programs in the greater area.*
>
> —Amigos

Amigos was one of the first CBOs in its region when it began 40 years ago. Although Amigos has various services to meet the many needs of the people of their community, they focus on their family support program. The family support program was founded on six basic assumptions: (1) to approach families from a health and well-being perspective, (2) to provide childrearing techniques that incorporate family and community cultural values, (3) to support parents to draw from their experiences to raise their children, (4) to help families make connections with other families, (5) to provide families with information about child development so that they react appropriately to their children, and (6) to empower parents to advocate for themselves. These assumptions speak to the respect they have for families, specifically parents. The words *connections, incorporate family,* and *empower* set out a "game plan" for Amigos' parent education programming that is not solely about providing parents with information but also about connecting parents to be empowered to become their children's biggest advocates.

Although Amigos is a well-established CBO, each aspect of their service is tailored for the family or set of families who participate in the services (e.g., new parent groups, literacy groups, tutoring, tax preparation, counseling, and financial support for school).

The New Mom Group: The New Mom Group is one of the best benefits of Amigos' programming. The group is designed for women who had children when they were 23 years of age or younger. The evening schedule accommodates the young mothers, who are encouraged to go to school or work during the day. The group meets year-round, providing a continuous source of support for the mothers, with free meals and child care for attendees, transportation, diapers, bus tickets, and access to support outside of the group. Topics of their nightly meetings mirror areas of conflict or concerns in the women's daily lives, ranging from relationship help to how to apply for a new job. The young mothers face a lot of struggles raising their children. Amigos' programming is able to help ameliorate many of these struggles through its holistic approach to support.

Ana, the group facilitator, will do as much as possible to help the women. She regularly offers to take them to doctors for birth control or medical services and to register for school if they have dropped out. She also connects the women with other organizations for additional support (e.g., help creating a résumé, tax support, or psychological therapy). She encourages the women to reach out and receive the support they need.

CBO APPROACHES TO PARENT ENGAGEMENT AND EMPOWERMENT

Direct observations of programs demonstrate that PEI and Amigos orient their programming in a manner that helps to uncover the unknown for parents through the respect they have for parents and the way in which they include parents in the programming. Programming is designed to help guide parents to become advocates and to foster self-pride. Finally, their unique, program-specific workshops enable relationships to bloom for continued transformation beyond the confines of the workshops—essential for their kids' lifelong social and academic success.

Uncovering the Education System

The education system means slightly different things to each CBO in terms of meeting parents where they are in understanding U.S. schooling practices and acquiring the proper services in a manner that will help them get to the next step. Parents at PEI are told how the American education system works, which is especially important for the parents educated outside of the United States. Amigos mothers, while predominantly educated in the United States, are still struggling with their place in the education system. Many were pushed out once they realized they were pregnant, and others struggled to go back once their first baby arrived.

PEI programming's first goal is to make the education system explicitly available. As Blanca (the director of PEI) noted, "Latina/o parents are not at a point to demand what they need." In other words, parents cannot speak up for themselves if they do not know what they need. The structured workshops help parents understand the institutional structure that pushed them out so that they can fight their way back in.

The second goal of PEI is to increase the number of students, especially Latina/o students, who attend a university. The direct educational focus is accomplished through their explicit nightly curriculum. The topics are organized in a manner where the immediate educational experience is presented—for example, homework—followed by those that one learns through informed networks of people—for example, requirements for attending a university, academic standards, and how the school system works. This approach allows parents to learn how each aspect of education sets the path to a university.

Parents' experiences and perspectives are welcomed and encouraged. For example, during discussion of California English Language Development Test (CELDT) testing, a mother mentioned that she heard the CELDT test was hard and that they should not label their children as English language learners. The facilitator used this opportunity to inform parents of their choices and possible outcomes of those choices. She explained that a child tracked into a dual-language path could fall behind through the additional testing that a child must pass before placement in English-only classes that emphasize high academic language.

Amigos' mothers need a different kind of educational approach. These women have experienced American schooling but schools have failed them. They were marginalized due to their new status as mothers. They need support to reconnect to their schooling so that their children can have educational role models.

Night workshops begin by asking the women to state their educational or career status. It serves as a constant reminder of the importance of school. When a woman is not enrolled in school, the facilitator offers help and reminds her that she will be limited in her possible income without a high school education. Prepared for this weekly question, many of the mothers enroll in school with Ana's help. This educational focus is somewhat subtle in that members rarely spend the evening discussing the nuances of school, but it is enough to demonstrate the value of school.

Unfortunately, although their own education is discussed, rarely do mothers bring up their children's education or development. If a mother has a particular question, she will address it in a group setting, but it is seldom a first thought.

Respect, Inclusion, and Voice

Parent voice and perspective are an integral part of both workshops. The PEI requires that parents speak a minimum of 50% of the time. Occasionally, a few parents are heard more than others, but the facilitator redirects until another parent speaks. She varies pedagogical techniques from one-to-one conversations, small-group work, and whole-class discussions. These practices ensure that all parents' perspectives are included.

Amigos' parent inclusion is less formalized but equally valued. The room is arranged in a circle so that all participants have an equal place and voice. The topics are based on the needs of the mothers in attendance. For example, one night a woman mentioned that she lost her job. This led to a discussion about résumés, the importance of working as opposed to living off welfare, and how to go about obtaining a job.

Developing Advocacy and Pride

At both CBOs, information is shared for educational advocacy, giving power to the information. Therefore, what PEI and Amigos do is to help support parents' sense of advocacy through developing a sense of pride.

PEI and Amigos strive to articulate the importance of parents' believing in themselves and recognizing how their confidence translates to their children's ultimate success. The theme of the second night at PEI is "promoting self-esteem and academics," and a part of the session is spent sharing the many things parents are proud of both for themselves and in their children. The parents answer with "*De mi mismo!*" (Of myself!) and "*Mi hija mayor esta en la Universidad*" (My eldest daughter is at the university). Parents smile as their greatest accomplishments are put on the "stage" for them to share. After sharing, parents sit a little more upright and are a lot more attentive. They are shown how this confidence connects to their children by emphasizing that if children focus on their strengths they will be up to the many educational challenges they will face. Such a simple exercise conveys so much meaning to all those in the room.

The practice of developing advocacy and pride is no more evident than it is on graduation night. On that night, parents are aware of their new role in their children's lives and discuss it with other parents. "*Nosotros, como padres, tenemos el obligación*" (We, as parents, have an obligation) (Carlos, parent from PEI). The fact that parents feel responsible demonstrates not only that they learned but, more importantly, that they are ready to advocate for their children.

Even the act of receiving a certificate of completion at the graduation ceremony serves as a reminder of their success, especially to the many parents who have never graduated. After the ceremony parents are heard discussing where to post their "diploma" (e.g., "*Yo, los voy a poner en la sala!*" [I'm going to put it in the living room!]). Parents are inspired to help their children to feel the same sense of accomplishment when they graduate from high school.

As a former teen mother, Ana knows the struggles that the women face and what it will take to overcome those struggles to succeed. Ana relies on herself to show the women that anything is possible. When asked about her role, Ana replied that "we're advocates." She noted that many parents "feel impotent" and that she leads workshops and helps parents "because I have a voice." She recalled a story in which a mother wanted to help out in her child's classroom but was afraid to do so because she was undocumented and would need to be fingerprinted in order to help. Ana helped her find a way so that the mother could engage more in her child's class.

Ana believes in the mothers but understands that they are young and that there is room for growth. It became evident one night that the mothers become upset over confrontation. When they started to complain, Ana removed herself from the table and returned minutes later, saying, "In life if you are not going to do something then don't complain. I did something." She confronted the people who were criticizing the mothers and they stopped. Ana made a point to tell the women they could do it, too.

One important aspect of the group is that each meeting, although facilitated by Ana, is very much led by the mothers who attend. One night Cynthia entered with a huge black eye. The women, knowing Cynthia and her history, started to ask about the eye. They could tell she was embarrassed, but they listened as she shared. They provided many suggestions for how she could remove herself from the situation. Their ideas nearly all came from personal experiences of past abuse. They could speak to what it was like to get out of abusive relationships. Ana acknowledged how proud she was that the women were able to remove themselves from such negative situations and that their choices meant their children would be better off.

Developing Strong Connections, Relationships, and Trust

A strong positive relationship between parents helps the CBO message carry on beyond the workshop. PEI parents have much in common with their immigration status, Spanish-speaking families, and children in school together. Amigos mothers are teen parents and share their vulnerability. These similarities plus time together creates a space for positive relationships to form.

According to PEI director Blanca, "From the initial orientation session, PEI makes a cultural and social connection to the families it serves and empowers them to be engaged in their children's education." PEI works to connect with parents on all levels, through their value of parents' cultural and social backgrounds. Frequently this is achieved. For example, during the graduation night two mothers began discussing the program and touched on their new relationship:

> *Estephanie: Comadre . . .* (directly translated to "co-mother")
> *Gloria: Ya hasta comadre!?!* (Now we are co-mothers!?!)

These two women did not know each other before they began the workshops, yet by the end of the series they became *comadres* (co-mothers), a term of endearment held for women who have a unique and trusting bond. Over such a short period of time, these women were able to build a strong relationship that went beyond a typical friendship.

The formation of friendships is even more common among Amigos mothers. Many mothers are required to attend Amigos workshops. While initially they do not know one another, they immediately realize they have something in common: teen motherhood. Friendships quickly form. Women regularly arrive to the workshops together or discuss shared plans for the weekend. Dona, one of the older mothers, even invited everyone to her son's birthday party.

Friendship between mothers is expected, but what was surprising was the development of strong bonds between Ana and the women. Having had her first child at the age of 16, Ana can relate to their struggles: "I was where they are at. I think I understand them more and validate them. I can have more empathy even when I have to be stricter . . . I hope." However, occasionally this closeness does cause struggles because of her high expectations. Ana expects a lot from the mothers since she was in their shoes and was successful. In many ways, this is a positive thing but occasionally Ana will provide the women with the answers to their struggles rather than giving them the tools to solve their problems themselves.

PROGRESS IS NOT WITHOUT SETBACKS

Each CBO acknowledges the strengths they see in their programming: the respect they have for the parents and understanding for their circumstances. Yet their work in the community is not without some strong challenges. Occasionally they continue to engage with schools or school personnel who are not supportive. Blanca recalls one particular situation with a principal who said to parents, "Are you going to be so selfish to keep [Title I] money for yourself instead of teachers?" Some principals do not yet see the power of parent knowledge, or perhaps they fear it. It was therefore difficult to encourage parents to participate when the principal stood at the door of the workshops and told parents they did not have to attend. In many ways, though, such opposition fuels PEI to continue.

 Institutions operate with a need for financial backing and CBOs are no exception. The recent recession had a major impact on Amigos. They laid off many workers while attempting to maintain all services, ultimately placing more responsibility and stress on the remaining workers. Funding and the changing economy will always be a source of stress for such programs. It is important to keep offering the workshops for free in order to remove potential barriers for parents, yet there are also limits to what each community can provide.

CONSTRUCTING SOCIAL CAPITAL DEEP IN THE COMMUNITY

Social capital refers to the "relationships and networks that transmit vital forms of resources and institutional supports" (Stanton-Salazar, 1997, p. 20) that are created through lasting relationships built on trust (Conchas, 2006). Putnum (2000) posited that the community holds many sources of social capital, specifically that there are people or groups within the community who hold the resources and can provide the institutional supports to which Stanton-Salazar (1997) referred. These findings suggest that CBOs are those sources of social capital.

 CBOs have the educational know-how and have positioned themselves in the way that they make their information accessible to the parents they serve. Recall PEI's topic schedule. Every week parents learned about the nuances of the education system (e.g., API scores and CEDLT testing) that most families, no matter their class standing, do not understand. Because of this, parents, and subsequently their children, recognize the early educational choices that can lead to university acceptance. And given that their children are so young, these parents have the chance to change their children's paths so that they are on the "right" track. This change is the strength of social capital because of the opportunity for social mobility afforded to the children once they become adults (Mehan, Villanueva, Hubbard, Lints, & Okamoto, 1996; Stanton-Salazar, 1997).

Likewise, this pattern is seen at Amigos. Of the mothers who were interviewed, five of the six reported near completion of a high school, GED, or technical program. The support to return to school was strongly facilitated by their participation in the New Moms Group. The facilitator went to great lengths to support the women in their process. This was crucial since many of the mothers, such as Dora, did not have familial support to further or complete their education because their academic success was beyond that of any member of their families. Completing high school and or the completion of additional training would nearly double their lifelong earning potential. In this regard, Amigos was able to serve as a source of social capital to those mothers.

Despite CBOs' varied approaches to parent education programs, they met the unique needs of the parents they served. Takahashi and Smutny (2001) highlighted that the benefit of CBOs is their ability to meet the specific needs of the community they serve. PEI and Amigos, because their services varied, were able to fulfill parents' needs by providing the unique educational know-how for academic success. PEI educates the predominantly immigrant population about the American school system. Given that the parents have limited, if any, experience with the American education system, PEI shared some crucial details about schooling that can and will better position their children. Likewise, Amigos' New Moms Group consists of young women who are trying to balance out their education and the responsibilities of being parents. Ana, the facilitator, serves as a model of the many possibilities available to these women. All parents have gained access to many intangible resources through their connection with PEI.

Approaches to parent education programming are partially about the specific education information parents receive, but they are also about how the information is obtained. How the information is shared impacts the possible formation of relationships that are necessary for the continued movement of information. Both organizations clearly demonstrate a respect for the parents. PEI demonstrates their respect through their dedicated input night and their parent speakers at graduation night. Amigos shows the mothers respect through the honest way that all subjects are approached, without judgment, to finding opportunities to have the women's voices heard in front of parents much older than them. In giving both sets of parents a voice, PEI and Amigos help parents develop a sense of pride and promote advocacy. The people who attend the workshops become more than classmates—they become friends and *comadres*. These relationships allow CBOs to become potential sources of social capital that enhance and elevate Latina/o parents' cultural wealth to shine bright in the city.

REFERENCES

Boger, R. P., Kuipers, J., & Beery, M. (1969). *Parents as primary change agents in an experimental Head Start program of language intervention.* East Lansing, MI: Head Start Evaluation and Research Center, Michigan State University.

Bourdieu, P. (1977). *Outline of a theory of practice.* Cambridge, England: Cambridge University Press.

Bronfenbrenner, U. (1974). Is early intervention effective? In F. G. Jennings (Ed.), *Teachers college record* (vol. 76, 279–303). New York, NY: Columbia University.

California Department of Education, Educational Demographics Unit. (2011). *Selected statewide data summarized by county.* Retrieved from http://dq.cde.ca.gov/dataquest/Cbeds1.asp?FreeLunch=on&cChoice=StatProf2&cYear=2010-11&cLevel=State&cTopic = Profile&myTimeFrame = S&submit1 = Submit

Conchas, G. Q. (2001). Structuring failure and success: Understanding the variability in Latino school engagement. *Harvard Educational Review, 70,* 475–504.

Conchas, G. Q. (2006). *The color of success: Race and high achieving urban youth.* New York, NY: Teachers College Press.

Conchas, G. Q., & Vigil, J. D. (2012). *Streetsmart schoolsmart: Urban poverty and the education adolescent boys.* New York, NY: Teachers College Press.

Delgado-Gaitan, C. (1992). School matters in the Mexican-American home: Socializing children to education. *American Educational Research Journal, 29* (3), 495-513.

Lareau, A. (2000). *Home advantage: Social class and parental intervention in elementary education* (2nd ed.). Lanham, MD: Rowman & Littlefield Publishers.

Mehan, H., Villanueva, I., Hubbard, L., Lints, A., & Okamoto, D. (1996). *Constructing school success: The consequences of untracking low achieving students.* San Diego, CA: Cambridge University Press.

National Center for Education Statistics (NCES). (2010). *High-poverty public schools: Where are high-poverty schools located?* Retrieved from http://nces.ed.gov/programs/coe/analysis/2010-section1b.asp

Portes, A., & Sensenbrenner, J. (1993). Embeddedness and immigration: Notes on the social determination of economic action. *The American Journal of Sociology, 98*(6), 1320-1350.

Putnum, R. (2000). *Bowling alone: The collapse and revival of American community.* New York, NY: Simon & Schuster.

Stanton-Salazar, R. D. (1997). A social capital framework for understanding the socialization of racial minority children and youth. *Harvard Educational Review, 67*(1), 1–40.

Stanton-Salazar, R. D., & Dornbusch, S. M. (1995). Social capital and the reproduction of inequality: Information network among Mexican-origin high school students. *American Sociological Association, 68*(2), 116–135.

Takahashi, L. M., & Smutny, G. (2001). Collaboration among small, community-based organizations: Strategies and challenges in turbulent environments. *Journal of Planning Education and Research,* 21, 141–153.

Trumbull, E., Greenfield, P., Quiroz, B., & Rothstein-Fisch, C. (1996). *Bridging cultures: Evaluating teachers' understanding of cross-cultural conflicts.* San Francisco, CA: WestEd.

Valdés, G. (1996). *Con respecto: Bridging the distinction between culturally diverse families and schools.* New York, NY: Teachers College Press.

Valenzuela, A. (1999). *Subtractive schooling: US-Mexican youth and the politics of caring.* Albany, NY: State University of New York Press.

Villenas, S., & Foley, D. E. (2002). Chicano/Latino critical ethnography of education: Cultural productions from la frontera. In *Chicano school failure and success: Past, present, and future* (2nd ed., pp. 195–225). London, England: Routledge/Falmer.

Woolcock, M., & Narayan, D. (2000). Social capital: Implications for development, theory, research, and policy. *The World Bank Research Observer, 12*(2), 225–249.

PART III

CRITICAL CASE STUDIES EXPLORING ETHNICITY, IDENTITY, AND IMMIGRATION

CHAPTER 8

When Does Resistance Begin?

Queer Immigrant and U.S.-Born Latina/o Youth, Identity, and the Infrapolitics of the Street

Cindy Cruz

> What one did was turn away smiling all the time, and tell white people what
> they wanted to hear. But people always accuse you of reckless talk when you
> say this.
>
> —James Baldwin, *A Talk to Teachers,* 1963

*Resistance in the form of traditional politics, such as mobilizing against school
policy, immigration, and using social media for civic engagement, do not often work
for lesbian, gay, bisexual, transgender, and queer (LGBTQ) Latina/o street youth.
In this ethnographic study of 57 LGBTQ homeless youth in a large U.S. city, the
author reframes Latina/o immigrant and U.S.-born youth narratives through a lens
of infrapolitics—reimagining what might count as resistance. Examining the small
and deliberate practices of youth toward their caseworkers, security guards, and
with one another aids researchers in identifying and recognizing resistance when
youth refuse the logic of domination and practice sharing knowledge in ways that
suggest new kinds of socialities. Reframing the relationships between the surveillance
and power of police, teachers, and other authorities and queer Latina/o youth as
infrapolitical allows social science and educational researchers to move away from
the deficit thinking and radical "othering" that is often found in educational policy
and research. The case study suggests that these new socialities have the possibility to
become spaces where youth can practice new sensibilities and ways of being as they
negotiate through the often hostile worlds they traverse.*

Lesbian, gay, bisexual, transgender, and queer (LGBTQ) Latina/o youth occupy
tight spaces of resistance, where multiple subjections, including being positioned

as an unaccompanied and/or undocumented minor, make moves against any kind of domination difficult. Resistance happens when youth say no to the alternatives they are offered in worlds where they are brutalized and oppressed. Queer Latina/o youth might resist using the smallest of gestures. Part of the work as teachers and researchers is to recognize and acknowledge the small acts of resistance that youth are making in the face of tremendous odds.

Feminist philosopher and popular education scholar Maria Lugones (2003) writes about resistance in "tight spaces," where a delicate spatiality is produced in off-stage practices. But these spaces are porous and Lugones argues that despite the constriction of this spatiality, it is neither permanent nor concrete for youth. "You are concrete. Your spatiality, constructed as an intersection following the designs of power, isn't" (p. 10). In this chapter, I activate a rethinking of resistance to portray the agency of LGBTQ Latina/o youth. It is in the careful observation of the often violent junctures of race, gender, citizenship status, and sexuality where the "tight spaces" of Latina/o youth resistance is encountered. Interfacing Lugones's theorizing of resistance with those by James C. Scott (1990) and Robin D. G. Kelley (1993), I begin by examining the everyday acts of resistance in tight spaces, where LGBTQ Latina/o youth often violate and inhabit this spatiality with great resistance.

This chapter reframes youth experiences that extend traditional notions of resistance, where the daily acts of resistance performed by Latina/o LGBTQ youth become important. Part of this reframing of youth resistance centers on Lugones's (2010) concept of resistant socialities, where an examination of the offstage practices of queer Latina/o youth offer researchers an opportunity to reexamine youth experiences in ways that perceive these alternative socialities as the breathing spaces, however tight, for youth to reclaim energy, regroup, and create safe space. As Lugones (2003) states:

> And if "you" (always abstracted "you") are one of the dominated, your movements are highly restricted and contained. And there may not be any you there under certain descriptions, such as "lesbian" or any other description that captures transgression. (p. 9)

Resistance in these instances is not about mediating the life circumstances of queer Latina/o youth, nor is it about the destruction of a system of oppression. It is the small deviation from the logic of oppression, however small and imperceptible these acts may be.

The queer body has always been perceived as infected, contaminated, and expendable (Cruz, 2011; Goldberg, 1991) and youth's talking back to power must be recognized. In this chapter, I will (1) define queer Latina/o youth resistance as infrapolitical, (2) describe how an infrapolitical frame offers queer Latina/o youth the possibilities of creative and strategic ways of developing alternatives for being and relating in their worlds, and (3) begin the discussion about how these offstage socialities are necessary for queer Latina/o youth to survive in worlds hostile to their existence.

INFRAPOLITICS AND QUEER LATINA/O YOUTH

Henry Giroux (1983) states that resistance is the complex and creative field through which class, race, and gender-mediated practices are often refused, rejected, and dismissed, particularly in schools. In my first experiences working with LGBTQ street youth, I was unable to see resistance. Resistance did not happen with picket signs in front of a school or city hall with LGBTQ street youth, nor was it organized in ways that suggested the organization of any kind of nascent social movement. Resistance for queer Latina/o youth and other youth of color occurred in such small and almost imperceptible ways that I was forced to ask myself, *When does resistance begin?*

Infrapolitics are defined as the dissident offstage practices that resist the everyday degradations and experiences of exclusion that make up the daily fabric of LGBTQ Latina/o youth lives. The young people I worked with often hung out together outside the doors of the school and on the sidewalks of the youth drop-in center. Young people gathered at the local bus stop, smoking cigarettes, flirting, or joking around with one another in Spanish and queered Spanglish, often calling out to passersby in dramatic fashion. There is always a strong security and police presence at community and youth social service agencies in the spaces where youth struggle to maintain a certain level of civility with staff and security. It is helpful to think about youth resistance in these spaces as offstage practices that take place just outside of the surveillance of authorities (Scott, 1990). These offstage practices are important in how we can reframe resistance by queer Latina/o youth.

During my tenure as a teacher with queer Latina/o students, I observed youth "talking" back to teachers, caseworkers, and police in bodily ways. Small acts of resistance looked like the exaggerated snap of fingers in someone else's face or a slow sashay of a student turning his or her back on an authority figure. Schools, even those places where the mission was centered on getting LGBTQ students enough credits to graduate, were counter spaces for these youth where an infrapolitics were in place (Kelley, 1993). Scott (1990) defined infrapolitics as the space of offstage practices and "dissident political cultures that manifest itself in daily conversations, folklore, jobs, songs, and other cultural practices" (Scott, 1990, quoted in Kelley, 1993, p. 77). Scott argued that these small acts of resistance are strategies created by subaltern communities to negotiate the incessant scrutiny and repression from those in power.

Perceiving resistance within the tight spaces of Latina/o youth infrapolitics allows researchers to move away from the discourses of delinquency and poverty that often frequent educational policy and research. This deficit approach to educational policy and research is often about "fixing" pathologized youth. These policies force change upon imperfect, non-English-speaking youth of color. Countering such research models requires another kind of infrapolitics. To divest oneself from the research models of radical "othering" requires educational and social science researchers to reframe the relationships of domination and oppression between queer Latina/o youth and police, teachers, social workers, and other authorities.

Thinking about LGBTQ Latina/o youth practices and small acts of resistance through an infrapolitical framework offers invaluable insight into the economic, political, and cultural patterns of power and resistance. Beginning with a *public transcript*, the public performance of deference and humility by the powerless, Scott (1990) argued that those with power uphold this public transcript through the maintenance of the symbols and practices of a multitiered social order. The *on-stage* practices of a public transcript maintain the illusion of particular social orders. The performances in the public sphere between those with power and those without reveal little information of how power is exercised between communities.

> A skeptic might well ask at this point how we can presume to know, on the basis of the public transcript alone, whether this performance is genuine or not . . . . The answer is, surely, that we cannot know how contrived or imposed the performance is unless we can speak, as it were, to the performer offstage, out of this particular power-laden context, or unless the performer suddenly declares openly, on-stage, that the performances we have previously observed were just a pose. (Scott, 1990, p. 4)

For queer Latina/o youth, the hidden transcript is the space of rest and leisure, a place to gossip about your caseworkers, teachers, and the ever-present security guards in Spanish. It is also a place for youth to exchange valuable information about how institutions, organizations, worksites, and in this case, schools and youth centers, work (see Conchas, 2001). If an on-stage performance is the public transcript, then the *hidden transcript* is the account that takes place offstage and beyond the surveillance of those in power (Scott, 1990).

I did my primary observations at a youth drop-in center, where I often hung out with the LGBTQ Latina/o youth who congregated on the sidewalk or on the roof where there were places to sit and relax. These were places where youth were allowed to smoke cigarettes, and it was a space out of sight of the center security and staff. These spaces were safe spaces where youth often shared stories, gossiped, and complained about their treatment from caseworkers and center staff.

For example, at one point I overheard a young trans-Latina tell a group of youth about her derisive treatment by center security: "They dragged me out with my skirt hiked up to my armpits, I am sure on purpose," and did not allow her to enter the building to see a mental health worker without an appointment. Having been homeless for over a week and unable to take care of her basic needs, the security guards escorted the youth roughly out of the center, exposing her body in ways that was meant to embarrass and reveal that she was transgender. The harassment of Latina/o trans-youths who came in for services became a point of contention for many of the youth clients seeking assistance. Because they often depended on these services from the drop-in center, it forced a public transcript of civility between trans-Latina youth and staff. The sidewalk and rooftop smoking area became some of the few secure places where youth could talk back about their ill treatment that was outside of the hearing distance of center staff and security.

In these ways, the hidden transcript helps researchers understand the eventual low turnout of youth as resistance. The emphasis on security in social services settings at this field site, even now, is immense. In a 2014 visit to this same youth center, staff reiterated the work of security as one "that keeps [city] out of the center." Youth, particularly trans-youth, stayed away in such numbers due to the presence of guards at each facility that some centers were forced to cut hours and staff, if not close operations altogether. Examining these security practices, is this show of force by center guards for the protection of youth from predatory adults or is it to protect the property of the community agency? This theme requires further research.

METHODOLOGY OF THE STREETS IN MULTIPLE LGBTQ SITES

The data for this case study come from a multiyear ethnography of LGBTQ homeless youth in a large city with one of the largest populations of homeless adolescents in the United States. I was a teacher and a street outreach worker for 5 years prior with this community of young people. I did HIV counseling at a youth community center and taught writing and community studies at a continuation school that served LGBTQ students who were at risk for dropping out of school. Although the official ethnographic work was conducted over a period of 2 school years, I had been engaged in learning and teaching in this community of youth for much longer and continue my relationships with youth, staff, and administration to the present.

The communities where I conducted my research with 57 youth between 14 and 21 years of age are places undergoing massive gentrification, where formerly working-class neighborhoods of apartments and small single-family dwellings co-existed with exclusive neighborhoods that extended east into the hills above the main streets. The major boulevard of the community was filled with small ethnic shops and eateries, tourist attractions, and new entertainment scenes for wealthy patrons, including shopping malls. The new development of this community also meant that more attention was given to loitering and vagrancy laws by police and security who made youth an easy target to harass and push away from new community development. New shopping and entertainment areas in gentrified neighborhoods did not want homeless youth hanging around the community's recent investments.

Some homeless Latina/o youth took advantage of empty and abandoned homes to sleep in, and others found cheap hotels and rooms to stay in for a week or less. Survival sex and prostitution have been one of the primary means homeless Latina/o youth have of exchanging sex for shelter, food, or money. The school and the youth drop-in center dealt with these issues through safe sex curriculums and HIV testing. Both sites were able to share resources with other youth agencies that provided caseworkers, HIV educational resources, and other mental health services. The school site, modeled after continuation schools typically found in the large urban district, offered credit accumulation courses to integrate students back into their comprehensive high schools. Rarely did students integrate back into their comprehensive high schools. Almost all students at the LGBTQ educational center stayed through graduation.

I observed and did semi-structured interviews and focus groups with 57 youth aged 14–21 who fit the following criteria:

- Youth must have experienced homelessness (as defined in the McKinney-Vento Homeless Assistance Act [42 USC 11434a]) for at least 1 night in the past 6 months.
- Youth must be between the ages of 14 and 21.
- Youth must self-identify as lesbian, gay, bisexual, transgender, or queer.

Thirty-seven of the 57 youth identified as Latina/o immigrant and the children of immigrants. Thirty-four of the 37 were young gay men and transgender youth. Three of my subjects were young lesbians. My role as researcher was multiple, where I was a teacher, an HIV counselor, and a referral service. I was attentive to the everyday conditions of youth lives. I learned much about the community agencies that offered services to youth and often hung out with youth to understand better the daily regimen of queer homeless youth. My focus on the bodily experiences of queer youth, including youth who had crossed international borders unaccompanied, helped me understand on a material level the lived experiences of being young, Latina/o, and homeless in a large city and the options youth are offered to resist, survive, and thrive.

THINKING ABOUT AGENCY AND ACTIVE SUBJECTIVITIES

When queer Latina/o youth share information with one another in offstage discussions to weigh their options against other youth's experiences with caseworkers, police, teachers, and social services, the concept of youth agency needs to be rethought. The agency enacted by youth is not one of an individual act but one with a set of histories and communities, such as the trans-Latina/o community, that contributes to how youth share and assess their own options. Lugones (2010) named this movement an "active subjectivity" rather than individual agency, stressing a "peopled sense" of youth worlds. In essence, agency for queer Latina/o youth needs to be reimagined as one that is collective, peopled, and intersubjective.

When I talk with youth, I cannot be exhausted or distracted. Access to these offstage spaces that youth create is not so easily established for researchers, whose questions and observations may be seen by youth as informing the powerful. Coded languages, like *caló* or the queer languages of youth, may be indecipherable and inaccessible to some researchers. Additionally, the boundary between the public and the hidden transcript is a "zone of constant struggle" (Scott, 1990), where our recognition of subordinate/dominant narratives and resistant/

conformist behaviors are not so concise. A researcher may not even comprehend, or worse, may deny or misinterpret certain kinds of behavior as resistance. As social scientists and educational researchers, not only are we responsible for the critique and deconstruction of deficit and race and culture of poverty models of achievement, but we are also unfortunately positioned to only recognize certain kinds of agency and active subjectivity in the public transcript.

RESEARCHING INFRAPOLITICS

There is a certain position a researcher must take when working with queer Latina/o youth. It is a belief that youth have something to say about their own experiences with oppression, that the insight that youth bring to a research event is illuminating and survivor-rich, and that the researcher has as much to learn from youth as they do from the researcher. Yet this stance should not be one of pity. Many stories that youth narrate elicit emotions that are not ones of empathy or even solidarity. Pity keeps researchers, teachers, and other youth advocates from a deeper engagement with the issues that are significant in a young person's story. There is no bridging the gap between a researcher and a youth participant when pity defines the relationship—pity objectifies. A youth will never be subject when pity defines the relationship between researcher and young person.

To research youth resistance is to take the stance that youth are not victims but are often witnesses and survivors of great trauma and oppression. In order to recognize their resistance later, I have to first recognize the stories that students narrate on their own terms. For example, a 17-year-old queer Latina/o youth, "Carlos," told his story of moving from his parents' home to a large city in the United States to pursue a relationship with an older adult:

> You don't want to know my story of how I got to [the city]. I just know I had a boyfriend who was crazy who tried force me to have sex with him. Ugh, I got away from him. Now that I am here in [a new city], I have a new man but he's crazy too. Just last week he even tried to grab me off the street right outside the center! I saw him on [street name], tried to talk with him and told him no, I am not going anywhere with you, *maricón*, and stepped right back in here. I usually hate the guards around here but I was glad they were on it that day. (Carlos, age 17, September 18, 2014)

When I hear stories from youth where a relationship with an adult figure is central, I have to acknowledge that this could be a story of sexual exploitation. In this fieldnote, Carlos tells a story of resourcefulness and shrewdness, where he talks back to his abusive partner and is able to avoid further strife by stepping back into the youth center. It is significant when youth say "no" to a potentially volatile situation. Yet there is a very real problem with domestic violence and sexual exploitation in the street youth community that must contextualize this narrative.

In Carlos's recasting of events, he refuses to be seen as powerless and without options. In this zone of constant struggle, my reading of the sexual exploitation of a young gay Latina/o becomes intimately tied to my recognition of his refusal to be defined as a victim.

In thinking through multiple interpretations of youth narratives, Lugones's (2003) conception of "world-traveling" becomes so helpful. World-traveling is the negotiation of mainstream life in the United States. for queer youth, immigrants, women of color, and others from nondominant communities, who occupy and move through multiple worlds in their everyday existence. An important part of world-traveling is the concept of the multiple, shifting self as it moves across worlds. World-traveling is frequently done unwillingly to often hostile worlds for women and men of color. In a "world" of sexual exploitation, a young person is deemed powerless and utterly victimized. In the previous example, Carlos refuses that "world" and instead reframes his story in a "world" where he tries desperately to maintain his dignity and resourcefulness. Yet researchers must also recognize this other "world" of exploitation. In these multiple and contradictory "worlds" that exist in this example, there is a healthy tension between how Carlos sees himself, how a researcher might see him, and how Carlos sees the researcher. Part of world-traveling is the ability to understand "what it is to be them and what it is to be ourselves in their eyes" (p. 17).

The researcher's role becomes crucial in this mediation of multiple narratives, selves, and worlds. The aim is to create different interpretations of youth experience and to forge new knowledge that is outside of the usual frames of public performances of power. It often means challenging both subject and researcher to see what other kinds of meaning can be made. Recognizing and validating the multiple narratives of this example is a critically important methodological move, where this queer Latina/o youth's story can be remediated as resistant, agentic, and sometimes even emancipatory, even when homeless young people take many risks for connection and for procuring basic needs. When you are 17, without a diploma or GED, unemployed (as are most youth in the United States), homeless, and LGBTQ, your options are few, with little social economic and cultural capital. What is left is the body and experience, with survival sex figuring prominently in almost every queer street youth narrative I have collected.

LGBTQ Latina/o youth take many calculated risks, such as the youth mentioned earlier, who weighed the chances of leaving home for a commitment of intimacy with the costs of potential exploitation. Despite guarantees of anonymity in the research interview process,[1] it may be that the youth testimony is deliberately designed to have multiple meanings, protecting the identities of the actors in this story. In order to make sense of vague and unclear narratives, researchers must also consider the resistant sociality in those tight spaces where meanings are developed.

YOUTH LEARNING THE SOCIALITIES OF RESISTANCE

Emphasizing the development of a collective identity among Black laborers in the Jim Crow South, Kelley (1993) discussed how workers in Birmingham, Alabama, organized their time and space with others. In these spaces of Black working-class culture, workers were able to "take back their bodies, to recuperate, to be together" (p. 84). Kelley theorized that places of rest and recreation, such as family organizations, churches, dance halls, parties, and bars, became spaces where Black laborers learned alternative socialities outside of the institutions of White supremacy. Organizing together for a dance, a party, or church reinforced the sense of shared community, knowledge, and cultural values for the Birmingham Black working class. In terms of LGBTQ youth socialities, where spaces like a continuation school for LGBTQ students or a youth drop-in center can—despite their problems—offer the possibility of alternative forms of mutuality and sociality. What happens in these youth spaces helps to explain the solidarity that queer Latina/o youth have shown in times of duress. In this case, resistance is not only about countering oppressive systems, but of building infrapolitical worlds that are essential for survival for LGBTQ Latina/o youth.

The Black workers in Kelley's study not only made these spaces to unmask themselves of the disguises of deference and humility, but they also practiced new ways of relating outside of oppressive restrictions. Both Lugones (2010) and Kelley (1993) suggested that these socialities can only be practiced in spaces where communities are able to define themselves outside the frameworks of their oppressors. In the offstage spaces where youth create, define, and rehearse more egalitarian ways of relating with one another, there is an implied pedagogy of teaching one another, sharing information, or finding ways to celebrate their mutual socialities.

For example, in a 2014 focus group interview I asked queer Latina/o street youth about their social media use. The youth shared that social media was an inexpensive way to communicate internationally, among other things. All youth interviewed carried smartphones, although none had contract cellular plans. One young gay male from a Central American country showed his focus group the application on his smartphone that allows free international calls. The other youth were not aware of this application, where they quickly "friended" one another through the application portal. In a matter of minutes, the youth shared his knowledge about the application, how it operated, and what kind of wireless connection you needed to use it. "You have to be in a Subway [restaurant], the big Target, or in a Verizon store to grab Wi-Fi without filters," the youth told the group. Not only did he offer the other participants a quick map of local places where unrestricted Wi-Fi was available, but he also demonstrated a quick lesson how to hack into a WEP (Wired Equivalent Privacy) network when needed. It was vital information shared among youth, an example of the practice of sharing knowledge that may prove to be invaluable when access to communication may be denied or unavailable. This practice of connecting to one another in joint activity with knowledge to share illuminates how queer homeless Latina/o youth participate in resistant socialities that often center on creative and strategic uses of technology in unintended ways.

DIFFICULTIES OF RESEARCH AS FAITHFUL WITNESSING

When I am part of an activity where queer Latina/o youth share important information necessary for their daily survival, as researcher I make the commitment to write and interpret these youth experiences as infrapolitical. It is a commitment recognizing resistance in all of its complex and intermeshing/intersecting ways. However, these experiences of youth and researcher always come from power-laden contexts. Despite Scott's (1990) assertion that the infrapolitics of subordinate groups cannot be known unless we can speak to an informant offstage, the presence of researchers, even those committed to pedagogies of faithful witnessing, may disrupt resistant youth socialities. Not all of my research events were as open or as trusting as the young queer Latina/os in my focus groups. In another of my engagements in this case study, I met "Gloria," a 14-year-old Latina lesbian. In this excerpt from my interview fieldnotes, she turns from telling a story about her body to a critique of power, representation, and research:

> I have been living on the streets for 6 days now. I've talked with caseworkers and social workers, those people at [the youth shelter] and I am ready to go home now. I just want to go home, take a shower, sleep in my own bed. I am tired of walking and walking and walking all over this place, my feet hurt, even my skin hurts. You want to test me, sure, go right ahead. What do I get for that? Do I get paid for this? What do I get for my little drop of blood?

Equating a body to its revenue-generating value to produce wealth is a discourse directed at immigrants, homeless women and men, teen mothers, and youth of color. Gloria implicates the research process as part of the mechanism for these neoliberal discourses. As a researcher, I was attempting to compile experiences of violence, homelessness, and the body. Gloria's response reflects how the process of knowledge production about the queer Latina body is reductive and predatory. She challenges the implicit discourse of a body's net worth in terms of dollars accumulated in a lifetime of earnings. The drop of blood is a vital part of that laboring body and the labor of that body is the only thing this young person has left to sell. She is also critical of the pedagogy in my research ("What do I get for that?") and its unequal exchange between subject and researcher.

Being a faithful witness is inadequate if it is reduced to only acknowledging the narratives that describe the trauma and perils of LGBTQ street youth defiance. It is not only about being a good listener with street youth, but also about acknowledging that researchers know very little about homeless queer youth if we only notice that they are homeless and hungry. We might know that she is particularly desperate to go home that night, or that we know the limitations of youth shelters and their availability of beds, and we might even recognize that she may have suffered at the hands of her family or schoolmates or partner. We might have learned something about the shape of her oppression. These are certainly important understandings of the conditions facing LGBTQ street youth.

However, it is critical that we challenge a social science epistemology that surmises "once we know" about queer Latina/o street youth, then this knowing offers something "better." Things are supposed to "get better" with better, more reflexive research. Perhaps witnessing faithfully has revealed how a resistant sociality is necessary in the lives of queer Latina/o street youth. In the tight spaces of their resistance, researchers might witness the opening of new creative strategies for organizing life and practicing new kinds of relating in their worlds that are outside the dynamics of oppression. Research, therefore, can be used to share knowledge with other youth and develop creative strategies to survive these often-hostile worlds.

In a fieldnote about a 16-year-old gay Latina/o, I began to understand how few options were left for youth leaving abusive environments:

> I interviewed a young Latina/o, 16 years old, who said he was looking for his brother in the streets of [the city]. "I know he's here and I need to find him," he told me, "because I can't live there at home without him." I also noticed that many of his fingers had been broken but healed, and that he had chewed all his fingernails down to the quick. "I've been looking for him for 2 weeks now. Do you know where I can find him?" he asked. The condition of his fingers made me think about his anxiety and his worry about his brother and the knowledge that he cannot live in his family's house without his brother there to intervene. I told him that eventually his brother would visit this youth center, and if he wanted to, he could leave a message for him at the front desk.

When young queer Latina/os decide that the uncertainty of the streets is a better option than staying home, I believe they are enacting one of the few possibilities left available for them. Most research on homeless adolescents shows that physical and sexual abuse is one of the main reasons that youth leave home for the streets (Bagley & Young, 1987; Buckner & Bassuk, 1997; Tyler & Melander, 2013). For this young man and his brother to leave home where domestic violence and abuse is part of their everyday experience, I want to name this as resistance, where resistance is a refusal of abuse and domination. In these tight spaces of agency, youth have little space to resist, yet these brothers have said no to abuse and further violence. I think it is important to note these rejections made by youth, where in the tight spaces of their positions, not only must we be attuned to these signs of abuse and violence, but we must also recognize these refusals and gestures as resistance.

DISCUSSION

In *Ideology, Culture, and the Process of Schooling,* Giroux (1981) argued that resistance is the translation of a critical or political understanding of collective experience into political struggle that contests the hegemonic practices of schools. Part of that contestation is an understanding by students that political struggle is also tied to larger struggles against the concentration of power in the capitalist state itself. Yet resistance in the form of traditional politics, such as mobilizing against school policy, immigration, and using social media for civic engagement in otherwise more formal arrangements, do not often work for LGBTQ Latina/o street youth. What I witnessed were small yet deliberate acts by youth toward their caseworkers, security guards, and teachers (Cruz, 2011). A theory of resistant socialities may be as simple as creating "a new story of the self" (Lugones, 2000, p. 180) for queer Latina/o street youth, whether in the tight spaces of the hidden transcript or on the roof of the youth center talking or testifying, which may offer the potential to create other ways of being and acting in the world outside the parameters of power.

I want to think about these socialities of queer Latina/o youth as these spaces where youth are able to practice other ways of relating in the world that are not part of the everyday struggle between youth and police and other authorities. Kelley (1993) suggested that for Black workers in the Jim Crow South, these spaces outside of White supremacy were necessary for this community to regroup, reenergize, and find other ways of being in the world that were not part of the public transcript. Let me make this idea portable, where queer Latina/o street youth also find refuge, regroup, and find creative ways of relating to others. These spaces are necessary for youth to survive and thrive despite the continued surveillance in a world where street youth are made invisible and expendable, and otherwise live disposable lives.

CONCLUSION

Resistance begins when youth learn to recognize and witness one another's practices of refusing to be dominated as they negotiate often hostile worlds. Thinking with the infrapolitical theorizing of Lugones (2003, 2010), Scott (1990), and Kelley (1993) helps researchers to recognize the gestures, practices, and narratives that make up queer Latina/o youth resistance. The socialities of resistance that youth develop for survival are vital spaces where the potential to learn new ways of negotiating these hostile worlds can also become places to learn multiple sensibilities and new ways of engaging their world(s) that offer liberatory possibilities. When queer Latina/o street youth move away or refuse to continue to engage with abusive partners, share technology and vital digital information with one another, or question the pedagogy of research, I argue that it is here that resistance begins.

Doing research under an infrapolitical framework also offers researchers a chance to acknowledge how research is infused with regulatory power and how social scientists and educational researchers can rethink our stance with or against power. It is the small acts of resistance that are necessary to recognize and to acknowledge how these refusals by youth make up the daily interactions between youth and security guards, social service agencies, and other authority. These refusals define the everyday experiences of queer Latina/o street youth, marking sites of power and resistance that are the core of homeless experiences. Instead of staying silent, invisible, and passive, youth talk back, share knowledge, and practice ways of knowing and being that have the potential for other kinds of emancipatory praxis.

NOTE

1. IRB did not allow any names, places, or information collected that could be linked back to the identities of the youth I interviewed. This may have freed youth to talk openly, yet the politics of the public/hidden transcript seemed a part of every interview.

REFERENCES

Bagley, C., & Young, L. (1987). Juvenile prostitution and child sexual abuse: A controlled study. *Canadian Journal of Community Mental Health (Revue canadienne de santé mentale communautaire)*, 6(1), 5–26.

Baldwin, J. (1963/1988). A talk to teachers. In R. Simonson & S. Walker (Eds.), *Multicultural literacy: Opening the American mind* (pp. 3–12). St. Paul, MN: Graywolf Press.

Buckner, J. C., & Bassuk, E. L. (1997). Mental disorders and service utilization among youths from homeless and low-income household families. *Journal of the American Academy of Child and Adolescent Psychiatry, 36*, 890–900.

Conchas, G. Q. (2001). Structuring failure and success: Understanding the variability in Latino school engagement. *Harvard Educational Review, 70*, 475–504.

Cruz, C. (2011). LGBTQ street youth talk back: A meditation on resistance and witnessing. *QSE: International Journal of Qualitative Studies in Education, 24*(5), 547–558.

Giroux, H. A. (1981). *Ideology, culture, and the process of schooling*. Philadelphia, PA: Temple University Press.

Giroux, H. A. (1983). Theories of reproduction and resistance in the new sociology of education: A critical analysis. *Harvard Educational Review, 53*(3), 257–293.

Goldberg, J. (1991). Sodomy in the new world: Anthropologies old and new. *Social Text, 29*, 46–56.

Kelley, R. G. (1993). "We are not what we seem": Rethinking black working-class opposition in the Jim Crow South. *The Journal of American History, 80*(1), 75–112.

Lugones, M. (2000). Multiculturalism and publicity. *Hypatia, 15*(3), 175–181.

Lugones, M. (2003). *Pilgrimages/peregrinajes: Theorizing coalition against multiple oppressions*. Lanham, MD: Rowan and Littlefield Press.

Lugones, M. (2010). Toward a decolonial feminism. *Hypatia, 25*(4), 742–759.

Plyler v. Doe. 457 U.S. 202. (1982).

Scott, J. C. (1990). *Domination and the arts of resistance: Hidden transcripts*. New Haven, CT: Yale University Press.

Tyler, K. A., & Melander, L. A. (2013). Child abuse, street victimization, and substance use among homeless young adults. *Youth & Society*. doi: 0044118X12471354.

CHAPTER 9

Uncertain Futures

Educational Attainment and the Children of Undocumented Mexican Immigrants in the Greater Los Angeles Area

Leo R. Chavez

> You become depressed, you become very depressed. You work so hard and now what? You start questioning yourself. Is it worth it? Was it worth it? And what now? You have two options. Either you take the college route because education is education, and I'm learning and I like what I'm learning, and I'm going to continue to learn. Or you take the other route, where you just say, that's it. I'm just going to start working. It wasn't worth it. My mom or my dad, or my neighbor, was right. Why am I still going to school if I am not going to be able to continue with my education? So two paths, you have to decide which one to take.
>
> —Lupe, 21 years old, brought to the United States from Mexico at age 8

This chapter examines postsecondary education and two related factors, Spanish and English language usage and income, among the children of Mexican immigrants in the greater Los Angeles area. Interviews with 1.5-generation children of Mexican immigrants, second-generation U.S.-born children of Mexican immigrants, and three-plus-generation Mexican Americans find that language, education, and income are interrelated aspects of integration. Contrary to much heated public discourse on immigration, language acculturation is occurring rather rapidly among the children of Mexican immigrants in the greater Los Angeles area and there are obstacles to educational attainment and income—specifically related to immigration status. These findings contribute to the larger immigration debate by showing that it is not the children of immigrants who do not want to learn English or succeed educationally. These young people face significant obstacles to social and cultural integration, which will not improve until a more permanent solution, such as national comprehensive immigration reform, occurs.

Lupe's comments reflect the depth of her anguish at her uncertain future as an undocumented child of immigrants in California. Ultimately, she decided to attend the University of California. Lupe's comment also suggests the struggles faced by the children of Mexican and other Latin American undocumented immigrants as they confront obstacles to their integration into U.S. society. Lupe underscores the significance of President Obama's 2012 policy for Deferred Action for Childhood Arrivals (DACA) and the post-2014 election policy to extend DACA deportation relief to those undocumented youth over 31 years of age who originally did not qualify for DACA. Often lost in the controversy over these policies is the fundamental disadvantage the children of undocumented immigrants, especially those undocumented youth themselves, face integrating into society.

This chapter examines postsecondary education and two related factors, Spanish and English language usage and income, among the children of Mexican immigrants in the greater Los Angeles area. The data examined are based on interviews with adult children of immigrants collected almost 10 years before DACA and its recent expansion, and yet they underscore the need for much broader, comprehensive immigration reform. The data are important because they show that the adult children of immigrants, whether they are legal immigrants, undocumented immigrants, or U.S.-born citizens, face many challenges to furthering their education and economic mobility. DACA may help alleviate some of the obstacles experienced by undocumented children of immigrants, who can work and not fear deportation while the program exists. Some of these young people we interviewed would have been included under the original DACA and others are now included under DACA's extension. Importantly, not all of these youth will choose to participate in DACA due to fears that they themselves or their families may face future issues of deportability. To understand why this fear exists, and to understand why a more comprehensive immigration reform is difficult to accomplish, I first begin with conceptualizing who the children of immigrants are. I then provide a brief discussion of the way public discourse and public policies have framed the lives of children of Mexican immigrants as a threat to U.S. society.

THE CHILDREN OF IMMIGRANTS

To appreciate what the obstacles to social integration are—and to consider their efforts to overcome them—we need to begin by asking, who are the children of immigrants? Children of immigrants include those brought to the United States as children and those who were born in the United States (second generation). Immigration and citizenship status further differentiates the children of immigrants. Those who were born outside the United States came either as legal entrants or unauthorized entrants, whereas those who were born in the United

States are citizens. A level of complexity is added by their parents, who themselves could be unauthorized immigrants, legal residents, or naturalized citizens.

The literature refers to the 1.5 generation as those who migrated at a young age (typically under 15 or 16 years old) in recognition of the fact that most or all of their schooling and much of their cultural and social development occur in the host country (Olivas, 2012; Portes & Rumbaut, 2001; Rincón, 2008; Rumbaut, 2004). According to the Pew Hispanic Center's research, there were 1.5 million undocumented children under age 18 living in the United States in 2008 (Passel & Cohn, 2009).

Although there are many similarities between the unauthorized 1.5-generation and the second-generation children of immigrants, there is an important difference between them—that is, their relationship to citizenship status (Bean, Brown, & Rumbaut, 2006). Catarina, a 21-year-old University of California student with a 3.9 grade point average, brought to the United States when she was 8 years old, makes clear the way she views the significance of being in the 1.5 generation and an unauthorized immigrant:

> In different ways, the way you see culture, how strong you feel about your ethnic identity, I find it that it's different from the people I've met, who are let's say, who consider themselves Mexican American. I'm not Mexican American, I was not born here and I feel very attached to my native country. I'm sure that within one generation like my family [this will change]. . . . Having the barriers that I had, or not having all the opportunities that I see that a lot of the [U.S.-born] students have and they might not be taking advantage for different reasons. I know I'm no one to criticize their decisions, but I think that's what really makes me consider myself a Mexican. I am immigrant, immigrant Mexican. Because you have to belong to a group, and let's say you don't have the opportunities that a Mexican American has, because you don't have the social security. So you have to make the decision, I don't fit in here, they don't want me in here, then I fit here, with Mexicans.

Most notably, some of the 1.5 generation experienced a condition of illegality because of their unauthorized entry into the United States. Because moving from illegal status to a legal permanent resident has become much more difficult as a result of changes in U.S. immigration law, most notably the 1996 Illegal Immigration Reform and Immigrant Responsibility Act, many 1.5-generation adults continue to live in the United States without proper documentation from the federal government (Bunis & Garcia, 1997).[1]

Illegal refers to unauthorized residents who entered the country without permission from government authorities, or they may have entered with permission—tourist or student visas—but then overstayed visa end dates. "Illegality," as Coutin (2007) observed, has meant that "individuals can be physically present but legally absent, existing in a space outside of society, a space of 'nonexistence,' a space that is not actually 'elsewhere' or beyond borders but that is rather a hidden dimension of social reality" (p. 9). A slight variation on Coutin's representation is that to be illegally present is not to be "outside of society" but to be allowed to participate in some aspects of society, schooling, for example, but not others, such as work. As a condition, being "illegal" contributes to subjective understandings of the world and to identity, and therefore should be kept as a concept and social identifier (Coutin, 2000; De Genova, 2002; Menjívar, 2006; Suárez-Navaz, 2004; Willen, 2007).

Cultural and social integration of the children of undocumented immigrants are is as easy to characterize as, say, labor market participation or income (Hirschman, 2013). Culture is neither a thing, nor a quantity, nor something that grows linearly by the year. Culture and culture change are more ephemeral, often captured indirectly. Moreover, changes in cultural beliefs and practices can occur in various directions at once, often making causal statements difficult. Individuals and groups learn from one another as they socialize; share and exchange ideas, styles and preferences; attend schools and religious services; and marry. *Assimilation, acculturation,* and *hybridization* (blending), and joining the "mainstream," are terms we use to capture the changes taking place among immigrants, their descendants, and other members of their communities and the nation (Alba & Nee, 2003; Chavez, 2006).

To integrate implies that people of different racial or ethnic backgrounds are brought together into unrestricted and equal association ("to become integrated"). Several factors influence integration, not the least of which is immigration status (Bravo-Moreno, 2009, 2012; Gonzales & Chavez, 2012; Massey & Pren, 2012). Because undocumented children grow up steeped in U.S. culture, their illegality poses fundamental dilemmas. They must often make critical life decisions within the constraints caused by their status, as Lupe's earlier comment illustrates. Importantly, the integration of the children of immigrants must not be viewed as an either/or situation, integrated or not integrated. Rather, integration is affected by a myriad of factors that are often in flux. Even the status of illegality is not fixed, because laws exist for regularizing an unauthorized status, although they have become much more restrictive over time.

President Obama's Deferred Action for Childhood Arrivals policy, which includes the more recent extension of that policy, allows undocumented immigrants brought as children, the 1.5 generation, to request a grant of relief from the Department of Homeland Security (Chavez, 2013; Gonzales & Terriquez, 2013). In addition, the U.S. Congress could pass immigration reform that would provide further, broader avenues for status regularization, as it did in 1986 with the Immigration Reform and Control Act (IRCA). IRCA resulted in 70% of the nation's undocumented immigrants between 1986 and 1988 moving into a legal status, typically legal permanent residency (Yoshikawa & Kholoptseva, 2013). The point here is that we must not consider illegality as the only factor affecting attachment to U.S. society, nor should it be the focus of policy on social and cultural integration of immigrants and their children (Jones-Correa & de Graauw, 2013).

At the same time, we must not minimize the effect that regularizing the status of undocumented 1.5 children of immigrants would have on their integration (Massey, 2013).

THE LATINA/O THREAT NARRATIVE

Over the last 50 years, the discourse on immigration in the United States has turned decidedly more alarmist, especially in relation to Mexican and other Latin American immigrants, what I have called the Latina/o threat narrative (Chavez, 2001). The often vociferous debate has expanded to include U.S.-born Latina/os, whose reproduction, both biological and social, has been characterized as a threat to the nation (Chavez, 2013). The threat is based on a set of beliefs: that Mexican and other Latinas are unable, or unwilling, to control their fertility; that Latina/os, led by Mexicans and Mexican Americans, are unwilling to integrate socially, are unwilling to learn English and U.S. culture, and are preparing to take over the Southwest United States (Bravo-Moreno, 2006; Chavez, 2004).

The Latina/o threat discourse places the children of Mexican immigrants in an ambiguous position, as their alleged threat is extended to Mexican Americans whose families have lived multiple generations in the United States. For example, American conservative political scientist Samuel P. Huntington (2000) raised the alarm of a Mexican takeover: "The invasion of over 1 million Mexican civilians is a comparable threat [as 1 million Mexican soldiers] to American societal security, and Americans should react against it with comparable vigour. Mexican immigration looms as a unique and disturbing challenge to our cultural integrity, our national identity, and potentially to our future as a country" (p. 22).

Political commentator Pat Buchanan also emphasized the threat of the growing Latina/o population on MSNBC (March 24, 2009): "Mexico is the greatest foreign policy crisis I think America faces in the next 20, 30 years. Who is going to care . . . 30 years from now whether a Sunni or a Shia is in Baghdad or who's ruling in Kabul? We're going to have 135 million Hispanics in the United States by 2050, heavily concentrated in the southwest. The question is whether we're going to survive as a country."

The politics surrounding immigration is also reflected in public policies and laws. Two examples from President Obama's administration make this point clearly. First, President Obama responded to public concern about immigration by increasing the threat of deportation for undocumented immigrants. In 2009, a total of 387,790 people were deported, a 5% increase over 2008, the last year under George W. Bush's administration (Medrano, 2010). However, in a dramatic change in policy, the Obama administration in August 2011 began reviewing all deportation cases in order to focus on criminals. Those who have not been convicted of a crime would possibly receive a suspension of deportation and be allowed stay and also be able to apply for work permits (Preston, 2011). Nonetheless, by the end of March 2012 the review of about 300,000 pending deportation cases had only resulted in 2,609 men and women being allowed to stay temporarily in the United States (Chavez, 2013).

Second, President Obama initiated the DACA program on June 15, 2012. DACA allows the Department of Homeland Security to grant relief to undocumented individuals who have been ordered to leave the country, or to grant relief to undocumented individuals who come forward but who have not undergone removal proceedings. DACA deferred forced removal for 2 years. To be eligible, an undocumented immigrant must have come to the United States under age 16; be under age 31 as of June 15, 2012; have lived continuously in the United States since June 15, 2007; have not committed a felony or significant misdemeanor; have not posed a threat to national security; and have pursued an education or military service. On November 20, 2014, President Obama expanded DACA to include those over 31 years of age who came to the United States. before turning 16 years old. Importantly, DACA does not provide a path to legal permanent resident status or citizenship. Individuals who come forward under DACA face possible deportation in the future, unless Congress passes comprehensive immigration reform and provides permanent relief—that is, a path to citizenship. Meanwhile, individuals who receive deferred action are considered in the United States under the color of law and can apply for employment authorization and government benefits such as a driver's license (Winograd, 2012).

The public debate over immigration and possible threats posed by the children of undocumented immigrants frames issues of education attainment as well as social and cultural integration. Lupe's comment at the beginning of this chapter indicates the despair some undocumented youth can feel given their limited choices for education and work. Interviewees such as Lupe would have been too old for the DACA program but may be eligible for the extension to those over 31 years of age. DACA would open the possibility for Lupe and others like her to possibly gain relief from deportation, work, and gain a measure of integration. Another interviewee, Amalia, spoke specifically about how she views integration and belonging:

> I think if you have obstacles to integrating, one, they don't want you to integrate. Obviously, they have the obstacles for you not to integrate, so you get to the point where you know what, I don't want to integrate, whether you will eventually want me to integrate for any reason, I am no longer willing to integrate. . . . After September 11, I felt American. And it's amazing because regardless of political inequalities, I think of my life and what would it have been if I had not been here. And here I am. There are obstacles, but it's better. It's better here even with the inequalities. I guess it's human nature. We just want something better.

The prevalence of the Latina/o threat narrative has led to counter-narratives, especially among the 1.5 generation, those known as The DREAMers, which refers to the Development, Relief and Education of Alien Minors Act (DREAM Act).[2]

Rather than passively accept this state of affairs, many undocumented students across the country have rallied under the banner "Undocumented and Unafraid" and formed a number of organizations, such as Immigrant Youth Justice League and The DREAM Act Coalition, with the goal of promoting federal legislation that would provide them with a way to legalize their status, allow them to attend colleges and universities, receive federal financial aid, join the military, and pursue other avenues for social integration.

This discussion of the narrative of threat aimed at Latina/o youth, public policies, and activism by the children of immigrants frames postsecondary educational attainment, as well as related factors such as language use and income.

IMMIGRATION AND INTERGENERATIONAL
MOBILITY CASE STUDY IN LOS ANGELES

To examine the language, education, and economic integration of the adult children of immigrants in the greater Los Angeles area, I drew from the Immigration and Intergenerational Mobility in Metropolitan Los Angeles (IIMMLA) project. IIMMLA's co-principal investigators were Rubén G. Rumbaut, Frank D. Bean, Susan K. Brown, Leo R. Chavez, Louis DeSipio, Jennifer Lee, and Min Zhou. Conducted in 2004, with support from the Russell Sage Foundation, we targeted the young adult children of immigrants from large immigrant groups in the five-county metropolitan Los Angeles area (from Ventura County in the north to Riverside and San Bernardino counties in the south—see Figure 9.1) and used a random telephone survey to gather information from 4,780 persons ages 20 to 40 who had at least one immigrant parent.

The study was designed to be a random probability sample of persons whose parents' national origin was Mexican, Central American (Salvadoran or Guatemalan), Chinese (from both the mainland and Taiwan), Filipino, Korean, and Vietnamese, residing in households with telephones in the greater Los Angeles area. Because of the centrality of the Mexican-origin group to the immigrant experience in Los Angeles, we oversampled the Mexican population.[3] This chapter will focus on the Mexican-origin respondents. The IIMMLA project surveyed adult Mexican immigrants (125), 1.5-generation children of Mexican immigrants (190), second-generation, U.S.-born children of Mexican immigrants (553), and three-plus-generation Mexican Americans (401).

EXAMINING SOCIAL AND CULTURAL INTEGRATION

Language, education, and income are interrelated aspects of integration. Saying they are interrelated does not mean they all move simultaneously, in lockstep fashion. The children of immigrants may acquire English proficiency relatively

Figure 9.1. Map of the Greater Los Angeles Area

quickly, but how this translates into educational and economic attainment is influenced by many factors, not the least of which are family dynamics; social attitudes, such as the Latina/o threat narrative; and immigration status.

Language

Language use is both emotional, a source of ethnic pride, and instrumental, key to educational and economic success. In terms of the former, Lupe pointed out that bilingualism has definite benefits and she would try to ensure her children could speak Spanish. As she said, "One is a culture thing. If you know Spanish and if you're Mexican, or that's your cultural background, you have to teach [children] some culture. It's essential for their identity, self-identity, self-esteem, and two languages, especially here, let's say in the United States, and in California, Spanish and English, that's plus."

Despite the emotional and even implicit economic benefits, the generation after Lupe's will probably prefer to speak English in even higher proportions. Nearly all the adult children of Mexican immigrants in the Los Angeles area grew up in homes where Spanish was spoken (Figure 9.2). Clearly, their parents were Spanish speakers who communicated to their children in their native language.

Figure 9.2. Language Use at Home Among Mexican-Origin Interviewees Growing Up and Now, in Percentages

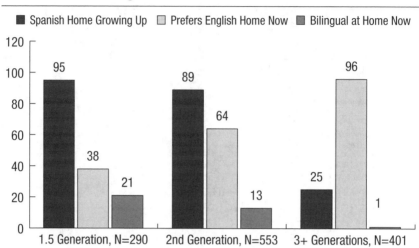

Source: Immigration and Intergenerational Mobility in Metropolitan Los Angeles (IIMMLA) project. Conducted in 2004 with support from the Russell Sage Foundation.

However, many of these adult children of immigrants now prefer to speak English at home, with the U.S.-born second generation (64%) almost twice as likely as the 1.5 generation (38%). Only 25% of those with three or more generations in the United States spoke Spanish at home when growing up, and now almost all (96%) prefer to speak English at home.

This shift from Spanish to English can occur rapidly, from migrant parents to their U.S.-born children and succeeding generations. Moreover, while the children of immigrants may speak Spanish, only about half said they spoke it very well (Figure 9.3). They do, however, indicate a higher level of comprehension than speaking. By the third-plus generations, there is a marked decrease in those who indicate they can speak, comprehend, and read very well in Spanish. Despite Lupe's desire for her children to be bilingual, the education system in California does not appear to function well to develop bilingualism or retention in speaking and reading Spanish. Rather, the children of Mexican immigrants move rapidly along a path of English acquisition. These patterns suggest linguistic acculturation is occurring among the Mexican-origin population in California. National data underscore the findings for the greater Los Angeles area; about 92% of the U.S.-born children of Latin American immigrants speak English well or better according to the 2000 U.S. Census.[4] Does this acquisition of English mean that the children of immigrants are moving rapidly in terms of educational attainment? If so, we would expect to see increased rates of postsecondary education across generations.

Figure 9.3. Mexican-Origin Interviewees who Speak, Understand, and Read Spanish Very Well, in Percentages

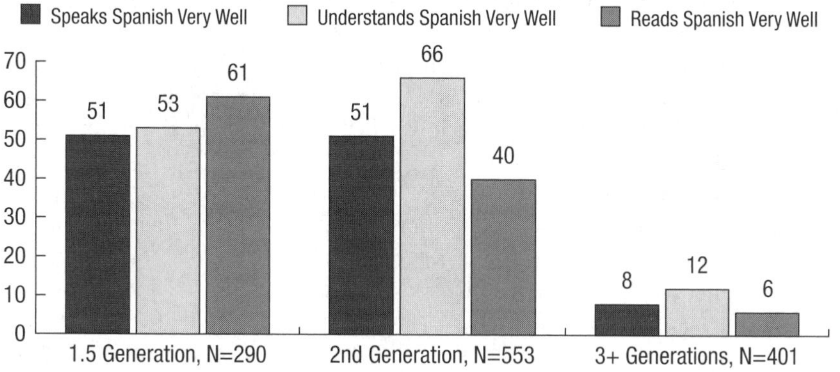

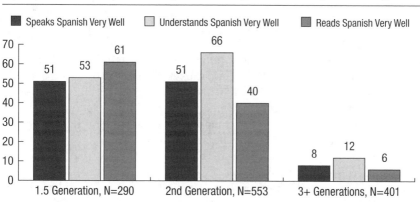

Source: IIMMLA, 2004.

Education

The most striking pattern in educational attainment is the difference between Mexico-born and U.S.-born children of Mexican immigrants. As depicted in Figure 9.4, many (37%) of the 1.5 generation did not finish high school, compared to only 19% of the second and later generations. Fewer (38%) of the 1.5 generation took courses at the college level or graduated with a college degree or advanced degree, compared to the second (53%) and third-plus generations (55%).

Figure 9.4. Educational Attainment, Mexican-Origin Interviewees, in Percentages

■ Speaks Spanish Very Well   ☐ Understands Spanish Very Well   ■ Reads Spanish Very Well

Source: IIMMLA, 2004

Each of the generations examined improved on their parents' educational attainment. The 1.5 generation surpassed their fathers' (19%) and mothers' (14%) high school completion rate, and were more likely to have moved beyond a high school education than their fathers (11.7%) and mothers (8.5%). When compared to national data, the 1.5 generation examined here surpassed Mexican immigrant high school graduation rates (24% in 2011) by 13 percentage points, but the actual graduation rates nationally would be lower if the 1.5 generation were excluded (Gonzalez-Barrera & Lopez, 2013).

The second generation was also more likely than their parents to get some or all of a post–high school education (23% of fathers; 20% of mothers). A similar pattern was evident for the third-plus generations; 36% of their fathers and 23.3% of their mothers continued their education beyond high school. Significantly, the third-plus generation's educational attainment was similar to that of the second generation, rather than a dramatic drop-off in educational attainment as suggested by the so-called immigrant paradox.

Although the children of immigrants have surpassed their parents' education levels, they still lag behind their White and Black counterparts in the Los Angeles area. As noted above, we also collected information from 406 third-plus generation Whites and 405 Blacks. Both Whites (75.9%) and Blacks (64.9%) were more likely to have some college or finished college compared to the little more than half of the 2nd generation and third-plus Mexican-origin subjects in the study.

Immigration status places obstacles to educational attainment for the 1.5 generation. Almost half of the 1.5 interviewees were unauthorized when they first came to the United States, and 19% were still undocumented immigrants at the time of the interview. In the United States, undocumented children have access to education at the primary and high school level as a result of the U.S. Supreme Court's 1982 decision in the *Plyler v. Doe* case (Olivas, 2012). Access to college, however, has had a more complicated history and varies by state. Some states do not allow undocumented students access to publicly funded colleges and universities, whereas others allow access but charge foreign student tuition, which is typically much more than in-state residency tuition, and block their access to financial aid. California currently allows undocumented students access to public colleges and universities and they pay in-state tuition (Abrego, 2008). However, until the temporary relief provided by DACA, undocumented young people who were educated in California and the United States could not work legally in the United States (Gonzales & Terriquez, 2013). Importantly, DACA offers only a temporary relief from this dilemma, and only comprehensive immigration reform, with a path to citizenship, can provide more permanent relief.

The interviews examined here were conducted before DACA and reflect the dilemma faced by the undocumented 1.5 generation, and seen in Lupe's comment at the beginning of this chapter. At the time, young people did not know if getting an education was worth it if they could not work legally. These obstacles to education and work are reflected in education and income findings. The 1.5-generation children of Mexican immigrants who came to the United States without authorization were less likely (33%) than those who entered legally (43%) to have had education beyond high school, compared to 44% of all immigrants in California in 2009, according to the American Community Survey (Chavez, 2013). However, only 11% of those in the 1.5 generation who were still undocumented immigrants at the time of the interview acquired any education beyond high school. They faced the dilemma Lupe spoke of and could not find a way to overcome the obstacles.

One last point on immigration status and how the Latina/o threat narrative concerns the U.S.-born children of undocumented immigrants. Because these children are U.S. citizens, they should have no problem going to school. All their parents should have to show is that they reside in the school's district, and they can do this with a utility bill, a rent receipt, or some other document with an address on it. However, there have been many cases of school administrators asking parents to prove that they are legal residents of the United States, a practice that has led some parents not to enroll their children into public schools. The problem is widespread enough to cause the U.S. Justice and Education departments to take action by issuing guidelines on appropriate identification required of immigrant parents (Phelps, 2014).

Effects on Income

Education and income are clearly interrelated. National data indicate that Mexican immigrants (including 1.5 generation) had a median personal income of $20,000 in 2011 (Gonzalez-Barrera & Lopez, 2013). However, the advantage of the data examined here is that we are able to tease out the relationship between generation and immigration status. The first two columns on the left of Figure 9.5 show the effect of entering

Figure 9.5. Post–High School Education and Personal Income, Mexican-Origin 1.5-Generation Interviewees by Immigration Status at Time of Entry into United States and Now, in Percentages

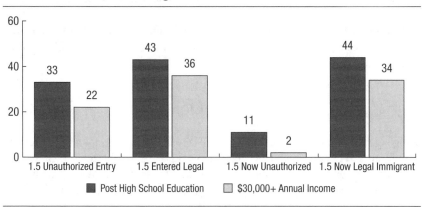

Source: IIMMLA, 2004.

the country without authorization compared to entering as a legal immigrant. There is a clear penalty paid for unauthorized entrants, who were less likely than legal entrants to have some postsecondary education and less likely to earn $30,000 or more.

Interviewees who continued as undocumented immigrants into adulthood fared much worse than those who are now legal immigrants. Only 11% of those in the 1.5 generation who were still undocumented at the time of the interview had some postsecondary education and only 2% had personal incomes of $30,000 or more. This pales in comparison to those who attained legal status, among whom 44% had some postsecondary education and 34% had incomes of $30,000 or more. (As an additional comparison, 34% of the second and 41% of the third-plus generations in the survey had $30,000 or higher incomes.)

The data clearly state that when undocumented 1.5-generation interviewees try to work or even just engage in everyday activities most citizens and legal residents take for granted, their illegality comes into question. As Lupita—another undocumented respondent—explains:

> I didn't want to break the law, but everything you do is illegal because you are illegal. Everything you do will be illegal. Otherwise you can't live. But I am still afraid. I don't want to jeopardize anything. I mean, I guess I am just ashamed. I looked [for work] in most restaurants and they would be like "Why do you want to work for us if you have a B.A.?" So, I am going to have to lie and I am going to have to tell them that I just dropped out of high school. But eventually they are going, it is going to come out, I know it. The people [working] at those places, like the cooks and the cashiers, they are either really young people, and I feel really old, like what am I doing there if they are all like 16, 17 years old. The others are like señoras who are 35 and have little kids; they dropped out of school, but because they have little kids they are still working at the restaurant. Thinking about that, it makes me feel so fucking stupid. And like the factories, too, because they ask me, "*Que estas haciendo aqui*? ["What are you doing here?"] You can speak English. You graduated from high school. You can work anywhere." They don't stop bugging me. (Quoted in Gonzales & Chavez, 2012, p. 264)

Catarina made a similar point, reflecting her frustration: "I know I can do so much more, but I can't because I can't live wherever. I can't choose where I live. I can't choose where I work."

CONCLUSION

Language acculturation is occurring rather rapidly among the children of Mexican immigrants in the greater Los Angeles area, and there are obstacles to educational attainment and income—specifically related to immigration status. Entering the country as an unauthorized migrant continues to negatively affect educational attainment and income. This pattern has not improved since this study was conducted; indeed, continued unauthorized status is far worse. These findings suggest that significant improvements in social and cultural integration will not occur until a more permanent solution to the obstacles faced by the 1.5 generation is found. More specifically, social and cultural integration would be greatly enhanced by opportunities to move from an unauthorized status to that of a legal permanent resident, the so-called path to citizenship. However, policymakers find it difficult to agree on comprehensive immigration reform because, in part, of the discourse of the Latina/o threat elaborated above.

The children of Mexican immigrants will continue to carry the burden of the inability of politicians to find a rational and comprehensive solution to the presence of undocumented immigrants. While they are learning the language and culture of the United States, the children of Mexican immigrants are not encountering a level playing field in education or the labor market. Short-term solutions such as DACA only alleviate the anxieties and obstacles for some of the 1.5 generation for a short period. More comprehensive solutions are needed to give the children of Mexican immigrants a better chance at a more substantive level of social and cultural integration. However, this would entail a new discourse, not one of threat but of contribution and belonging.

The problem is that continuing the present course is not a solution. For the children of undocumented immigrants, their subjective understanding of their place in society is that of being "unwanted" and "discardable." They view society as willing to leave them in a political and social limbo, one in which they are present physically but not present legally. Even citizen children of undocumented immigrants often feel they carry the stigma of their parents' immigration status (Chavez, 2013). These are not unwarranted beliefs, but the result of experiencing life in the United States, a life in which their future goals are often placed on hold. Their lives are sidetracked and derailed seemingly without concern by the larger society.

To repeat Amalia's poignant lament above: "Obviously, they have the obstacles for you not to integrate, so you get to the point where you know what, I don't want to integrate, whether you will eventually want me to integrate for any reason, I am no longer willing to integrate." Such despair among the children of undocumented immigrants reflects the very real obstacles to their educational mobility and social and cultural integration. Although finding policy solutions that would reduce these obstacles is mired in many fundamental disagreements over immigration, and obscured by the Latina/o threat narrative, one thing the whole nation should agree on is that these young people are part of the future in the United States. As such, their future opportunities for educational and economic mobility and integration should be enhanced, and not limited, for their own good and for the good of the nation.

NOTES

1. The 1996 Illegal Immigration Reform and Immigration Responsibility Act is available at http://www.uscis.gov/ilink/docView/PUBLAW/HTML/PUBLAW/0-0-0-10948.html.

2. The DREAM Act provides a 6-year-long conditional path to citizenship that requires completion of a college degree or 2 years of military service. To qualify, a person must have entered the United States before the age of 16; been in the United States at least 5 consecutive years prior to the bill's enactment; must have graduated from a U.S. high school, obtained a General Educational Development Test diploma, or been accepted into a college or university; must be between the ages of 12 and 35 at the time of the application; and must have a good moral character. However, the DREAM Act has been in Congress, in some form, for years without passage. Each time the DREAM Act comes up for a vote in Congress, The DREAMers' hopes are raised, only to be deflated (Abrego, 2006, 2011; Negron-Gonzales, 2009; Olivas, 2012; Ramirez, 2008).

3. The sample included individuals other than these national groups who are not considered here, including U.S. Whites, African Americans, other Latin Americans than those mentioned above, other Asians, and Middle Easterners.

4. IPUMS-USA, Census 2000, 5% Extract. Children Ages 6–15.

REFERENCES

Abrego, L. J. (2006). "I can't go to college because I don't have papers": Incorporation patterns of Latino undocumented youth. *Latino Studies 4*, 212–231.

Abrego, L. J. (2008). Legitimacy, social identity, and the mobilization of law: The effects of Assembly Bill 540 on undocumented students in California. *Law & Social Inquiry, 33*(3), 709–734.

Abrego, L. J. (2011). Legal consciousness of undocumented Latinos: Fear and Stigma as barriers to claims-making for first- and 1.5-generation immigrants. *Law & Society Review, 45*(2), 337–370.

Alba, R. D., & Nee, V. (2003). *Remaking the American mainstream: Assimilation and contemporary immigration*. Cambridge, MA: Harvard University Press.

Bean, F. D., Brown, S. K., & Rumbaut, R. (2006). Mexican immigrant political and economic incorporation. *Perspectives on Politics, 4*, 309–313.

Bravo-Moreno, A. (2006). *Migration, gender and national identity: Spanish migrant women in London*. Oxford: Peter Lang.

Bravo-Moreno, A. (2009). Socio-cultural belonging in legal limbo. In T. Rahimy (Ed.), *Representation, expression and identity: Interdisciplinary perspective* (pp. 53–68). Oxford: Inter-Disciplinary Press.

Bravo-Moreno, A. (2012). Negotiating identities in school settings: "Latinos" in Madrid and Buenos Aires. In L. Wikander, C. Gustafsson, & U. Riis (Eds.), *Enlightenment, creativity and education: Polities, politics, performances* (pp. 209–230). Rotterdam, the Netherlands: Sense Publishers.

Buchanan, P. (2009, March 24). Buchanan on MSNBC. Retrieved from http://www.youtube.com/watch?v=4F-eMlO_rXE.

Bunis, D., & Garcia, G. X. (March 1997). New illegal-immigration law casts too wide a net, critics say. *Orange County Register, 31*, 1.

Chavez, L. R. (2001). *Covering immigration: Popular images and the politics of the nation*. Berkeley, CA: University of California Press.

Chavez, L. R. (2004). A glass half empty: Latina reproduction and public discourse. *Human Organization, 63*(2), 173–188.

Chavez, L. R. (2006). Culture change and cultural reproduction: Lessons from research on transnational migration. In J. Stockard & G. Spindler (Eds.), *Globalization and change in fifteen cultures: Born in one world and living in another* (pp. 283–303). Belmont, CA: Thomson-Wadsworth.

Chavez, L. R. (2013). *The Latino threat: Constructing citizens, immigrants, and the nation* (2nd ed.). Palo Alto, CA: Stanford University Press.

Coutin, S. B. (2000). Denationalization, inclusion, and exclusion: negotiating the boundaries of belonging. *Journal of Global Legal Studies, 7*, 585–594.

Coutin, S. B. (2007). *Nations of emigrants: Shifting boundaries of citizenship in El Salvador and the United States.* Ithaca, NY, and London, England: Cornell University Press.

De Genova, N. P. (2002). Migrant "illegality" and deportability in everyday life. *Annual Review of Anthropology, 31*, 419–447.

Gonzales, R. G., & Chavez, L. R. (2012) "Awakening to a nightmare": Abjectivity and illegality in the lives of undocumented 1.5 generation Latina/o immigrants in the United States. *Current Anthropology, 53*(3), 255–281.

Gonzales, R. G., & Terriquez, V. (2013) How DACA is Impacting the lives of those who are now DACAmented: Preliminary findings from the National UnDACAmented Research Project. Immigration Policy Center, Center for the Study of Immigrant Integrant, University of Southern California. Retrieved from http://www.immigrationpolicy.org/just-facts/how-daca-impacting-lives-those-who-are-now-dacamented

Gonzalez-Barrera, A., & Lopez, M. H. (2013). A demographic portrait of Mexican-Origin Hispanics in the United States. *Pew Research Center Hispanic Trends* (May 1). Retrieved from http://www.pewhispanic.org/2013/05/01/a-demographic-portrait-of-mexican-origin-hispanics-in-the-united-states/

Hirschman, C. (2013). The contributions of immigrants to American culture. *Daedalus, 142*(3), 26–47.

Huntington, S. P. (2000, December). The special case of Mexican immigration: Why Mexico is a problem. *The American Enterprise*, 20–22.

Jones-Correa, M., & de Graauw, E. (2013). The illegality trap: The politics of immigration & the lens of illegaity. *Daedalus, 142*(3), 185–198.

Massey, D. S. (2013). America's immigration policy fiasco: Learning from past mistakes. *Daedalus, 142*(3), 5–15.

Massey, D. S., & Pren, K. A. (2012). Unintended consequences of US immigration policy: Explaining the post-1965 surge from Latin America. *Population and Development Review, 38*(1), 1–29.

Medrano, L. (2010, August 12). Obama as border cop: He's deported record number of illegal immigrants. *The Christian Science Monitor*, p. A24.

Menjívar, C. (2006). Liminal legality: Salvadoran and Guatemalan immigrants' lives in the United States. *American Journal of Sociology, 111*, 999–1037.

Negron-Gonzales, G. (2009). *Hegemony, ideology & oppositional consciousness: Undocumented youth and the personal-political struggle for educational justice.* Institute for the Study of Societal Issues, Working Paper No. 36. Berkeley, CA: University of California.

Olivas, M. A. (2012). *No undocumented child left behind: Plyler v. Doe and the education of undocumented school childen.* New York, NY: New York University Press.

Passel, J. S., & Cohn, D. (2009). *A portrait of unauthorized immigrants in the United States.* Washington, DC: Pew Hispanic Center.

Phelps, T. M. (2014, May 9). Anti-immigrant school bias called "troubling." *Los Angeles Times*, A9.

Portes, A., & Rumbaut, R. G. (2001). *Legacies: The story of the immigrant second generation.* Berkeley, CA: University of California Press.

Preston, J. (2011, August 23). U.S. issues new deportation policy's first reprieves. *The New York Times*, A15.

Ramirez, E. (2008, August 13). Should colleges enroll illegal immigrants? *U.S. News & World Report.* Retrieved from http://www.usnews.com/articles/education/2008/08/07/should-colleges-enroll-illegal-immigrants.html

Rincón, A. (2008). *Undocumented immigrants and higher education: Sí se puede.* New York, NY: LFB Scholarly Publishing.

Rumbaut, R. G. (2004). Ages, life stages, and generational cohorts: Decomposing the immigrant first and second generations in the United States. *International Migration Review, 38*, 1160–1205.

Suárez-Navaz, L. (2004). *Rebordering the Mediterranean: Boundaries and citizenship in southern Europe.* New York, NY: Berghahn Books.

Willen, S. S. (2007). Toward a critical phenomenology of "illegality": State power, criminality and abjectivity among undocumented migrant workers in Tel Aviv, Israel. *International Migration 45*(3), 8–38.

Winograd, B. (2012, November 16). DACA approvals surpass 50,000. *Immigration Impact.* Retrieved from http://immigrationimpact.com/2012/11/16/breaking-daca-approvals-surpass-50000/

Yoshikawa, H., & Kholoptseva, J. (2013, March). *Unauthorized immigrant parents and their chidren's dedvelopment: a summary of the evidence.* Migration Policy Institute. Retrieved from http://www.migrationpolicy.org/pubs/COI-Yoshikawa.pdf

CHAPTER 10

The Promise and Reality of *Plyler v. Doe*

Community Resistance to the School-to-Deportation Pipeline

Edelina M. Burciaga

E: So you're the only one in your family right now [*without papers*]?

S: Yeah, and it would take a while for her [*his mother*] to apply for me. Because she got it. And on top of that, it would be 8, 10 years on top of that. But I'm still in that waiting place, like Dr. Seuss. He says are you waiting for snow to snow? Can you imagine, sitting, staring at snow, waiting for the snow to do its thing? To snow? Waiting for time to pass. How do you wait for time to pass?

—Samuel, undocumented college student

In 1982 the Supreme Court of the United States held in Plyler v. Doe *that undocumented immigrant children had the right to attend public schools, stating that education "plays a fundamental role in maintaining the fabric of our society." The* Plyler *decision legally established the K–12 school system as a safe haven for undocumented immigrant children. In recent years, however, an increasingly hostile anti-immigrant climate and collaboration between local police, including school police, and immigration officials has resulted in eroding the rights of undocumented immigrant youth in schools. Drawing on 8 months of participant observation of the Coalition for Safer Schools, this chapter highlights how community members are building a foundation for long-term change in school policies and practices that disproportionately impact youth of color, including undocumented immigrant youth.*

Cracks in the Schoolyard—Confronting Latino Educational Inequality, edited by Gilberto Q. Conchas, with Briana M. Hinga. Copyright © 2016 by Teachers College, Columbia University. All rights reserved. To reprint any portion of this chapter, please request permission from Teachers College Press via Copyright Clearance Center, http://www.copyright.com

Dr. Seuss's *Oh, The Places You'll Go!* is a favorite gift at graduation time because it captures the journey of an unnamed protagonist as he decides to leave his town for bigger and better adventures. A sense of hope and anticipation permeates the story as the protagonist experiences the ups and downs of life. Yet in fall 2010 when I interviewed Samuel, a 23-year-old undocumented college student, the sense of optimism the book is meant to invoke did not capture his imagination. Instead, what resounded with him was the idea of the waiting place—where people are caught in limbo—as he referred to this idea more than once during our interview. Unauthorized immigrant youth like Samuel are often referred to in the sociological literature as the undocumented 1.5 generation, signaling their place between the first generation who migrated as adults and the second generation, who are similarly children of immigrants but are born in the United States (Gonzales, 2009; Portes & Rumbaut, 2001).

While not all members of the 1.5 generation are undocumented, what distinguishes this group from other members of the 1.5 generation who arrived as children to the United States is that they remain in the country without legal permission. Samuel, for example, immigrated here at the age of 7 with his mother and has lived in the greater Los Angeles area for over 15 years. In that time he graduated from high school and college, pursued a passion for activism and poetry, and lived his life as any other young person in the United States might. Still, Samuel is in the country without legal authorization, creating what he termed his own waiting place—during our interview he poignantly compared this place to the in-between space that many undocumented immigrant youth experience on a day-to-day basis.

Approximately 11.1 million undocumented immigrants, primarily from Mexico and Central America, currently live in the United States, the result of years of unauthorized migration and increasingly restrictive immigration laws and policies (Passel & Cohn, 2011). About 1.7 million are like Samuel; they are under the age of 30 and arrived before the age of 16, spending the better part of their lives in United States (Passel & Lopez, 2012). These 1.7 million undocumented youth and young adults have developed values, identities, and aspirations that are influenced by growing up American and are also impacted by the practical reality of living "illegally" in the United States. In the past 10 years, the experiences of the undocumented 1.5 generation have captured the scholarly imagination. Focusing primarily on the personal and academic challenges faced by high-achieving college-bound and college-enrolled undocumented youth—often referred to as "DREAMers"—this growing body of literature expands understandings of the immigrant experience by highlighting the profound impact of legal status on the incorporation and mobility prospects of the undocumented 1.5 generation (Abrego, 2006; Gonzales, 2007, 2009, 2011).

Yet what happens to undocumented immigrant youth who do not fit the ideal profile of a DREAMer? Like any social group, undocumented youth are not a monolith. Like their citizen peers, some undocumented youth find themselves caught up in a school culture that criminalizes young people of color (HoSang, 2006). However, distinct from the experiences of citizen youth of color, instead of finding themselves on a school-to-prison track, undocumented youth often end up on the school-to-deportation track. While recent studies have followed the efforts of "DREAMers" to mobilize for policy changes to increase higher education access—such as the passage of the Development Relief and Education for Alien Minors (DREAM) Act and Deferred Action for Childhood Arrivals (DACA) (Abrego, 2006; Burciaga, 2012; Nicholls, 2013; Seif, 2004, 2011)—much less is known about mobilization for policy changes outside of these areas.

This chapter fills the aforementioned gap by highlighting community efforts in Orange County, California to stem the tide of the school-to-deportation pipeline. As immigration enforcement becomes increasingly localized, the mobilization of this particular community has important theoretical and practical implications for Latina/o communities and policy change. While access to higher education is a key policy issue for Latina/o communities, undocumented immigrant youth, like many youth of color, face multiple structural challenges. Among these is the real threat of deportation created by increased cooperation between schools and law enforcement. This chapter highlights how undocumented youth organizing is evolving away from notions of merit and deservingness toward a more humanistic frame based on *respect* and *dignity* for all undocumented immigrants. The practical implications of focusing on this particular community is to highlight the potential of intersectional organizing—that is, recognizing the multiple identities and spheres that undocumented youth inhabit—for bringing together multiple groups and organizations for policy change. In addition, we learn how communities can mobilize seemingly neutral laws and policies to benefit undocumented immigrants—individuals who are typically viewed as living outside the law. In the sections that follow, I provide a brief history of the legal complexities that shape the lived experience of undocumented youth. I then discuss how undocumented youth experience the law and the threat of deportation in their daily lives. I highlight one community's ongoing efforts to change school policy as a way to address the school-to-deportation pipeline, and to reframe the criminalizing discourse that has emerged in recent years not only about undocumented immigrants, but also about youth of color.

THE LEGAL LANDSCAPE FOR THE UNDOCUMENTED 1.5 GENERATION

In 1982, the Supreme Court of the United States held that undocumented immigrant children had a right to a public education through high school graduation. The case reached the Supreme Court as the result of a Texas law seeking to charge undocumented children tuition to attend public primary and secondary schools (López, 2005; Olivas, 2011). Despite a 5–4 decision, reflecting a deeply divided Court, the *Plyler* precedent has endured over the course of 30 years, and the Court's rationale is echoed in today's political discussions about the undocumented 1.5 generation (López, 2005; Olivas, 2011). Justice Powell, who wrote the Court's decision, argued that denying undocumented immigrant children access to a public education would create a "lifetime hardship on a discrete class of children not accountable for their disabling status" (*Plyler v. Doe* in López, 2005, p. 17). The Court's opinion reflected a tacit acknowledgment of the importance of education for creating a pathway to upward social mobility, or in the case of undocumented children, at the very least avoiding a state-sanctioned downward trajectory.

In addition, the decision underscored the innocence of undocumented children in making the decision to migrate to the United States. These themes continue to shape how politicians and policymakers frame the undocumented 1.5 generation's experience. While *Plyler* is generally considered a historic legal victory for Latina/os, one of the most influential legacies of the *Plyler* decision is to open the door to an uncertain future as undocumented young people come of age (López, 2005; Olivas, 2011).

Some of this uncertainty has been eliminated through the announcement of administrative relief during President Barack Obama's second term. First, in 2012, he announced Deferred Action for Childhood Arrivals (DACA), which I detail later in the chapter. Most recently, in 2014 he announced an expansion of administrative relief for the parents of U.S. citizen children, known as Deferred Action for Parental Accountability (DAPA). It should be noted that both of these programs only offer a temporary stay of deportation, meaning that eligible immigrants cannot be deported. Although some of the benefits associated with these types of programs, such as receiving a work permit, are significant, these types of programs by no means eliminate the fear and stigma associated with being undocumented. In the absence of comprehensive immigration reform, through a pathway to citizenship and full legal inclusion, undocumented immigrants have had to negotiate an increasingly hostile political context.

The 1986 Immigration Reform and Control Act (IRCA) marked the last successful effort at comprehensive immigration reform. IRCA provided legal residency to nearly 3 million immigrants, of whom about 2.3 million were Mexican migrants. While IRCA provided a pathway to citizenship, the legislation also ushered in stricter immigration policies focused primarily on enforcement, both along the border and in receiving communities. In the nearly 30 years since IRCA was passed, most immigration initiatives have focused on some aspect of enforcement as opposed to incorporation. These initiatives include employer sanctions, harsher border control, and increased deportation quotas. For example, the 1996 Illegal Immigration Reform and Immigrant Responsibility Act (IIRAIRA), considered one of the most draconian pieces of immigration legislation, included specific provisions to increase the size of the border patrol each year through 2001, and to allow states to determine whether or not to grant driver's licenses to undocumented immigrants and other "benefits" reserved for citizens.

Following September 11, 2001, immigration legislation continued its trajectory toward increased enforcement and anti-terrorist measures. In fact, in the past 10 years or so, the criminalization of unauthorized immigration and immigrants has become so intimately connected that legal scholars have a coined a new term, *crimmigration* law (Kanstroom, 2012). While all undocumented immigrants are subject to this hostile environment, the undocumented 1.5 generation is often seen as an exception to this harsh treatment. Echoing the *Plyler* ruling, the Development Relief and Education for Alien Minors (DREAM) Act provides a pathway to citizenship for undocumented immigrant young people who meet certain requirements. Although the DREAM Act has been introduced several times since 2001, each time it has failed to pass. Furthermore, with each introduction, including in 2007, 2009, and 2010, the language of the DREAM Act has become more restrictive and focused primarily on rewarding "deserving" undocumented young people, and thereby pushing undocumented young people who do not fit this paradigm deeper into the shadows.

The legal landscape for the undocumented 1.5 generation shifted once more at the federal level when in June 2012 President Obama announced the Deferred Action for Childhood Arrivals (DACA) program. Legally this program grants a temporary stay of deportation for 3 years for eligible undocumented young adults who came to the United States before the age of 16.[1] Symbolically DACA represents the first major federal effort since the 1986 IRCA reform that formally acknowledges, albeit with a temporary legal remedy, the continued presence of undocumented immigrants in the United States. For undocumented young adults who meet the DACA eligibility requirements, not only is there a temporary reprieve from deportation, but they also do not continue to accrue a period of unlawful presence, *and* they are eligible to apply for authorization to work legally. DACA applications are accepted on a rolling basis, and a snapshot of all 465,000 DACA applications as of June 2013 suggests that approximately 1%, or about 5,000 applications, had been denied. The most common reason for denial of a DACA application is an inability to provide sufficient evidence of *educational enrollment* and continuous presence in the United States (Singer & Svaljenka, 2013). Undocumented youth and young adults, who for some reason or another face challenges in school, are effectively shut out of the DACA program.

In 2014, President Obama expanded administrative relief to include parents of U.S.-born children with DAPA. Estimates suggest that an additional 4 million undocumented immigrants will be eligible for work permits and a temporary stay of deportation under this initiative. Grassroots members of the immigrant rights community cautiously celebrated this victory because it means fewer families will face the devastating effects of deportation. However, significant portions of the undocumented immigrant community, including the parents of DACA recipients, are left with no recourse and, more importantly, will continue to face the day-to-day fear of deportation.

The introduction of forms of immigration relief like DACA and DAPA highlight a growing understanding in the undocumented immigrant community that immigration reform and reward will continue to hinge on definitions of "deserving" and "undeserving" immigrants, a discourse that while not unique to the undocumented Latina/o community, is troublesome (Maira, 2009). The prevalence of this type of discourse emphasizes the necessity for studies like this that examine community efforts to reclaim the deserving/undeserving paradigm, and to actively fight the threat of deportation.

In the next section, I describe the research methods and specifically outline how the Santa Centro Coalition for Safer Schools ("the Coalition") employed a multiprong approach to stem the school-to-deportation pipeline, and how this approach is changing the discourse *and* practice in the Santa Centro schools, an integral aspect of reclaiming power in the school setting.

THE CASE STUDY ON STOPPING JUVENILE DEPORTATIONS

This case builds on an ongoing ethnography of undocumented youth community organizing in the greater Los Angeles area, and the interview data shared here were collected in 2010 with undocumented youth activists. Four years later, some of these same activists became key organizers in the fight to the stem the school-to-deportation pipeline in the Santa Centro School District. I chose to focus on the emergence of the Coalition to gain both a better understanding of the evolution of these particular activists and undocumented youth organizing more broadly. To my knowledge, the Coalition was one of the few groups to connect immigrant rights to school discipline and to actively build a strategic coalition to stop juvenile deportations. In order to understand how the Coalition approached the work of stopping juvenile deportations, I conducted a case study of the group's organizing over the course of 9 months. I collected data primarily through participant observation at Coalition meetings, retreats, and events between June 2013 and February 2014. The ethnographic observation included in this study was part of a larger team-based data collection process tracking community change through the Santa Centro Community Health Initiative (SCCHI). My initial observation started with a subgroup of the SCCHI, which met weekly to discuss education issues affecting students and families in the school district. A community organizer facilitated this group, and attendees included parents, staff of other community-based organizations, and occasionally students. Around the same time that I began attending these meetings, a separate but related group focused on issues facing young men of color also began to meet regularly and to sponsor events and forums about school discipline and restorative justice. Realizing their shared interests in creating schools that were student focused, these two groups, along with a labor-organizing group working with parents and an LGBTQ organization working with youth, eventually joined to form the Coalition for Safer Schools. These groups were also joined by other community-based organizations, including an immigrant rights organization, a youth-focused organization, and staff representing the SCCHI. The community change efforts of both the SSCHI and the Coalition continue, although my role as an evaluation team member has ceased.

This study captures the Coalition at a key moment in its development: during its emergence when organizations were collectively negotiating a strategic platform. This is important because these early negotiations have informed the Coalition's strategy for long-term change in the Santa Centro School District. Theoretically, capturing the Coalition at this moment in its development highlights how mobilization by and with undocumented youth is expanding to include a broader swath of the undocumented population, which we still know very little about. To better explain how the Coalition organized, and how it continues to work to create safer schools by empowering immigrant youth and parents, I coded detailed fieldnotes for the emergence of strategies, tactics, framing of the issue, and counter-discourses. The findings presented below suggest that the Coalition was able to use a change in California school funding law to push the Santa Centro School District to make a measurable commitment to implementing student-centered discipline policies, but the broader mission of the Coalition continues to be to change district culture and practice.

THE COALITION AS THE CASE STUDY SITE

While the Coalition emerged in December 2013, the groundwork for the group's work was laid long before as several of the conveners had spent years organizing, working, and living in the community of Santa Centro and the surrounding areas. The Coalition's individual members came from a variety of organizations, including those focused on immigrant rights, labor organizers, undocumented youth groups, faith-based organizations, and the LGBTQ community. This wide array of perspectives strengthened the Coalition's approach to defining and identifying key aspects of safe schools and has continued to be an asset for the group as their work is ongoing. In addition, several of the individuals involved in the Coalition claimed what scholars refer to as "intersectional identities," meaning that their lived experience was grounded in multiple identities, and this was reflected in the Coalition's organizing.

In this chapter I show how this kind of intersectional organizing not only validated individual members' lived experiences, but also created a bridge for framing restorative justice as important for all students, not just those students who are disciplined. I then discuss how the Coalition engaged in a process of reframing the discourse on school safety, and how this framing empowers not only immigrant students, but also all students. Finally, I show how the Coalition used a change in California school funding policy to push the district to make a measurable commitment to creating a positive school climate.

INTERSECTIONAL ORGANIZING AND BUILDING
THE COALITION FOR SAFER SCHOOLS

The emergence of the Coalition for Safer Schools reflected an important development in community organizing for the Santa Centro Community Health Initiative, as reforming school discipline became a crosscutting issue for several of the groups working within the SCCHI. Individually organizations were doing important work in the areas of education, parent leadership development, youth development, immigrant rights, and LGBTQ rights. Because of the years that many organizers of the Coalition had already spent working together, there was recognition early in the process of the development of the Coalition that their individual work could be more powerful if they coalesced around the issue of school discipline, a leading issue in the Santa Centro School District.

Gina, a parent organizer, shared at the second formal meeting of the Coalition, "What we realized is that youth were working on their own, and educators were working on their own, and they were parents, and then we decided to have the one-on-ones, and then we thought 'hey, we should just have one group'"(fieldnotes, January 13, 2014). Lisa, a youth organizer working with an LGBTQ organization, added, "And the elements of the campaign are all the issues and the suggestions for the work and the platform are a reflection of what we have learned from the community" (fieldnotes January 13, 2014).

During these initial meetings, members of the Coalition spent a considerable amount of time discussing their own experiences in school as well as relaying the experiences of the communities they worked with. Both Gina's and Lisa's comments, and the larger group discussion during these meetings, reflect the Coalition's early commitment to developing a representative platform that not only was based on a strategic alliance, but also reflected the lived intersectional experiences of the communities they worked with.

In addition to drawing from the experiences of the community members they worked with, organizers drew from their own experiences to inform the strategic platform of the Coalition. Several of the key organizers in the Coalition are either immigrants themselves or the children of immigrants. Two of the youth organizers are undocumented and continue to be directly involved in undocumented youth organizing in Santa Centro and countywide. Although these two undocumented young adults were college graduates and working as community organizers, each of them had either been or had grown up around undocumented youth who faced challenges in school and in their neighborhoods. During strategic planning meetings, they drew from these experiences to help the Coalition make the connection between school discipline and the criminalization of immigrants.

Drawing from the UCI Law School report *Second Chances*, youth organizers Andres, Mateo, and Rogelio discussed with the group the connection between school discipline and juvenile deportations: "If we look deeper we see that a lot of youth end up on probation or violations of probation and one the major reasons is school related.

. . . [O]ne of the top five reasons is school related, gang related, and zero-tolerance policies." For Gina, a parent and labor organizer, this brought up memories of her own youth, and she shared, "Growing up here in Santa Centro we always grew up with gang injunctions and there was always someone there saying, 'here are the rules' [related to the gang injunction] and when I moved to Altama [a nearby city], that wasn't there." Through these types of exchanges, individual members drew from their own experiences and those of the communities they worked with to forge deeper connections with one another. This resulted in a strategic platform that was reflective of the multiple individual experiences of Coalition members.

The work of the Coalition for Safer Schools was not viewed by organizers as a single-issue initiative, but was considered a part of a larger movement to empower immigrant communities. At the January strategic planning meeting, Gina and Lisa bantered about "taking *all* the issues to the county, the state, and the country" (fieldnotes, January 13, 2014). Although their sentiment was lighthearted, it conveyed an implicit understanding in the group that reform in the district was tied to broader struggles for humane treatment of immigrants, regardless of age or status. By the end of their second formal strategic meeting, Coalition members had identified implementing restorative justice as an alternative discipline practice as the primary mechanism for changing district practice and culture. Advocating for the implementation of restorative justice became the anchor of the Coalition's strategic platform, and in the sections that I follow I detail how advocating for a restorative justice approach is a part of the Coalition's broader goal of reframing discourse about youth and color, and I highlight how the Coalition was able to secure a policy victory.

Restorative Justice and the Platform to Reframe the Discourse on Safety

The work of the Coalition for Safer Schools sought to reclaim the safety discourse by reclaiming what a "safe school" means for immigrant and Latina/o families. Drawing from the experiences of immigrant and Latina/o youth in the district, and reflecting a broader trend nationally, school safety in the district had become synonymous with increased enforcement primarily through the presence of school-based police officers. Exacerbating the police presence are school-based disciplinary practices based on zero-tolerance policies—one of the most harmful disciplinary practices in the district, and statewide, the employment of a "willful defiance" standard for assessing student behavior. Willful defiance is when a student fails to comply with any request that a school teacher or administrator makes—this can include talking back or even in some cases not adhering to a school dress code by wearing baggy pants. The standard itself is relatively subjective, and teachers and school administrators have broad discretion to designate a student as willfully defiant.

At a January meeting of the Coalition, Gina, a parent and labor organizer, relayed the following story to demonstrate precisely how subjective the willfully defiant standard can be: "Maria shared with me that her son is a big boy and he is always getting into trouble because of his appearance, even though he is younger, and she feels he is being criminalized" (fieldnotes, January 13, 2014). Although this story is brief, it demonstrates how discipline standards in the district had become so subjective that a larger physical presence could be perceived as a discipline problem. For the members of the Coalition, this story was demonstrative of the larger problems in the district that resulted from a willful defiance discipline standard.

At a December retreat, the coalition identified "willful defiance" as one of the most harmful practices that was feeding the school-to-deportation pipeline. Mateo, a youth and immigrant rights organizer, shared:

> This is an article from 2012 about OC. About willful defiance and how that is handled. . . . One of the biggest reasons—58% of youth are pushed out under willful defiance. There is huge racial disproportionality around willful defiance. African American and Latina/o youth and youth with disabilities, and ELLs are the highest groups that are suspended. This usually leads to expulsion.

Mateo was making the connection for retreat attendees between the practice of willful defiance and other more serious consequences like expulsion. Mateo was also highlighting how students of color—and relatedly undocumented youth—can end up on the road to the probation department, which in Orange County could lead to a referral to Immigration and Customs Enforcement (ICE). Making this initial link between the practice of willful defiance and broader, more negative consequences was the first step in identifying which policies and practices the Coalition needed to target to begin to reframe the discourse on school safety. Early in the process, the Coalition identified a long-term goal of eliminating willful defiance as a standard for discipline in the district. They were encouraged by the success of parent and youth organizers in Los Angeles, who were able to get the district to adopt a resolution that eliminated willful defiance as a discipline standard.

Beyond willful defiance, the Coalition also identified bullying as a key sticking point in terms of discipline. In this particular aspect the Coalition's organizational diversity proved to be an asset because members of the LGBTQ organization—a group of students who are normally the target of bullying and harassment— provided integral context to the discussion about bullying. During the discussion about bullying, the group talked about how both the bullied and the bullies should have the opportunity to be "made whole" again. Again, Mateo shared that

> there is a bunch of research that has been done between trauma and other behaviors. They may be acting out in class and are being criminalized in their classroom. The policies will change some of that climate in the schools. . . . So that someone stops and says to them, what is going on? Rather than acting out or bullying or shutting down.

Here Mateo and the group were working through how to address bullying in a way that honored those who were bullied and also recognized the trauma and experiences that might lead a youth to engage in bullying. A few of the organizations that formed the Coalition were researching alternatives to zero-tolerance–based policies like willful defiance, and after identification of the Coalition's key policy priorities, the group decided to pursue restorative justice as a framework for changing *both* district policy and to begin to change the district's culture around school discipline.

For the group a restorative justice approach to school discipline *in contrast* to zero-tolerance policies included both "trauma informed services and transformative healing," according to youth organizer Raul. When the Coalition first started to meet, the Santa Centro School District had implemented Positive Behavioral Intervention and Supports (PBIS). While this type of school discipline is an alternative to zero-tolerance policies, careful research by youth members and organizers found that this type of discipline was compliance driven, meaning that it still resulted in disproportional suspensions and expulsions of youth of color in the district (fieldnotes, February 4, 2014). For the Coalition and its members, this highlighted the imperative of their overarching policy platform, which was to get the district to commit to implementing restorative justice.

For Coalition members, the implementation of restorative justice was not only about introducing an alternative discipline practice, but was part of a larger project to create long-term and lasting change in the district. As Raul suggested at a meeting, "We need to get the district to see that this is not just a policy, but that this is a way to stop the suspension and expulsion of students." For Coalition members, implementing restorative justice was a way to introduce other practices that can lead to healing the trauma that many of youth of color and undocumented immigrant youth experience. Such practices include healing circles—spaces in school for youth to talk about trauma and to develop alternative ways to express their pain as opposed to "acting out." Following several more meetings, the group decided on a simple yet powerful definition of safe schools, and this includes a place where students could expect to be treated with "dignity and respect" (fieldnotes, January 13, 2014). In addition to introducing the concept of dignity and respect, the Coalition recognized that new accountability structures would need to be introduced to the district. To this end, the Coalition began to develop a language for a school discipline policy focused on positive school climate.

Focusing their efforts on developing a comprehensive school climate policy that, in the words of one Coalition member, addressed "the whole general environment, the feeling, the tone, the values, the way it educates and deals with problems" (Veronica, Coalition member), the Coalition was providing a template and plan for their advocacy work. The positive school climate policy envisioned and drafted by the Coalition included challenging the district to (1) implement alternatives to discipline (to address both those who were bullying and being bullied) and to eliminate the willful defiance practice, and (2) develop a school climate advisory council consisting of parents, students, allied teachers, and school staff.

Drawing from the experiences of other school districts like Los Angeles Unified School District, Coalition members realized that getting the Santa Centro School District to adopt a comprehensive school climate policy would take time and long-term advocacy. The group's coalescence coincided with major shifts in California education policy, and the Coalition decided to capitalize on this shift by focusing their efforts on using these policies to move their agenda forward.

The Coalition's organizing occurred during a major change in California school funding as the state adopted the Local Control Funding Formula (LCFF), which provides additional funding to districts educating a high number of certain populations of students, including students who are eligible for free and reduced-price lunch, English language learners, and students with disabilities. Under the LCFF, each district is expected to develop a Local Control and Accountability Plan (LCAP) in collaboration with parents and the public. Within the construct of the funding law, the state identified eight priority areas, one of which was school climate. The Coalition seized on the opportunity presented by the LCFF to help the district define and identify the elements of a positive school climate for not only undocumented immigrant youth but for all youth.

Regaining Local Control and the Empowerment of Immigrant Communities

In October 2013, organizations that eventually formalized their relationship as the Coalition for Safe Schools held a community forum to discuss the LCFF and its implications for the Santa Centro School District. More than 150 parents, students, school staff, and community members attended the forum. A key issue that emerged was that parents and students wanted the district to create a positive school climate through restorative justice programs. During the forum, Ismael, a youth organizer, shared the following:

> We are here today because almost half of the students in Santa Centro are forced to leave school because of disciplinary policies. These youths are being unjustly criminalized or marginalized for not speaking English or being undocumented. This county has the highest rate of deportation and most of these youth come from Santa Centro or Altama. For these reasons we want to implement restorative justice programs in the schools in Santa Centro. (Fieldnotes, October 29, 2013)

Following formal presentations by parents and other community members, the forum was opened up for comments and thoughts on how to improve education in the Santa Centro School District.

Students and parents echoed the need to use the LCFF funds to create a positive school climate. According to Jessica, a mother of five children in the Santa Centro School District: "When they go to school, they bring additional problems, because they reflect the situation that they are living, because many of them were adopted by relatives. In school, because of being so strict, the employees don't take the time to find out what's behind their behavior." Barbara, also a parent of children in the district, shared:

> What I would really love is for a part of these funds to go to mental health for our kids, or young people. It's very important. The students in junior high and high school have many needs like the lady mentioned: bullying, racism, anorexia, emo kids. All of these groups need it. The parents work. They need a lot of help. Let's focus, please. Let's not just have small programs. (Fieldnotes, October 29, 2013)

Building on this momentum, in December when the Coalition formalized, they connected the LCFF to their organizing work through one of the eight state priority areas identified in the law, improving school climate. The Coalition used this mechanism, which requires school districts to identify goals and actions for reducing school suspension and expulsion rates, to advocate for language in the plan that included restorative justice approaches, trauma-informed services, and respect.

In preparation for a summer adoption of the district LCAP, the Coalition ramped up their organizing and sought to educate the broader community about the connections between school discipline policies, suspension and expulsion, and the negative impact for *all* youth, but especially for undocumented youth who could face deportation. In December 2014, Coalition members sponsored a town hall to raise awareness about the record number of deportations in the county. At the town hall meeting, participants were broken up into smaller groups and were taken through a simulation of how an undocumented youth could end up in the juvenile justice system as a result of a school-related offense. Several of the community members noted that the process was "confusing and intimidating." Petra, a graduate student in social work, noted, "I have worked with youth in probation and even then it was still confusing; there were a million choices. I can imagine being a youth and not understanding this and it being complicated. Definitely very intimidating" (fieldnotes, December 8, 2014). Similar to the LCFF forum, for community members not working regularly with the Coalition, the Juvenile Justice Town Hall highlighted the way that the juvenile justice system disproportionality impacted undocumented youth. More important, it underscored the imperative of changing district policy on school discipline. Following the forum, the Coalition formalized as a group and had several meetings where members were brought up to speed about the LCFF.

Manuel, a community organizer with a faith-based group, took the lead for facilitating Coalition members' knowledge and understanding of the LCFF law. Manuel, who had been working as the organizer for the education subgroup of the SCCHI, participated in regular statewide calls about LCFF and what to expect. At the December retreat, during a discussion to highlight current opportunities for advocacy, Manuel explained that the LCFF requires that districts provide more funding for students that are low-income, learning English, and foster youth. Organizations are pushing for transparency and accountability down to the site level, and one of the eight areas is school climate. In the development of the plan, the district needs to involve stakeholders, and this includes parents and students. On July 14, districts will adopt the local accountability plans and will submit them to county education offices for approval. (Fieldnotes, December 14, 2014)

To prepare for the July adoption of the local accountability plans, in April 2014 the Coalition organized a forum that provided an opportunity to help parents, youth, and concerned community members understand the LCFF law. Not only did the forum educate the community about the LCAP, but it also drew on the considerable knowledge in the room by asking youth, parents, and community members to define what a safe school climate was for them. Parents, youth, and community members resoundingly supported "restorative practices for all," reflecting an inherent understanding that a school and district culture that respects students will lead to student success.

The work of the Coalition over the next few months centered primarily on getting the Santa Centro School Board to agree to allot $10 million of the LCAP funding to implement restorative justice practices in all schools in the district. Early in their organizing model, the Coalition prioritized a popular education model to facilitate parent and youth knowledge and advocacy for restorative justice practices. The forum was just one indication of the group's commitment to empower community through knowledge of restorative practices and the LCFF law.

In addition to large community education events, as the Coalition gained momentum, the group's weekly meetings grew in size. With each meeting more parents and youth were in attendance—a key development. Two months after the forum, the Coalition, now a vibrant mix of parents, youth, and community members, attended the Santa Centro school board meeting. Youth and parents held bright orange signs that stated "Safe Schools = Restorative Practices for All," "Safe Schools = Parent Leadership," and "Safe Schools = Reducing Arrest." The Coalition proposed a safe schools platform that included (1) reducing suspensions; (2) interventions for school arrest; (3) parent, youth, and community voice; (4) restorative justice in all schools; and (5) cultural sensitivity and LGBTQ training for all. This broad platform reflected the intersectional-organizing model discussed in the previous section. Both youth and parents testified at the school board meeting. By the end of the meeting, the board agreed to allocate $4 million to restorative justice practices in the entire district—a significant victory for the Coalition and the Santa Centro community.

DISCUSSION AND CONCLUSION

By strategically using the Local Control Funding Formula law, the Coalition was able to push the Santa Centro School District to make a measurable commitment to creating a positive school climate by providing funding for restorative justice. The Coalition still has a long road ahead of organizing for implementation and accountability, and yet focusing on a policy win highlights how undocumented youth and concerned community members can assert agency within a larger bureaucratic structure that at times seems impenetrable and opaque. This chapter highlights three key mechanisms that facilitated this policy victory. First, by emphasizing the complexity of the undocumented immigrant experience—meaning that undocumented immigrants are not defined by their status alone—the Coalition was able to draw from multiple narratives to create connections across organizing platforms. Rather than see certain identities, like identifying as LGBTQ, as taking away from the core issue of safe schools—as is often the case in single-issue or identity movements—the Coalition integrated this experience into the broader discourse of school safety to create a more inclusive and empathetic definition of safe schools.

The second way the Coalition managed to secure a policy win was by reclaiming the discourse and understandings about the experiences of undocumented immigrant youth and youth of color. The Coalition seized on school safety language, which historically has been used to hyper-criminalize youth of color, including undocumented immigrant youth, and instead introduced student- and parent-centered meanings of school climate. The Coalition introduced the idea of restorative justice to community members and the district, including concepts like the impact of trauma on youth's behaviors, making students whole again, and treating students with respect and dignity. This shift signals the Coalition's long-term agenda to change district culture and practices on school discipline. The Coalition is part of a statewide movement to eliminate the willful defiance standard in school districts across the state. This movement, and the Coalition, is using recent changes in school funding law to challenge California school officials to treat all students, regardless of race or legal status, with respect and dignity.

Finally, the Coalition took advantage of the LCFF law. School funding schemes are notoriously opaque, but through educational forums and community meetings the Coalition engaged a popular education campaign to help parents, youth, and community members understand how the funding law could work in their favor. By focusing their efforts on getting the school district to commit funding to restorative justice, the Coalition will be able to hold the district accountable as they move forward with goal of implementing restorative justice in all schools. Although this was a significant policy victory, the work of implementation is just starting. The Coalition continues to meet with parents, youth, and community members to develop their vision of restorative justice in the school district, to identify benchmarks for success, and to figure out ways to hold the district accountable.

At the beginning of this chapter, Samuel, an undocumented college student, reflected on the experiences of undocumented youth who, though raised in the United States, remain in a legal limbo, even with the announcement of DACA. The organizing model and strategies employed by the Coalition for Safe Schools, of which Samuel is a key organizer, reflects this shift in the larger immigrant rights narrative. By framing demands for school safety within a larger discourse of *respect* and *dignity*, they are drawing from and contributing to a discourse that seeks to humanize immigrants and the immigrant experience. Perhaps more important— especially within the school context—a discourse of dignity and respect as well as practices of restorative justice requires that schools be held accountable for creating school cultures that do not recognize the humanity of undocumented youth and the humanity of all students.

NOTE

1. Other requirements include: (1) continuous presence in the United States from 2007; (2) under the age of 31 as of June 15, 2012; (3) physical presence on June 15, 2012; (4) entered the United States without inspection before June 15, 2012; (5) currently enrolled in school, high school graduate, GED, or honorable discharge from armed forces or Coast Guard; and (6) no felony or serious misdemeanor convictions and do not pose a serious threat to national security.

REFERENCES

Abrego, L. (2006). "I can't go to college because I don't have papers": Incorporation patterns of Latino undocumented youth. *Latino Studies, 4*(3), 212–231.

Burciaga, E. (2012). *Education not deportation: Undocumented student activism in the Obama years. Sociological Quarterly, 55*(1), 143–167.

Gonzales, R. G. (2007). Wasted talent and broken dreams: The lost potential of undocumented students. *Immigration Policy in Focus 5*(13), 1–11.

Gonzales, R. G. (2009). *Young lives on hold: The college dream of undocumented students.* New York, NY: The College Board.

Gonzales, R. G. (2011). Learning to be illegal undocumented youth and shifting legal contexts in the transition to adulthood. *American Sociological Review, 76*(4), 602–619.

HoSang, D. (2006). Beyond policy: Ideology, race and the reimagining of youth. In P. Noguera, J. Cammarota, & S. Ginwright (Eds.), *Beyond resistance! Youth activism and community change: New democratic possibilities for practice and policy for America's youth* (pp. 3–21). New York, NY: Routledge.

Kanstroom, D. (2012). *Aftermath: Deportation law and the new American diaspora.* New York, NY: Oxford University Press.

López, M. P. (2005). Reflections on educating Latina/o and Latina undocumented children: Beyond *Plyler v. Doe. Seton Hall Law Review, 35*(3), 631–656.

Maira, S. (2009). "Good" and "bad" Muslim citizens: Feminists, terrorists, and US Orientalisms. *Feminist Studies, 13*(2), 189–204.

Nicholls, W. (2013). *The DREAMers: How the undocumented youth movement transformed the immigrant rights debate.* Palo Alto, CA: Stanford University Press.

Olivas, M. A. (2011). *No undocumented child left behind:* Plyler v. Doe *and the education of undocumented schoolchildren.* New York, NY: New York University Press.

Passel, J., & Cohn, D. (2011). *Unauthorized immigrant population: National and state trends, 2010.* Washington, DC: Pew Hispanic Center.

Passel, J., & Lopez, M. H. (2012). *Up to 1.7 million unauthorized immigrant youth may benefit from new deportation rules.* Washington, DC: Pew Hispanic Center.

Portes, A., & Rumbaut, R. G. (2001). *Legacies: The story of the immigrant second generation.* Berkeley and Los Angeles, CA: University of California Press.

Seif, H. (2004). "Wise up!" Undocumented Latina/o youth, Mexican-American legislators, and the struggle for higher education access. *Latina/o Studies, 2*(2), 210–230.

Seif, H. (2011). "Unapologetic and unafraid": Immigrant youth come out from the shadows. *New Directions for Child and Adolescent Development, 2011*(134), 59–75.

Singer, A., & Svaljenka, N. P. (2013). DACA: Coming of age at a time of immigration reform. Retrieved from http://www.brookings.edu/blogs/up-front/posts/2013/06/19-daca-immigration-reform-singer-svajlenka

CHAPTER 11

Conclusion: Reflections on Critical Achievement Cases Toward a Critical Hope

Filling the Cracks in the Schoolyard

Briana M. Hinga & Gilberto Q. Conchas

The preceding chapters offer various methodologies and findings to illuminate both injustice and hopeful possibilities through education. Together, the studies inform ways to understand assets and agency of Latina/o youth, their families, and their communities. Such studies counter a deficit perspective on Latina/o youth and provide windows into a critical hope toward equitable transformation in the education system and beyond the schoolyard. In this closing discussion, we use a frame of critical hope to discuss how such work can expose and fills cracks in the schoolyard.

Critical hope synergistically includes three components: material hope, Socratic sensibility, and audacious hope (Duncan-Andrade, 2009). Material hope centers on material resources and conditions in the lives of youth—partly as a means to acknowledge needs and set up supports (Duncan-Andrade, 2009; Syme, 2004). Socratic sensibility explains the importance and pain associated with examining injustice (Duncan-Andrade, 2009; West, 2004). Audacious hope involves authentic caring and empathy along the struggle (Duncan-Andrade, 2009; Valenzuela, 1999). In the words of Tupac Shakur as analyzed by Duncan-Andrade (2009), critical hope means understanding and celebrating the tenacity and will of urban youth. The cases of achievement in this volume illuminate the will, tenacity, and other incredible assets of Latina/o communities—and highlight methods and practical examples that foster such strength toward critical hope and transformative change. In doing so, the achievement cases foster a critical hope because they acknowledge injustice while pushing for transformation (Duncan-Andrade, 2009; West, 2004).

The chapters illuminate several methods and pathways to critical hope through critical investigation into taken-for-granted norms and practices—from individual-level consciousness, to policy reform, and community-based reform efforts. In all, the chapters reveal the importance and promise of disrupting deficit notions of Latina/o communities and instead working with these communities toward critical solutions.

RACE, RACISM, AND INEQUALITY

In the first section, *Critical Case Studies Centering on Race, Racism, and Inequality*, the first set of chapters highlight the need for change at both the consciousness and structural levels. Chapter 2 focuses on the component of critical consciousness in multicultural education among college students. The chapter highlights problematic (and often taken for granted) perceptions that can perpetuate inequality if not checked and addressed through Socratic sensibility. The chapter reminds us of the importance of preparing future educators and leaders to critically reflect on their assumptions of race to work toward a critical consciousness in their practice. The chapter explains that applied change in classrooms will require transformation in perceptions and experiences of future leaders. Toward this goal, the chapter solidifies the importance of a well-structured curriculum that challenges future educators and leaders to reflect on their perceptions, in both theory and practice.

Chapters 3 and 4 call attention to the importance of material hope within marginalized communities to overcome inequalities. Chapter 3 calls attention to the different levels of material hope that must be addressed for equitable college access. The study reveals the importance of both organizational and student-level efforts that shape college choice, transition, and navigation of pathways for Latina/o students who aspired to earn a bachelor's degree. The chapter also illuminates the importance of understanding intersectional, historical underpinnings of organizational and student-level efforts through the lens of critical race theory in education (CRTE). CRTE provides a frame to challenge deficit assumptions of Latina/o college-going that impact each level of college access.

The case study presented in Chapter 4 draws attention to how individual strengths can be leveraged when material hope, in this case—in the form of an after-school venue—supports community building. The sense of community leads into audacious hope, in the form of "brotherhood." Such community building supports a forum for engagement and achievement for Black and Latino males. This chapter underscores the importance of community building, which marginalized communities are not always afforded when pinned against one another—rather than struggling together toward transformative change.

FAMILY, CULTURAL RESOURCES, AND COMMUNITY STRENGTHS

The second section—*Critical Case Studies Documenting Family, Cultural Resources, and Community Strengths*—highlights the assets within communities by focusing on cases where communities are organized and share their knowledge. Chapter 5 discusses the PRAXIS Project, which uses participatory research within a school-based, university-affiliated research collaborative to understand and respond to the dropout crisis in the United States. This is an example of the vast intelligence and key change that results from inviting youth into the process of transformation. After all, who are more expert in the needs and assets of youth within a given community than the youth themselves?

Chapter 6 highlights the need to understand and work with motivational assets Latina/o youth use to achieve success in high school, despite the odds. The chapter celebrates commitment to earning a high school diploma and focuses on the need to examine and leverage the combination of academic and social supports from family ties, peer groups, and institutional agents that also contribute to youth's engagement and persistence in school. Chapter 7 further provides insight into how the knowledge of parents and communities can be leveraged through community-based organizations that work with communities to promote school readiness. This chapter clearly delineates the growth of Latina/o parental cultural wealth deep in the concrete jungle.

EXPLORING ETHNICITY, IDENTITY, AND IMMIGRATION

The third section, *Critical Case Studies Exploring Ethnicity, Identity, and Immigration*, targets specific components of material hope faced by many members of the Latina/o community. These chapters push toward understandings of policy- and practical-level transformation, within specific challenges that society places on identity formation for many Latina/o youth. Chapter 8 reframes the relationships between the surveillance and power of police, teachers, and other authorities and queer Latina/o youth as infrapolitical allows social science and educational researchers to move away from the deficit thinking and radical "othering" that is often found in educational policy and research.

Chapter 9 uncovers material obstacles to social and cultural integration for Latina/o immigrants, which will not improve until a more permanent solution, such as national comprehensive immigration reform, occurs. This study runs contrary to a deficit-oriented public discourse on immigration. The study shows children of Mexican immigrants in the greater Los Angeles area acquire English quickly. Further, the study argues that practical solutions would be better focused on reforming immigration status processes that actually hinder educational attainment and income. In other words, structures must be in place to foster the hard work and will of immigrants to succeed in schools. In Chapter 10, we see how in recent years, however, an increasingly hostile anti-immigrant climate and collaboration between local police, including school police, and immigration officials has resulted in eroding the rights of undocumented immigrant youth in schools. Drawing on almost a year of participant observation of the Coalition for Safer Schools, this chapter highlights how community members are building a foundation for long-term change in school policies and practices that disproportionately impact youth of color, including undocumented immigrant youth.

FILLING THE CRACKS IN THE SCHOOLYARD

The methodological developments and outcomes considered in this volume reveal overlooked Latina/os' educational experiences, perspectives, struggles, and vast assets. We hope that organizing this discussion within the three themes—Race, Racism, and Inequality; Family, Cultural Resources, and Community Strengths; and Exploring Ethnicity, Identity, and Immigration—raises productive understanding, discussion, and movement toward fundamental components of educational experiences for Latina/o youth that must be taken into account when working toward a more equitable education system. These categories help organize and clarify the need for change at levels of consciousness, policy, and on-the-ground education reform. The use of critical research to shatter deficit notions and work toward realistic needs of communities, using assets within communities to work toward change, shines through such organization. At the same time, each category is intertwined and informs the others. Taken together, the categories move us toward a more in-depth understanding of how to move toward critical hope.

When considered together, the chapters also illuminate that transformational education research need not be associated with one method of research only or a finite set of theoretical frameworks. The book is not meant to claim a specific set of experiences that Latina/o youth face. Rather, this book highlights how different types of methodological approaches can paint a more vivid picture of problems and promises in current and possible systems, often faced by Latina/o youth, that can go unacknowledged in normative evaluations. Research in Latina/o education still has many areas of inquiry left unexplored, and this volume proposes several considerations for scholars to engage in ongoing discussion. After all, as the Latina/o population continues to expand and gain traction in political, social, and economic spheres, educational researchers will need to consistently devise new approaches to their research.

Some of the methodologies in this book have the objective of challenging others to reassess negative cultural assumptions about Latino communities and families. For example, Chapter 2 speaks to the importance of critical reflection for educators and leaders. This objective is both important in the academy and in policy. Additionally, beyond informing perceptions of Latina/os, research can also be an important instrument to inform and shape education policy on, namely, the factors and influences that promote success instead of failure (Conchas, 2006). For example, Chapter 9 describes that full integration of Latina/o immigrants will not happen without comprehensive immigration reform. Moreover, research in this book shows how work within communities toward applied change can have immediate and direct impact, as well as inform the broader scope of future change.

A focus on Latina/o youth in this volume comes at a time when Latina/os occupy an important and growing presence in the United States. As we know, the strength of Latina/o growth (and the wonderful assets of this community) within the country is not matched with an increasing prosperity for Latina/o students through education. Inequalities in Latina/o student experiences show themselves in many ways. For one, "the academic achievement gap" is a term commonly used to describe the disparity in educational achievement for Latina/o youth. For example, a grave and stagnant gap in scores (for 4th- and 8th-graders in standardized tests of reading and math) exists between Latina/o and White students (Hemphill, & Vanneman, 2010). Another disparity exists in terms of school completion. The dropout rate of Latina/o students is nearly three times the rate of white students—18% versus 8% (California Department of Education, 2015). Dropout rates are even higher for Latina/o students in urban schools. In Los Angeles schools, for instance, the Latina/o dropout rate approaches 35%. Bleak statistics persist, despite several reform efforts (Fry, 2014).

The need for critical research and reform efforts rings clear with such persistent inequalities. Echoes of failed reform efforts seem to be a product of Albert Einstein's eloquent notion that "we can't solve problems by using the same kind of thinking we used when we created them." To change systematic outcomes within the current educational paradigm, we need new ways of looking at the problem and different methodologies toward reform. Critical methodologies, as exemplified in this book, investigate the problem and solution from fresh perspectives. In the general sense, critical methodologies expose approaches that challenge taken-for-granted norms and illuminate structures of power and domination within the current system.

NEW DIRECTIONS OF LATINA/O CRITICAL HOPE

In line with a conception of critical hope, methodologies in this book have opened up questions about (1) how the assessments we use contribute to (and limit) the way we understand the problem, (2) whose perspectives should be taken into account as we investigate the problem, and (3) how a broader, historically contextualized look at our current situation informs our understandings. As part of this perspective, critical methodologies frame inquiries by not only investigating what is not working but also by actively promoting and learning from instances of success or "achievement cases."

As seen in this book and over time, critical education research has been instrumental in uncovering previously unheard and non-mainstream educational experiences faced by Latina/os. Using critical research methodologies, educational researchers have challenged educational practices that otherwise assume "neutral" schooling and learning conditions. Critical methodology describes research that challenges conventional knowledge bases and methods that claim scientific objectivity.

As the case studies in this book exhibit, diverse theoretical frameworks and methodologies have been instrumental to researchers seeking to understand—from a variety of perspectives—the educational conditions faced by Latina/os in various educational contexts. In some cases this involves research that has used innovative methods, theories, and methodologies. In other cases, established methods viewed through a different conceptual lens have yielded findings that produce new knowledge about Latina/os and their oppressive and emancipatory relations in K–12 and postsecondary institutions.

Whether theoretical or applied, it can be argued that most educational scholars aim to have an impact on educational practice. However, the dissemination format for which the academy rewards merit—that is, peer-reviewed journals—is not accessible or widely available to practitioners, community organizers, and policymakers. Since the objective of critical research in Latina/o education is in large part to effect applied transformative change to the system, then what is recognized as valid research in the academy is sometimes at odds with researchers seeking to disseminate their research to lay audiences or engage in action-research methodologies (Ginwright, Noguera, & Cammarota, 2006). Indeed, research can be disseminated to both academic audiences and practitioners simultaneously, but given the reward structure in academe, this is not always practical. Without a doubt, peer-reviewed research gains integrity in the review process that is lacking in non-peer-reviewed research, so it would be dangerous to rid educational research of some sort of rigorous standards.

On the other hand, research using critical methodologies precisely critiques the epistemological origins of current academic standards for what constitutes "valid research" and dissemination practices. Many of the scholars explicitly seek to have broader impact with their research and in the research process. The discipline of education research merits examination in how the purpose of research is defined, how it is rewarded, and who is the audience. After all, for transformation to occur, we need to look at the situation in new ways, from new perspectives, and through the lens of community members most impacted by inequalities.

As bell hooks (1996) noted, "There must exist a paradigm, a practical model for social change that includes an understanding of ways to transform consciousness that are linked to efforts to transform structures" (p. 118). This volume provides a step in this direction by displaying how many different forms of critical research can inform the perceptions and critical consciousness of future educators, speak to needed policy reform, and pave the way for programs founded in critical hope. In other words, the Latina/o achievement cases included here reveal methods to foster critical hope, as linked to the material structural transformation of educational structures. We hope others can look to the methods and findings within this book to dismantle deficit notions of Latina/o youth, foster the diverse assets and potential within Latina/o communities, and move forward in critical hope.

REFERENCES

California Department of Education. (2015). DataQuest: Demographics Unit—2015: Dropout rate by age and major ethnic group.

Conchas, G. Q. (2006). *The color of success: Race and high-achieving urban youth.* New York, NY: Teachers College Press.

Duncan-Andrade, M. R. (2009). Note to educators: Hope required when growing roses in concrete. *Harvard Educational Review, 79*(2), 181–194.

Fry, R. (2014). *U.S. high school dropout rate reaches record low, driven by improvements among Hispanics, blacks.* Washington, DC: Pew Hispanic Center.

Ginwright, S., Noguera, P., & Cammarota, J. (2006). *Beyond resistance! Youth activism and community change: New democratic policies for practice and policy for America's youth.* New York, NY: Routledge.

Hemphill, F. C., & Vanneman, A. (2010). *Achievement gaps: How Hispanic and White students in public schools perform in mathematics and reading on the National Assessment of Educational Progress* (NCES 2011-459). Washington, DC: National Center for Education Statistics, Institute of Education Sciences, U.S. Department of Education.

hooks, b. (1996). *Killing racism: Ending rage.* New York, NY: Henry Holt and Company.

Syme, S. L. (2004). Social determinants of health: The community as empowered partner. *Preventing chronic disease.* Retrieved from http://www.cdc.gov/pcd/issues/2004/

Valdes, G. (1996). *Con respeto: Bridging the distances between culturally diverse families and schools.* New York, NY: Teachers College Press.

Valenzuela, A. (1999). *Subtractive schooling: U.S.–Mexican youth and the politics of caring.* Albany, NY: State University of New York Press.

West, C. (2004). The impossible will take a little while. In P. Rogat (Ed.), *The impossible will take a little while: A citizen's guide to hope in a time of fear* (pp. 293–297). New York, NY: Basic Books.

About the Contributors

Nancy Acevedo-Gil is an assistant professor in the Department of Educational Leadership and Technology at California State University, San Bernardino. As a Chicana scholar, she applies critical race theory and Chicana feminist theories to examine the educational experiences of students of color and low-income first-generation college students. Acevedo-Gil addresses the transitions from high school to college, as well as challenges and promising practices in community colleges, such as developmental education.

Alejandra S. Albarran holds a doctorate in education with a dual focus in learning, cognition and development, and educational policy and social context from the School of Education at the University of California. Her work takes an ecological perspective toward understanding how family, community, economic structures, and culture impact children's educational trajectories. Specifically, her research investigates community efforts to support Latina/o parents' understanding of the school system.

Edelina M. Burciaga is a PhD candidate in sociology at the University of California, Irvine. Her areas of interest include immigration, sociology of education, and the sociology of law. Her dissertation explores the influence of state and local immigration laws and policies in the incorporation of the Latina/o undocumented 1.5 generation. Prior to attending graduate school, she worked as an attorney advocating for educational equity in Massachusetts.

Leo R. Chavez received his PhD from Stanford University and is currently a professor in the Department of Anthropology at the University of California, Irvine. He is author of *Shadowed Lives: Undocumented Immigrants in American Society* (2013), *Covering Immigration: Popular Images and the Politics of the Nation* (2001), and *The Latino Threat: Constructing Immigrants, Citizens, and the Nation* (2013).

Gilberto Q. Conchas is professor of educational policy and social context at the University of California, Irvine. He is author of *The Color of Success* (2006), coauthor of *Small Schools and Urban Youth* (2008), coauthor of *Streetsmart Schoolsmart* (2012), and coeditor of *Inequality, Power, and School Success* (2015). He has also been a visiting professor at the University of Southern California, San Francisco

State University, University of Washington, the University of Barcelona, and the University of California, Berkeley.

Isiaah Crawford serves as provost and is a professor of psychology at Seattle University. He received his BA in psychology from St. Louis University and completed his doctoral studies in clinical psychology at DePaul University. He is a well-published scholar in the areas of human sexuality and health promotion, and his work has been nationally recognized with several awards, including two from the American Psychological Association.

Cindy Cruz is an associate professor in the Department of Education at the University of California, Santa Cruz. Her research on LGBTQ street youth narratives and *testimonios* (testimonies) centers on the theories, pedagogies, and methodologies of U.S. women of color thought.

Briana M. Hinga is an assistant professor of clinical education at the Rossier School of Education at the University of Southern California. She completed her PhD in education at the University of California, Irvine. Her research illuminates how history, social structure, schooling practices, policies, perceptions, and actions interact to shape educational opportunity. She focuses on partnerships with communities, students, and schools to design and evaluate learning environments that foster possibility and social justice.

Eduardo Mosqueda is an associate professor of education at the University of California at Santa Cruz. His research primarily examines the relationship between the English proficiency of language-minority students, their access to rigorous courses, and their performance on standardized mathematics assessments. He has authored or coauthored articles in *Equity & Excellence in Education*, the *Journal of Urban Mathematics Education*, and the *Journal of Science Teacher Education*.

Leticia Oseguera is an associate professor of education policy studies at Pennsylvania State University. Her research focuses on underserved youths' transitions to postsecondary education.

Louie F. Rodriguez is an associate professor of educational leadership at California State Univerity, San Bernardino. His work focuses on equity issues in urban schools and communities, particularly how students respond to institutional culture. He is author of *The Time Is Now: Understanding and Responding to the Black and Latina/o Dropout Crisis in the U.S.* (2013). He earned his master's and doctorate from Harvard.

Kip Téllez is a professor and former chair in the Education Department at the University of California at Santa Cruz. Combining his interests in English language teaching and teacher education, he has published articles in journals such as the *Journal of Teacher Education, Teaching and Teacher Education*, and the *Bilingual Research Journal*. He currently serves as editor for *Teacher Education Quarterly*. A recently published book, *Teaching English Learners* (2011), is designed to help teachers consider the wide implications of their work.

Irene I. Vega is a doctoral candidate in sociology at the University of California, Los Angeles. Her research interests are in international migration, racial and political group formation, and educational inequality. Her work has appeared in the *American Behavioral Scientist, Equity and Excellence in Education*, and the *Journal of Hispanic Higher Education*.

Index